JOSSEY-BASS TEACHER

Jossey-Bass Teacher provides educators with practical knowledge and tools to create a positive and lifelong impact on student learning. We offer classroom-tested and research-based teaching resources for a variety of grade levels and subject areas. Whether you are an aspiring, new, or veteran teacher, we want to help you make every teaching day your best.

From ready-to-use classroom activities to the latest teaching framework, our value-packed books provide insightful, practical, and comprehensive materials on the topics that matter most to K–12 teachers. We hope to become your trusted source for the best ideas from the most experienced and respected experts in the field.

THE COMPLETE GUIDE TO SPECIAL EDUCATION

Proven Advice on Evaluations, IEPs, and Helping Kids Succeed

Second Edition

LINDA WILMSHURST
Ph.D., ABPP
ALAN W. BRUE
Ph.D., NCSP

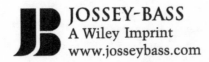

JOSSEY-BASS
A Wiley Imprint
www.josseybass.com

Published by Jossey-Bass
A Wiley Brand
One Montgomery Street, Suite 1200, San Francisco, CA 94104-4594—www.josseybass.com

Readers should be aware that Internet Web sites offered as citations and/or sources for further information may have changed or disappeared between the time this was written and when it is read.

Jossey-Bass books and products are available through most bookstores. To contact Jossey-Bass directly call our Customer Care Department within the U.S. at 800-956-7739, outside the U.S. at 317-572-3986, or fax 317-572-4002.

Jossey-Bass also publishes its books in a variety of electronic formats. Some content that appears in print may not be available in electronic books.

Library of Congress Cataloging-in-Publication Data

Wilmshurst, Linda.
  The complete guide to special education: proven advice on evaluations,
  IEPs, and helping kids succeed / Linda Wilmshurst, Alan W. Brue.—2nd ed.
    p. cm.
  Rev. ed. of: A parent's guide to special education. c2005.
  Includes bibliographical references and index.
  ISBN 978-0-470-61515-7 (pbk.)
  1. Special education—United States. 2. Special education— United States—Law and legislation.
I. Brue, Alan W. II. Wilmshurst, Linda. Parent's guide to special education. III. Title.
  LC3981.W55 2010
  371.9073—dc22

                                                                                    2010018018

Printed in the United States of America
SECOND EDITION
PB Printing 10 9 8 7

CONTENTS

ABOUT THIS BOOK

In the Best Interests of the Child

Our book, based on the perspectives of two school psychologists, focuses on how to optimize children's experiences in the educational system. Although we dedicate our book to children with special needs, we believe that all children, parents, and teachers can benefit from our recommendations and suggested interventions. In regard to children who require special education services, we provide explanations of the laws, procedures, and policies that are involved in identification and assessment of these children and, ultimately, in providing interventions for them.

Children live in a world that can provide rich resources to maximize their learning or minimize barriers to their success. If a child has a disability, then support from family, educators, extended family, the community, and even governmental laws can provide the resources needed for success. Our goal is to provide concerned parents and educators with the information they need to help make success a reality for all children.

ABOUT THE AUTHORS

Linda Wilmshurst, Ph.D., ABPP, is a Diplomate in Clinical Psychology (American Board of Professional Psychology) and is licensed as a psychologist and school psychologist in North Carolina. Linda has practiced psychology as a clinical child and adolescent psychologist and school psychologist for many years in both Canada and the United States. Linda is an associate professor in the psychology department at Elon University, where she teaches courses in child and adult psychopathology, developmental psychology, psychology in the schools, and introductory psychology. In her current research projects, she is investigating resilience, self-concept, and time perception in college students with ADHD. Linda is the author of a number of books, including *Child and Adolescent Psychopathology: A Casebook*; *Abnormal Child Psychology: A Developmental Perspective*; *Essentials of Child Psychopathology*; and *A Parent's Guide to Special Education*, which she co-authored with Alan Brue.

Alan W. Brue, Ph.D., NCSP, received his master's, specialist, and doctoral degrees in school psychology (with a specialization in gifted education) from the University of Florida. He works as a school psychologist for the Bartow County School System in Georgia and as a core faculty member in the Harold Abel School of Social and Behavioral Sciences at Capella University, where he teaches and develops graduate courses in psychopathology, child and adolescent psychology, learning theories, intellectual and behavioral assessment, and research methods. In addition, Alan has worked as director of professional standards for the National Association of School Psychologists and as a radio broadcaster. Co-author of *A Parent's Guide to Special Education* (with Linda Wilmshurst), he has extensive knowledge of assessment, special education laws, and school organization, and is keenly aware of the needs of children and parents. Alan is a Nationally Certified School Psychologist.

ACKNOWLEDGMENTS

I thank my children, Luke and Rachel, for their continued support and inspiration and Rachel for providing the artwork for some of the figures. I thank my co-author, Alan, who makes collaboration an effortless and rewarding experience. This book is dedicated to all the children and youth with special needs who continue to amaze me with their ability to master difficult challenges and to the parents and teachers who support them in making their accomplishments possible. May our book provide information that will guide your efforts and provide increased opportunities for children and youth to overcome the challenges that they face and achieve the success that they deserve.

—Linda Wilmshurst

Jett, I love you. Thank you for always being there; you are inspiring. I thank Linda Wilmshurst for continuing to be a great writing partner; our collaboration has been a very enjoyable process. I thank my family—mother, Doris, and sisters, Laura and Jennifer—for their ongoing support. To Dr. Thomas Oakland, the finest mentor and role model one could ever have, I am very grateful to you for your support and for your words of wisdom. My thanks go to Dr. Scott Smith, Wanda McPherson, R. David Freeman, and my school psychologist colleagues at the Bartow County School System for their assistance with the RTI forms. My thanks also go to Dr. Laren Winter and my teaching colleagues at Capella University for their dedication to training outstanding future school psychologists. And finally, I send special thanks to the students, parents, and teachers whom I have worked with and learned from over the years. This book is for you.

—Alan W. Brue

INTRODUCTION

COLLABORATION VERSUS CONFRONTATION: SPEAKING THE SAME LANGUAGE

To begin, let's meet Jeremy, a second grader who is not performing as expected academically or socially.

> Jeremy is not doing well in school. He does not complete his seatwork, and he seems to have problems getting along with the other children. His teacher is concerned because he seems to be falling behind. When she meets his parents for the first time at the first parent-teacher interview of the term, they are shocked that he is not doing well academically, given that he is a bright and engaging youngster who seems to gets along very well with everyone he meets.

The teacher is probably a bit nervous about meeting Jeremy's parents and having to give them less-than-positive news. She may be thinking, "What went wrong? Why is this child not succeeding? I must be able to do something that can change the situation. Have I tried everything? Maybe if I just give him more time, he will catch up."

At the same time, Jeremy's parents may also be a bit nervous meeting the teacher for the first time and hearing what she has to say about their child. After they listen to the initial summary, they may be asking themselves, "What went wrong? Why is my child not succeeding? We must be able to do something that can change the situation. Have we tried everything? Maybe if we just wait a bit longer, things will work themselves out."

In this scenario, both Jeremy's teacher and his parents are concerned about Jeremy, who is not doing well. After the initial interview, the parents also share the teacher's concern about Jeremy's school performance. How can all of them best help him?

This book has been inspired by our work with children who have special needs and the parents and teachers who are concerned for their welfare in a system that can become bogged down with legalese language, definitions, and terminology that can confuse and alienate those who most want to do the best thing. The book provides information rarely covered in other special education books, such as an introduction to the assessment process, assessment instruments used by school psychologists, and checklists that can help parents and educators obtain a better understanding of why a child may be experiencing problems.

OVERVIEW OF THE BOOK

The book is divided into five parts.

In Part One, we provide an overview of the different types of disabilities that children may have that qualify them for services under the Individuals with Disabilities Education Improvement Act of 2004 (IDEA 2004) and how these disabilities are assessed or evaluated. Response to intervention (RTI) is a relatively new concept. RTI is a method used to maximize student achievement and reduce problematic behaviors. The process allows schools to identify at-risk students, implement research-based interventions, and monitor student responsiveness to the interventions and progress in school and will be discussed at length in this section.

What do assessments evaluate, and what do they mean? Part Two will provide information about the many types of assessments conducted by school psychologists or private psychologists and explain how to make sense of the results. We discuss assessments for intelligence, achievement, learning, emotion, behavior, and executive functions. We end this part with a sample psychological report and comments on how to interpret and understand its findings.

In Part Three, we provide guidelines for successful interventions that can be used in the classroom or at home for children who experience problems with executive functions, self-esteem or social skills, behavior and discipline, or homework and project completion.

Communication and navigation are the topics of the chapters in Part Four, in which we discuss how to hold meaningful meetings with members of a child's Individualized Education Program (IEP) team and address the new emphasis on transitions in IDEA 2004.

In Part Five, we present the laws and regulations that govern special education and related services for students who qualify. We discuss IDEA 2004 and provide comparisons with services available through Section 504 of the Rehabilitation Act of 1973. We also offer insight about the No Child Left Behind Act, which affects all children.

In the appendixes, readers will find a wealth of information, including lists of educational acronyms and what they mean, helpful Web sites and resources for parents and teachers, and contact information for state departments of special education. The screening checklists for child problems will be a welcomed aid for teachers and parents who have concerns but are not sure whether their concerns warrant further action. We also provide samples of actual plans and forms that are typically part of the special education process. In another appendix, we list procedural safeguards that help ensure that parents of children with special needs know their rights under the law.

PART

One

Understanding Disabilities

CHAPTER

1

DIFFERENT DISABILITIES, COMMON GOALS

In 1975, the U.S. Congress passed the first bill for children with disabilities, called the *Education for All Handicapped Children Act,* which has subsequently been renamed the *Individuals with Disabilities Education Improvement Act* (IDEA 2004). However, in adopting the initial version of the act, many state public educational systems excluded children with physical disabilities and impairments (for example, children who were deaf, blind, or physically handicapped), and children with learning disabilities and emotional disabilities, from special education services. Prior to this time, children with mental retardation and speech and language difficulties had been recognized as needing increased services, but those with learning disabilities were not formally recognized for federal funding until the passing of the law in the mid 1970s. In 2003, approximately 6 million children (roughly 13 percent of all school-age children) were receiving some form of special education services (U.S. Department of Education, 2003).

The number of students with disabilities (ages three to twenty-one) who received special education services in the United States in 1976–77 was 3.7 million (8 percent of the school population); however, in 2005–06, that number had increased to 6.7 million students, representing 14 percent of the school population (U.S. Department of Education, Office of Special Education Programs, 2006). Critics of special education point to this increase as evidence of a tendency to over-identify children with special needs. However, the Association of State

Units on Aging (2005) reports that the number of individuals with disabilities between age twenty-one and sixty-five represents 19 percent of the U.S. population. The fact is that due to technological advances, increased awareness about disabilities, and pharmacological interventions, many individuals survive today and are recognized as disabled who would not have been recognized in the past. Furthermore, comparing actual percentage rates for school-aged children reveals that 10.4 percent of the school-age population were receiving special education in 1980 compared with 13.4 percent in 2003, which represents an increase of only approximately 3.4 percent over a twenty-four-year span.

WHO ARE THE CHILDREN WHO RECEIVE SPECIAL EDUCATION SERVICES?

Children who receive special education and related services represent children between three and twenty-one years of age who have a wide range of difficulties, disabilities, and special needs that interfere with their learning. The following list will provide a profile of characteristics that may apply to children who receive special education services:

- Children with special needs differ in ability levels, strengths and weaknesses, ages, learning styles, pace of learning, and personality or temperament.

- Students who receive special education services represent a wide range of social, economic, and cultural backgrounds.

- All students who receive special education assistance qualify for services based on their unique learning needs.

- Students who receive special education services will be provided with an individualized education program (IEP) that is specifically designed to meet their learning needs by incorporating modifications in instructional design or materials or other adaptive methods.

- In addition to modifications to their learning program, students may also require support services such as speech-language therapy, adaptive physical education, physical or occupational therapy, or counseling services.

- While some children may require minimal adjustments to achieve success, others with chronic health problems or multiple disabilities may require more complex adaptations and accommodations.

- Some students may experience cognitive deficits, such as intellectual delays that may range from mild to severe mental retardation, and therefore may require more time and repetition to consolidate information.

- Other students may not have cognitive impairments; however, they may experience impaired learning due to a variety of processing problems that interfere with their perception, reception, expression of information, or ability to recall information.

- Some students may require adaptations that accommodate their physical disabilities, such as wheelchairs or other devices, in order to improve their mobility in the classroom.

- Other students may require technical and assisted devices to adapt the educational program to sensory impairments such as vision or hearing problems.

- For some students, emotional or behavioral problems can be a barrier to learning and school success.

- While some students may require special education services for a limited amount of time in order to reduce the gap between their academic performance and their grade level, other students may require special education services throughout their school enrollment.

Although most people support the notion of special education services to improve educational opportunities for children with disabilities, there continues to be controversy and discussion about how the process should be funded and the best way to deliver services and monitor the success of programs.

WHAT SCHOOL ADMINISTRATORS ARE SAYING AND THE QUESTIONS THEY ARE ASKING ABOUT SPECIAL EDUCATION

A Public Agenda survey of over 850 superintendents and principals (Farkas, Johnson, Duffett, Foleno, & Foley, 2001) revealed that in times of increasing need and accountability (teacher shortages and high teacher turnover, overcrowded schools, higher academic standards) and decreasing budgets, administrators struggle to balance the needs of special education and regular education programs. In addition to voicing financial concerns, administrators have criticized the bureaucratic process of administering special education (which has become extremely paperwork-heavy and time-consuming) and the need for increased research to determine whether special education programs are actually effective. One of the major questions revealed by the survey was whether special education programs are a dumping ground for difficult students.

WHY DO WE NEED SPECIAL EDUCATION?

Critics of special education have asked some of the following questions: Couldn't we just get rid of special education if teachers were better trained to work with all children and give more consistent discipline? Would special education be needed if parents did a better job of disciplining their children? If special education is working, then why are so many children still enrolled? (Johnson, Duffett, Farkas, & Wilson, 2002).

By the time you finish reading this book, we hope that you will have found the answers to the questions posed in the box and any other questions that you may have. As you will see, administrators, teachers, and parents are all somewhat frustrated with the special education process, which means that in understanding how the process works, it is important to see the different concerns that each of the players brings to the table in order to create the best possible opportunities for a child. While some critics of special education are prepared to throw the baby out with the bathwater, others suggest shifting the emphasis from the process to the results. Horn and Tynan (2001) suggest that it is time to make special education special again by working to improve outcomes for children in special education and empowering students through compensatory mechanisms that will allow them to become more successful in regular education. For those of us who work in special education, that is always the goal. The movement toward response to intervention (RTI), which will be discussed in Chapter Four, is another attempt to focus on early intervention strategies that can increase opportunities for success in the regular classroom in a shorter period of time than would be required if a full assessment were necessary.

Another question that critics have asked is why special education classrooms are populated mostly by male students. Unfortunately, being male is a risk factor for many disabilities and a significantly higher proportion of males than females have attention deficit disorder, learning disabilities, oppositional defiant disorder, and conduct disorder. As a result, it would not be surprising to see more males than females in special education programs. Of the parents surveyed in the Public Agenda report described in the next section (Johnson et al., 2002), two-thirds had a male child in special education and only one-third had a female child in special education.

WHAT PARENTS ARE SAYING ABOUT SPECIAL EDUCATION AND THE QUESTIONS THEY ARE ASKING

Researchers from the Public Agenda report (Johnson et al., 2002) surveyed over 500 parents of children with special needs to obtain an in-depth look at how parents perceive the experiences and special education services that their children receive from the public education system. Results from that survey suggest the following:

- The majority of parents did not side with the critics who believe that educators are too eager to place children in special education; on the contrary, over half complained that information about special education was hard to come by and that schools were slow to volunteer the information.

- Once their child was in a special education program, 84 percent of parents felt that their child's teacher really cared about their child; 77 percent felt a part of their child's special education team; and almost 70 percent felt that their child's teachers were knowledgeable about their child's disability and how to work with it. A majority also felt that teachers were capable of managing their child's behavior and discipline.

- A majority of parents reported that their child spent the better part of the day in the regular class, regardless of the extent of disability, and most were supportive of this arrangement because it satisfied social and academic needs. However, parents also voiced concern that for special needs children, academics were often emphasized at the expense of social development, which is very important for these children.

- Parents were mixed in their feelings about how children with special needs were accommodated during standardized or statewide testing and exit exams. Many felt that if accommodations were not provided, their child would never pass.

- Many parents were less than satisfied with the number of services available and felt that they had to persist in order for services to be provided. Parents indicated a number of stumbling blocks and barriers within the special education process, including the process itself, paperwork, bureaucracy, and difficulty in getting help quickly.

WHAT SPECIAL EDUCATION TEACHERS ARE SAYING ABOUT THEIR PROFESSION

The Council for Exceptional Children (CEC) conducted an Internet survey during 1998–99 to obtain perceptions of special education teachers about the status of special education programs in their schools. Almost 200 teachers from thirty-two states responded to the survey. On average, the respondents had been teaching students with disabilities for five and a half years and had a caseload of twenty students. A majority reported that they were spending increasingly more time on paperwork and meetings and less time for teaching their students. A large majority (83 percent) indicated that they did not have enough time to spend on each individual student. Many also complained about IEPs and the legalese of IEP forms, and teachers in both general education and special education said they wanted easier access to modified textbooks for students with disabilities rather than having to spend time adapting existing materials for individual students enrolled in special education programs.

Over 1,500 special education teachers responded to a more recent survey conducted by the Texas Center for Educational Research (TCER) in 2006. Educators who responded had an average caseload of twenty-five students, the majority of which (57.9 percent) were categorized as learning disabled; smaller percentages of students had disabilities in areas of emotional problems (9 percent), mental retardation (7.6 percent), autism (4.3 percent), speech and language (4.1 percent), and developmental delay (1.3 percent). Thirty-five percent of respondents had a master's degree or higher. In response to a severe shortage of special education teachers nationally and high turnover rates in the profession, the survey looked at how special education teachers felt about their job and special education in particular. Although the respondents were generally satisfied, approximately one-third of the respondents stated that they planned to leave their positions in the following year.

Why would special education teachers be inclined to leave their profession? Frustration with paperwork and non-teaching responsibilities were high on the list of reasons. The special education teachers who responded to the TCER survey indicated that they spent an average of 57.9 hours a month (approximately 1.4 weeks per month) engaged in non-teaching activities (for example, planning, paperwork, meetings, and committees). In addition, they specified other needs:

- More release time for professional development
- Adequate classroom space and equipment

- Access to reliable computers in order to complete paperwork

- Adequate support regarding legal issues

- Opportunities to meet with other special education teachers in the district

For the majority of special education teachers, elements that would increase job satisfaction included more time to work with students; improved classroom facilities; and a supportive school environment. Supportive school environments were described as having

- Teacher involvement in the decision-making process

- A campus administrator who provides information and advice and helps resolve classroom issues

- Policies that are consistently applied

- A principal who understands the challenges of working in special education

- Evaluative feedback to improve teaching

- An administrator who considers student and teacher capabilities when placing students

- A principal who is knowledgeable about special education laws

As a result of their survey, TCER made two recommendations on how to improve special education services and the quality of the school environment:

1. Find ways to inform parents and general education teachers about special education topics.

2. Create more opportunities for teachers to spend uninterrupted time with their students in adequate classroom facilities.

CHILDREN WITH DISABILITIES IN EDUCATION: ACHIEVING COMMON GOALS

As we have seen in this chapter, administrators, teachers, and educators all share the common goal of providing the best possible educational opportunities for children; however, it is also clear that special education can be a complex and frustrating process for all concerned. For parents, obtaining information about special education services available in their child's school is often a major stumbling block. For special education teachers, working in a school environment in which administrators and general education teachers are aware and supportive of special education could make the difference in whether they remain as special education teachers or leave the profession. Special education teachers want more time to work with children individually. Administrators want to be able to hire high-quality special education teachers and retain them in the face of high turnover rates in the profession. And in the middle of it all is the special needs child, who just wants to learn and be successful in school.

In the next chapter, we will provide an overview of the different disabilities that qualify a child for special education services and how these disabilities are labeled and defined by educators. In Chapter Three, we will provide in-depth discussion of some of the more common disabilities, such as learning disabilities, attention deficit hyperactivity disorder, autism, Asperger's disorder, emotional disorders (including bipolar disorder), and behavioral disorders; how these disabilities are defined and labeled by clinicians who may be involved in helping a student; and suggestions for how to assist students with disabilities at home and at school. In Chapter Four, we will discuss response to intervention and how it works.

CHAPTER

2

WHAT ARE THE DIFFERENT DISABILITIES, AND HOW ARE THEY CLASSIFIED?

Thirteen different categories of disabilities are recognized by IDEA 2004. If children experience difficulties that fall within one of the thirteen categories and their education is significantly affected as a result of their disability, then they may qualify for special education and related services.

REASONS FOR NAMING THE PROBLEM

One of the goals in education is to include children with special needs in the regular education classroom as much as possible. Therefore, children with special needs will most likely have ongoing contact with regular education teachers, and these teachers may not have experience in working with children who have a particular disorder. Usually, a psychologist or school psychologist conducts an assessment and diagnoses a child to determine which diagnostic category best describes the child's problems. The child may have an emotional problem, a learning disability, an intellectual disability, or some other disabling condition recognized by IDEA 2004. Every child is different, and even children whose diagnosis falls within the same category can be very different from one another.

But just what do these terms mean? Let's take a child with an emotional disorder, for example. The term *emotionally disturbed* does not really provide a great deal of information about that child. If the problem is of an emotional nature, it could be anything from a specific phobia to depression—any emotional problem that interferes with the child's ability to learn. However, the term *emotionally disturbed* does name the category under which the child will receive services. That category, which is directly related to a diagnosis such as depression or generalized anxiety disorder, helps others to understand some of the child's problems and helps school personnel better understand the child's needs. Naming a child's problem and giving it a label often means giving the child access to and assistance from a variety of school personnel.

The names of the thirteen categories are presented in Table 2.1, along with the different types of school personnel who might be involved with the child. Use this information only as a guide, because some school districts, particularly those that are small, do not employ all these personnel. As you can see, children with complex problems may require support from a wide variety of resources. When parents come to a school meeting, it is sometimes overwhelming to them when all the individuals involved in helping their child attend the meeting to report on the child's progress. Having an understanding of what to expect and knowing that everyone is there to help the child can help alleviate these feelings.

DIDYOUKNOW

School psychologists have the highest entry-level education of any school personnel. To be credentialed in their state, they must acquire an advanced graduate degree, obtain supervised experience in the schools, complete a supervised, full-time, one-year internship, and pass a state or national examination (or both). A school psychologist may also be a Nationally Certified School Psychologist (NCSP), board-certified by the American Board of Professional Psychology, or licensed for private practice.

TABLE 2.1   WHAT'S IN A LABEL?

Disability	School Personnel Who May Be Involved
Autism	Regular education teacher, special education teacher, autism specialist, school psychologist, speech-language pathologist, occupational therapist, physical therapist, assistive technology specialist, adaptive physical education teacher
Deaf-blindness	Regular education teacher, special education teacher, vision teacher, school psychologist, assistive technology specialist
Deafness	Regular education teacher, special education teacher, school psychologist, assistive technology specialist, interpreter if sign language is used
Emotional disturbance	Regular education teacher, special education teacher, school psychologist, school counselor, behavioral specialist
Hearing impairment	Regular education teacher, special education teacher, audiologist, speech-language pathologist, interpreter, school psychologist
Intellectual disability	Regular education teacher, special education teacher, school psychologist, speech-language pathologist, occupational therapist, physical therapist, assistive technology specialist, adaptive physical education teacher
Multiple disabilities	Regular education teacher, special education teacher, school psychologist, school counselor, speech-language pathologist, occupational therapist, physical therapist, assistive technology specialist, school nurse, adaptive physical education teacher
Orthopedic impairment	Regular education teacher, special education teacher, physical therapist, occupational therapist, school psychologist, adaptive physical education teacher
Other health impairment	Regular education teacher, special education teacher, school psychologist, school nurse
Specific learning disability	Regular education teacher, special education teacher, disability school psychologist, occupational therapist, assistive technology specialist
Speech or language impairment	Regular education teacher, special education teacher, speech-language pathologist, school psychologist
Traumatic brain injury	Regular education teacher, special education teacher, school psychologist, school nurse, occupational therapist, adaptive physical education teacher
Visual impairment (including blindness)	Regular education teacher, special education teacher, vision teacher, assistive technology specialist, mobility instructor, school psychologist, adaptive physical education teacher

NEGATIVE ASPECTS OF CATEGORIZATION

Let's address some of the drawbacks of categorizing a child's problems. Some argue that there are many reasons why we should not place children's academic or behavior problems in specific categories; we will address some of those concerns in this section.

Lowered Teacher Expectations

Teacher expectations may be lowered for a child who is identified as having a disability. Low expectations can turn into a self-fulfilling prophecy in which a teacher with low expectations for a child's performance and growth discourages that child. As a result, children may achieve at a lower level. Children with a learning disability, for example, may be perceived as not being smart, being lazy, difficult to teach, and unable to learn a lot of information. While children with a learning disability require special teaching techniques and accommodations such as teacher notes, additional time to complete assignments, or a peer tutor, these changes to their program do not mean these children are necessarily difficult to teach. The truth is that children with a learning disability *can* learn a lot of information, but it may take them longer to learn it since they may process information either differently or more slowly than children without a disability.

You can help your child by making sure that the teacher's expectations remain high. In Chapter Sixteen, we'll talk about the contents of an individualized education program (IEP), which will create yearly goals for the child. If the child does not qualify for special education services, we encourage parents and teachers to get together on a regular basis to ensure that the expectations that are set for the child are appropriate and that home and school have the same set of expectations. Throughout our book, we will discuss ways to maximize parent-teacher communication.

DIDYOUKNOW

The book *Pygmalion in the Classroom: Teacher Expectation and Pupils' Intellectual Development,* written by Robert Rosenthal and Lenore Jacobson (2003), states that when teachers expect children to do well and show intellectual growth, they do, but when teachers do not have these expectations, performance and growth are not encouraged as much and may actually be discouraged in a number of ways. This effect is known as the Pygmalion phenomenon.

A Label's Long-Lasting Effects

Categorizing a problem and giving it a name, or label, sometimes results in that name lasting a long time, sometimes for life. Even when it no longer applies, the person may still be perceived by herself or others as having the characteristics associated with that problem. While most children who are blind or intellectually disabled, for example, will retain these problems into adulthood, a child with a health impairment may not. These children may outgrow their impairment and no longer show signs of their medical condition as an adult. In a similar manner, children with a learning disability may learn to cope with their disorder to the extent that its impact on them is limited.

Insufficient Time to Rule Out Other Problems

Labeling a child's problem too quickly may prevent a school psychologist or a physician from investigating other potential problems. For example, many disorders look like attention deficit hyperactivity disorder (ADHD). Problems such as anxiety, depression, or a learning disability can all resemble ADHD. While it is possible to have ADHD and some of these disorders at the same time, it is also possible that problems of inattention and concentration may have other causes. A thorough evaluation by a school psychologist is needed to determine what is potentially wrong with a child and decide how the school can help the child learn in the best possible way. The school psychologist may ask a parent, teacher, and even the child to complete questionnaires to assist in ruling out certain problems. In addition, a physician should be consulted to rule out medical issues as the cause of the problem.

Child's Reaction to the Problem

Most children don't like to be different. They don't like to stand out in any way, whether in their clothing, their hairstyle, or the car their parent uses to drive them to school. A child's knowledge that he has a disability can lead to certain self-perceptions, such as becoming self-conscious or lowering self-esteem or becoming anxious about being different. Some parents are torn between telling their child about the disability and protecting the child by withholding information. Other parents discuss the problem with the child so that he understands why he is struggling and that he may have to work a little harder than his peers. The truth is that most children know they are having problems, so protecting them from knowing isn't really an issue. We feel that it is important to talk to your child about his disability, and if you are not sure what to say, ask the school psychologist for advice. It's okay to name it. Children are like most people, who feel better if they leave a doctor's office with a diagnosis rather than thinking they have a mysterious illness.

Explaining the nature of the disability will help your child to understand why he will be getting extra help in school, while his friends may not be. Assure the child that he has not done anything wrong. Explain that each child learns differently and that some children may learn more slowly than others or have problems with remembering or understanding if they are distracted or if feelings get in the way. You can also mention that academic ability is like athletic or musical ability; some children have it, while others do not, and even those who have it must work hard to improve. Children who do not understand the nature of their disability run the risk of thinking that they are stupid or bad, and this can often lead to great frustration and lowered self-esteem. Helpful ways to bolster a child's self esteem can be found in Chapter Thirteen.

It is important that the child understand that teachers and parents are there to help inside and outside of the classroom. Sometimes having the child read a book about children who overcome obstacles (or reading one to him) can be helpful in motivating the child not to give up.

Parent Concerns

When a child is found to have a disability, parents sometimes feel ashamed and think they are the cause of the problem. Some disabilities have a genetic basis; others occur because of disease or accidents. Regardless of the cause, if your child has a disability, there is no reason for you to blame yourself. Many parents feel a variety of emotions when they find out that their child has a disability. Sadness is the emotion we encounter most often because, depending on the disability, parents realize that the vision they had for their child's future has been altered or dramatically changed. If you feel this way, we want you to know that you are not alone. And so that you do not feel alone, we suggest that you seek out a support group in your area. If there isn't one, you may find one on the Internet. We believe that a support group can provide you with comfort from other parents who are experiencing the same feelings that you are. These parents may have been working with teachers and other professionals for many years and probably have a wealth of information that may benefit you. You may learn about interventions that have worked for others, and while they are not guaranteed to work for you or your child, they may be worth trying. We will also include our own recommendations for interventions later in the book. If you are interested in a support group, some are listed in Appendix H. You may also wish to contact one of the many organizations listed in Appendix H, since they often provide referrals to support groups. We hope that you will take advantage of all they have to offer.

Regular Education Teacher Concerns

Some teachers, especially if they have not previously taught a child with a given disability, may feel somewhat responsible for a child's difficulties with learning. They may blame themselves for not finding the right way to teach a child in order to help the child learn. They may be reluctant to report a child's problems because they are still trying to find a solution themselves. In such cases, teachers should be encouraged to discuss the difficulty with an administrator or a special education resource teacher in order to obtain input and advice. An administrator may sit in on a class and provide valuable insight that will help the teacher in the initial stages while a child is awaiting an evaluation. Teachers may be frustrated when a child is not completing the work because they may be afraid of holding the rest of their class back, given a curriculum that needs to be covered in order to meet their annual goals. It is very important for the regular teacher to work with both the special education teacher and the child's parents to develop consistent expectations for the child and to provide a common set of goals. In Part Three, we also provide numerous resources for teachers to address problems with executive functions, for improving behavior and discipline problems, and for increasing a child's self-esteem and social skills when working with children who have special needs.

POSITIVE ASPECTS OF CATEGORIZATION: THE THIRTEEN CATEGORIES OF DISABILITIES

Categorizing a child's problem helps school personnel to understand and effectively meet the child's needs. The more specific the understanding is, the more specific the intervention can be. Children with a disability may require the services of specific school personnel such as an occupational therapist or a physical therapist. These personnel can work together with teachers to provide an atmosphere that is conducive to the best learning situation possible for a child.

Let's take a look at the special education categories and discuss some of the accommodations or programs that may be available in each area.

AUTISM

Children with autism require a structured, individualized curriculum that emphasizes functional skills, language and communication, and behavior management.

Speech therapy is often necessary, and occupational therapy (OT) and physical therapy (PT) may be needed if fine or gross motor weaknesses are noted. The child with autism likely will have a case manager who has experience in working with children with autism, because it takes some coordination of the various specialties to provide adequate services to these children.

DIDYOUKNOW

Until recently, the Centers for Disease Control and Prevention (CDC) have reported that the exact number of children in the United States who currently have autism or a related disorder is unknown. More recently, however, CDC (2009) reports have suggested that more and more children are being identified as having an autistic spectrum disorder (ASD). The recent CDC findings will be addressed in Chapter Three. Recent figures suggest that nearly 80,000 children and adults aged six through twenty-one are classified as having autism under IDEA. You can read more about the report at http://www.cdc.ncbddd/autism/.

Deaf-Blindness

Children who are deaf and blind require assistance with orientation and mobility. This special training helps children to learn how to move around safely, efficiently, and independently. An example of training in orientation would be helping a child understand how to navigate around the house or classroom. Mobility, on the other hand, involves actually moving. Once a child has become oriented to a home or classroom, getting from one place to another becomes the goal. This can be accomplished by crawling, walking, or using a wheelchair.

Deafness

Children who are deaf may need a sign language interpreter. Many children who are deaf use sign language to receive information and to communicate. What goes on in the classroom is conveyed by an interpreter to the child, and what is expressed by the child is conveyed to the teacher and other children. Other accommodations may include lecture notes, visual and written instructions, written exams, visual behavioral cues, or amplification equipment.

Emotional Disturbance

Children with an emotional disturbance may have a variety of diagnoses. Those with anxiety, depression, schizophrenia, or bipolar disorder fall within this category. While many children with emotional disturbance do well in the general education classroom, some of them have severe behavioral difficulties that require a more restrictive setting. They may have frequent outbursts, throw chairs or desks, or be physically or verbally aggressive. In cases of severe behavior problems, it is best that children be in a setting that is very structured and includes fewer peers. Some children with emotional disturbance may require individual or group counseling.

Hearing Impairment

Children with a hearing impairment who don't meet the definition of deafness still need assistance—for example, auditory training, instruction in oral and total communication (the use of all available means of communication), or hearing aid training. While these children may have fewer communication problems than a child who is deaf, they may still have difficulties because of the hearing loss. Accommodations may include lecture notes, visual and written instructions, written exams, and visual behavioral cues.

Intellectual Disability (Formerly Mental Retardation)

Recently, the American Association on Mental Retardation (AAMR) changed its name to the American Association on Intellectual and Developmental Disabilities (AAIDD, 2007). The change reflects the intent to replace the term *mental retardation* (MR) with *intellectual disability* (ID), which is the more common term used throughout Europe and Canada. However, the term *mental retardation* can still be found in major sources of classification, including IDEA 2004 and the *Diagnostic and Statistical Manual of Mental Disorders* (DSM-IV-TR; American Psychiatric Association, 2000). We will use the term *intellectual disability* (ID) throughout this book to refer to both designations. Children with an intellectual disability will have significant weaknesses in both intellectual functioning and adaptive behavior. According to the DSM-IV-TR, children with an intellectual disability fall in one of four categories: mild, moderate, severe, or profound. It may be necessary to implement significant modifications to the general curriculum, depending on the severity of the disorder. Adaptive skills, which are skills needed to live, work, and play in the community, include self-care (dressing, toileting, bathing), communicating with others, social skills, and academic skills.

Children with an intellectual disability may qualify for participation in a work program or vocational training.

> ## DIDYOUKNOW
>
> Approximately 2 percent of the population meet the criteria for ID, although 85 percent of those with ID will fall within the mild range. You can read more about intellectual and developmental disabilities and syndromes of congenital abnormalities that are known to be associated with an intellectual disability on Medline Plus at http://www.nlm.nih.gov/medlineplus/developmentaldisabilities.html.

Multiple Disabilities

Children with multiple disabilities have special needs depending on the nature of the different disabilities that exist. These children often have extreme educational needs that require the coordination of special education services involving various school personnel and health professionals.

Orthopedic Impairment

Children with an orthopedic impairment may have a range of needs. An orthopedic impairment may be caused by a congenital anomaly (something unusual at birth), disease, or other causes. A missing limb or clubfoot would be an example of a congenital anomaly. Bone tuberculosis is an example of an orthopedic anomaly caused by disease, while cerebral palsy or an amputation would fall in the "other" category. The services and expertise of a physical therapist are critical in assessing a child's continuing needs and tracking progress, which should occur on a regular basis.

Other Health Impairment

Children in the "Other Health Impairment" category are affected by a chronic or acute health problem. Many disorders fall in this category, including ADHD, asthma, epilepsy, leukemia, sickle cell anemia, and diabetes. It is difficult to suggest typical interventions because the range of disorders is so broad, but accommodations might include permission to complete tests and assignments in a small-group setting, extra time to complete tests or assignments, or permission to make up work when school is missed for medical appointments.

Specific Learning Disability

Children with a learning disability have a significant weakness in one or more of seven areas: reading, reading comprehension, math calculation, math reasoning (solving problems), writing, listening comprehension (understanding what is heard), or speaking. These children need extra help, support, and encouragement. They often have difficulty learning at the same pace as others. Children with a learning disability may need additional time to complete assignments, a quiet place to work, abbreviated assignments, or tutoring. The accommodations needed will depend on the age of the child and the severity of the disability. Unlike students who have intellectual impairments that cause global difficulties in learning, children in this category have at least average intelligence but encounter academic problems in "specific" areas.

Speech or Language Impairment

Children with a speech or language impairment are likely to be diagnosed with some type of communication disorder. They may have problems with stuttering or articulation, or they may have a noticeable language or voice impairment. In the schools, speech-language pathologists (SLPs), also called *speech therapists* or *speech teachers,* work with children who have a variety of speech and language disorders. The disorders may be congenital or acquired and may include feeding and swallowing disorders in infants and children, language-based learning disabilities, selective mutism, or right-hemisphere brain damage. SLPs may help children to attain normal speech patterns, eliminate a lisp, speak more intelligibly, or learn to retrieve words more easily.

DIDYOUKNOW

Speech-language pathologists who hold their "C's" (Certificate of Clinical Competence) must possess a graduate degree, perform supervised clinical observation and practice, complete a clinical fellowship, and pass a national examination.

Traumatic Brain Injury

Children with a traumatic brain injury (TBI) have an acquired brain injury that affects specific parts of the brain. The external physical force that caused an open or closed head injury may have resulted in total or partial functional disability. Depending on the part of the brain that was injured, there may be impairments in functions such as cognition, language, speech, memory, attention, reasoning, abstract thinking, judgment, motor abilities, or psychosocial behavior. The specific personnel needed and accommodations implemented to assist a student with TBI will depend largely on the severity of the head injury and which functions are impaired.

Visual Impairment (Including Blindness)

Children with a visual impairment or blindness may have partial sight or be completely blind. While some children are born with an impairment or blindness, others have acquired it through an accident or disease. Children with visual impairment may need books and textbooks on tape, Braille books, training in computer and typing skills, or assistance in getting around school. Teacher assistants and peer helpers may work with visually impaired children, especially those who are younger or who have recently become disabled.

FOR MORE INFORMATION

An appropriate diagnosis allows parents and teachers to access a wealth of information, including recent research and suggestions for effective interventions. A list of organizations that you can contact for more information is available in Appendix H. If you have access to the Internet, visiting an organization's Web site opens a world of information to you, free of charge. You will find tips, resource guides, treatment suggestions, and other helpful resources to assist you in better understanding a child's diagnosis and particular needs. For example, the Web site of the Council for Exceptional Children (CEC: http://www.cec.sped.org) includes an Information Center on Disabilities and Gifted Education, where you will find fact sheets, information on research-based interventions, links to discussion groups, links to relevant laws, and more.

DIDYOUKNOW

The Council for Exceptional Children (CEC) is the largest international professional organization dedicated to improving educational outcomes for individuals with exceptionalities, children with disabilities, and the gifted.

CHAPTER

3

SPECIFICS ABOUT SPECIFIC DISABILITIES

Understanding a child's disability begins with the recognition that disabilities are classified in various ways by different sources.

THE DIFFERENT WAYS THAT DISABILITIES ARE CLASSIFIED

As we discussed briefly in Chapter One and will discuss in more detail in Chapters Eighteen, Nineteen, and Twenty, federal law classifies disabilities according to different laws and acts: the Americans with Disabilities Act of 1990 (ADA); the Individuals with Disabilities Education Improvement Act of 2004 (IDEA 2004); and Section 504 of the Rehabilitation Act of 1973. Title I of the Americans with Disabilities Act (ADA) prohibits employment discrimination on the basis of disability. ADA is a civil rights law that was developed to protect individuals with disabilities by prohibiting discrimination in employment or public services and may affect areas such as education, housing, transportation, and employment. According to ADA, an individual is considered disabled if they have either a physical or mental impairment that severely limits major life activities. Accommodations under ADA may include but are not limited to alterations such as redesigned equipment or structural areas to ensure reasonable access to facilities (for example, wheelchair ramps) or information, such as telecommunication devices for individuals who are deaf (for example, telecommunication devices for the deaf: TDY).

DIDYOUKNOW

The ADA Amendments Act became effective January 1, 2009. The Equal Employment Opportunity Commission (EEOC) is responsible for revising existing federal regulations to ensure that they comply with ADA. To this end, the National Center for Learning Disabilities (NCLD) is recommending that a clinical diagnosis of specific learning disabilities (SLD) or attention deficit hyperactivity disorder (ADHD) by definition refers to individuals who are substantially limited in a major life activity and as such should be considered an impairment that would consistently meet the definition of disability and thus confer eligibility to receive accommodations in the workplace and when taking standardized tests such as the LSAT, GRE, or GMAT.

Under Section 504 of the Rehabilitation Act of 1973, a handicapping condition exists if there is a physical or mental impairment that significantly limits major life activities. *Major life activities* include walking, seeing, performing manual tasks, speaking, breathing, learning, and working. Section 504 pertains to adults in the workforce or school-age youth (that is, those under twenty-two years old). Under Section 504, ADHD could be considered a handicapping condition.

Unlike ADA, IDEA 2004 specifically defines disabilities in terms of *educationally handicapping conditions*. Children and youth between three and twenty-one years of age who have had an individualized evaluation can be deemed eligible for special education and related services by a multidisciplinary team if they qualify for services in one or more of thirteen designated categories. In addition, children aged three through nine years who evidence developmental delays may also qualify for services.

Under IDEA 2004, *special education* refers to instruction that is specifically designed to meet a child's educational needs on the basis of the child's unique disability. *Related services*, such as speech-language, physical, or occupational therapy, can also be provided at no cost to parents if it is determined that these related services are required in order to help the child benefit from special education services.

Infants and toddlers with disabilities (birth through two years of age) and their families receive support services through an early intervention system. IDEA 2004 supports early intervention for infants and toddlers with disabilities due to developmental delays (in cognitive, physical, communication, social-emotional, or adaptive functioning) or for those who have a diagnosed physical or mental handicapping condition. As was noted previously in the discussion of intellectual disability, adaptive functioning can include daily living and self-help skills, such as a child's ability to feed or dress himself.

Developmental Delays

IDEA 2004 allows each state and local educational agency (that is, a school district) to classify children between the ages of three and nine as *developmentally delayed* without having to specify one of the thirteen disability categories. Under IDEA 2004, the classification of developmental delay can be retained until a child's ninth birthday; however, this is at the discretion of the state educational authority.

ADDITIONAL INFORMATION ON FIVE CHALLENGING DISABILITIES

In Chapter Two, we introduced the thirteen categories of disabilities specified by IDEA 2004. Although the categories are consistent across states, each state may have slightly different ways of determining eligibility under each of these categories. For example, while all states require evidence of below-average IQ and impaired adaptive functioning as part of the eligibility criteria for an intellectual disability (ID), the actual scores used to determine whether a child qualifies for the program may vary from state to state. In addition, even though a child may meet criteria based on IQ and adaptive functioning, if his academic skills do not fall within a specified range, he still may not qualify for services.

DIDYOUKNOW

Children who have an intellectual disability may be classified with different names in different school districts or states, depending on the name of the program—for example, educable mentally handicapped (EMH), educable mental retardation (EMR), or intellectual disability (ID) are all possible classifications based on program titles. Also, in some states, an IQ below 70 is required for the designation, while in other states, a child with an IQ of 75 or even 80 may qualify in this area.

Educational and Clinical Classifications: Differences Between Systems

Educators use educational classifications of disabilities that focus on how a disability will affect a child's ability to learn, with the goal of developing an individualized education program (IEP) to address specific learning needs. Mental health practitioners, however, classify disabilities according to clinical criteria outlined in the *Diagnostic and Statistical Manual of Mental Disorders (DSM-IV-TR)* developed by the American Psychiatric Association (APA, 2000) and are more concerned with diagnosis as a means of identification and appropriate treatment planning to resolve mental health issues.

In the remainder of this chapter, we will focus on five of the thirteen categories of exceptionality—autism, emotional disturbance, ID, SLD, and ADHD, which encompass some of the most challenging and complex concerns for parents and teachers. We will provide information about prevalence rates, associated features, and mental health issues for these disorders.

Autism

Autism is a neurological disorder listed in the *DSM-IV-TR* (American Psychiatric Association, 2000) under the main category of pervasive developmental disorders (PDD).

Defining Criteria   IDEA 2004 recognizes three primary features of autism that result in severe and pervasive difficulties in the majority of daily activities, including learning:

1.   Restricted range of social interaction

2.   Impaired communication skills

3.   Persistent pattern of stereotypical behaviors (for example, rocking, hand flapping), interests, and activities (for example, nonfunctional routines, such as lining up objects or spinning parts of objects)

An expanded list of these symptom categories is available in Appendix B. Onset of autism is usually evident in one of these three areas before a child reaches three years of age.

Prevalence and Cause   Autism is one of five disorders classified under the category of pervasive developmental disorders (PDD) in the *DSM-IV-TR* (APA, 2000). According to the *DSM-IV-TR,* autism is a rare disorder with the "median rate" of children with autistic disorder being five cases per 10,000 with rates raging from "2 to 20 cases per 10,000 individuals" (p. 73). The disorder is far more prevalent (four times more common) in males than females. However, results of a survey conducted in 2006 by the Autism and Developmental Disabilities Monitoring (ADDM) Network sponsored by the Centers for Disease Control (CDC, 2009) reported a prevalence rate of 1 percent or one child in 110 for children in the United States as having an autistic spectrum disorder (ASD) based on the eleven sites sampled across the United States.

DIDYOUKNOW

The category of autistic spectrum disorders (ASD) used in the ADDM survey (CDC, 2009) included children who met criteria in the *DSM-IV-TR* (APA, 2000) for autistic disorder, Asperger's disorder, or pervasive developmental disorder–not otherwise specified (PDD–NOS). The category of PDD–NOS is reserved for individuals who do not fully meet the criteria for one of the other types of PDD. This category has come under criticism due the fact that children can be diagnosed in this category if they only have "some" symptoms of autism (Scheeringa, 2001).

The majority of children with autism (approximately 75 percent) have some degree of intellectual disability. Others who are referred to as having High Functioning Autism will score above an IQ 70. Significant controversy exists regarding how children develop autism, and no single gene or genetic link has been established.

Associated Characteristics   Children with autism must demonstrate a number of symptoms in each of the four areas described:

Language and communication skills. Language is likely delayed, if present at all, with minimal use of nonverbal communication (for example, pointing, directed eye gaze). If language exists, it is rarely used to initiate or sustain communication with others. Speech patterns are odd (for example, monotone) or demonstrate echolalia (repeating what someone else has said). Children with high-functioning autism (HFA) may "talk at others" on topics of high interest to themselves while ignoring their audience.

Play, imitation, and social interaction. Children with autism often seem to be in a world of their own and do not spontaneously participate in social interaction. Youngsters with autism do not develop age-appropriate play (for example, make-believe) or peer relationships and are often more intent on playing with parts of objects (spinning a wheel on a car) than interacting with others. Instead of forming attachments to people, children with autism may form strong attachments to inanimate objects, such as a plastic spoon or button.

Stereotypical and repetitive behavior patterns. Children with autism are often preoccupied with objects, repetitive movements or activities, or rigid adherence to routines and rituals that have little function in the real world, such as spending considerable time lining up objects (for example, toy cars) in a row. Often, it is difficult to disengage these children from their intense focus on repetitive motor movements such as hand flapping or twirling (called *self-stimulation*), which prevents them from engaging in their social world.

Children with autism are often highly resistant to any changes in their schedule or routines, regardless of how minor. While some professionals believe that autistic children hold on to the predictable because they are overwhelmed by external stimuli, others believe that these behavior patterns result from children being under-responsive to their environment.

Learning and development. Skill development can be uneven, and some children with autism demonstrate higher-functioning skills in specific areas, exhibiting hyperlexia (reading at an advanced rate) or an unusual ability to perform mathematical calculations. These skills are sometimes referred to as *savant skills*. Even when children with autism have elevated skill levels, they often lack comprehension; for example, a child might be able to perform calculations but have no number sense.

DIDYOUKNOW

Behavioral problems in children with autism can interfere with learning. Problems sometimes include hyperactivity; difficulties with maintaining attention; aggressiveness; self-injurious behaviors; or temper tantrums, especially in younger children.

Autism and Asperger's Disorder   Asperger's disorder shares deficits in two of the three areas noted for autism: impaired social reciprocity and stereotypical and repetitive movements. However, one criterion for Asperger's disorder is that an individual does not have language, cognitive, or adaptive delays. As a result, children with Asperger's disorder often score well above children with autism on IQ tests, and some may have an above-average or superior IQ. Although Asperger's disorder is listed as a separate disorder under pervasive developmental disorders in the *DSM-IV-TR,* the disorder is not mentioned by IDEA 2004. Because their language skills are not impaired and they function at a higher level, children with Asperger's disorder are often diagnosed at a much older age than those with autism. Because Asperger's disorder shares similar features to autism but at a much higher level of functioning, many clinicians prefer to think of these two disorders as the *autistic spectrum disorders (ASD),* in order to reflect the idea of a continuum with higher and lower levels of functioning.

Educational Planning   Educational programs for children with autism emphasize early intervention and focus on increasing skills in communication and social, behavioral, and adaptive functioning. Often, it may be necessary to address behavioral issues before an educational plan can be put in place. A *functional behavioral assessment* (FBA) is often helpful in pinpointing behaviors to be targeted for change. A functional behavioral assessment sometimes uses a chart referred to as an ABC chart (for antecedents, behaviors, and consequences), which shows what triggers the behavior (antecedent) and what the outcome is (consequence). Once problem behaviors are identified, a *behavioral intervention plan* (BIP) can be developed to help alter behavior patterns and develop more appropriate ways of responding. Examples of an FBA and a BIP are presented in Table 3.1.

Children with autistic features represent a wide range of functioning. Therefore, no single program or educational plan will meet the needs of all children with autism. However, all programs should emphasize the importance of consistently reinforcing common goals in the home and at school. A summary of key intervention strategies and the reasons that these strategies are important is available in Table 3.2.

What the Research Says About Treatment   At a minimum, successful early intervention should include individualized and systematic instruction, intense programming effort, and parent involvement in the educational process. Although controversy exists regarding which is ultimately the best program, two programs

TABLE 3.1   A SAMPLE FBA AND BIP

George is not successful academically because he does not complete his schoolwork. Based on observation and interviews, the resulting FBA and BIP were developed by the school psychologist to help George increase his productivity in the classroom.

Problem Behaviors Identified	High number of off-task behaviors (looking around the Identified room, staring into space, playing with his pencil, talking to his peers)
Antecedents: Conditions occurring before the behavior occurs	Teacher is working with another student. Teacher is writing on the blackboard.
Behavior: Conditions that occur after the behavior takes place	Teacher reprimands George for not having his class work finished. Teacher sends unfinished work home.
Consequences: What is the function of the behavior?	George does not have to finish his work in class (escape/avoidance). George's mother helps him with his homework (attention/ avoidance).

Based on the previous FBA, the following BIP was developed:

Specific Goals	1. Increase on-task behavior. 2. George will complete his seatwork assignments with 80 percent accuracy. 3. George will do his homework independently, with 80 percent accuracy.
Interventions	1. George will receive one "star" for each completed in-class assignment. 2. George will remain after school to complete missing in-class assignments. 3. George will receive one "star" for each completed homework assignment. 4. Parent will sign completed homework sheet. 5. Stars can be traded in for free time or to purchase items at the school store.

TABLE 3.2 KEY AREAS FOR INTERVENTION AT SCHOOL AND AT HOME

Area to Target	Rationale
Consistency and predictability	Children with autism will likely overreact to any changes in their program, even minor changes.
High degree of structure	Structure will increase predictability, reduce anxiety resistance, and optimize the learning environment.
Maximum use of visual supports to illustrate verbal comments	Language is often impaired; children with autism tend to perform better on tasks that use manipulatives (blocks, shapes) or rely on their stronger visual skills.
Breaking down complex tasks into small steps	Children with autism have difficulty with abstract concepts or those that require sequential processing.
Reinforce tasks completed at school with similar tasks at home	This will increase the opportunity to generalize information across situations rather than isolate learning into specific situations.

have documented research support of their positive impact on learning potential: the UCLA ABA Program developed by Ivar Lovaas and the Treatment and Education of Autistic and related Communication-Handicapped Children (TEACCH) Program, developed in the early 1970s by Eric Schopler at Duke University in North Carolina.

THE ABA PROGRAM THREE-YEAR GOALS

This intense behavioral program involves forty hours per week over a three-year period in the clinic and home environments.

- Year One: Increase compliance, decrease inappropriate behavior

- Year Two: Increase social play and language

- Year Three: Emotion expression and pre-academic skills: refining skills for integration into school system

Children in the ABA program had very positive outcomes; almost half of the children were promoted to the second grade and required little or no special education support.

The TEACCH program focuses on intentional communication, with the belief that children will learn to communicate in order to reach their goals. For example, if a child is thirsty and the only way he is going to get a drink is to say "juice," then he will learn to communicate. Instead of teaching language as an academic subject, this program focuses on developing a child's awareness of the practical use of language. The program also includes visual charts and displays to help children better understand abstract concepts such as time and space.

WOULD YOU LIKE TO LEARN MORE ABOUT THESE PROGRAMS?

Readers can find more information about the ABA program at http://www.lovaas.com and about the TEACCH program at http://www.teacch.com.

Emotional Disturbance

The IDEA 2004 definition of emotional disturbance focuses on emotional or behavioral problems that interfere with educational performance in one of five areas:

1. An inability to learn that is not explained by intellectual, sensory, or health factors

2. An inability to develop or maintain interpersonal relationships with peers or teachers

3. Age-inappropriate behaviors

4. Pervasive mood of unhappiness or depression

5. Tendency to exhibit physical symptoms or fears associated with school or personal problems

IDEA 2004's definition of emotional disturbance also includes the category of *schizophrenia,* a severe emotional disorder, although this disorder is rarely diagnosed in children.

HOW COMMON ARE EMOTIONAL DISORDERS IN CHILDREN?

The Surgeon General's report on Children and Mental Health (U.S. Department of Health and Human Services, 1999) states that almost 21 percent of children (one in five) in the United States between the ages of nine and seventeen have a diagnosable mental disorder. In the 2000–01 academic year, the U.S. Department of Education reported in its twenty-fourth annual report to Congress that approximately 472,000 children and youth were receiving special education and related services for emotional disturbance.

Associated Characteristics Fears, anxieties, and aggressive behaviors are common reactions of children to specific events such as worries related to school success or peer pressure. However, children with emotional disturbance display more severe and more frequent emotional responses to most situations. While some children exhibit *externalizing behaviors* (for example, acting out, aggression, or behavioral problems), other children respond primarily by *internalizing* their feelings (through depression, anxiety, or physical discomfort). Some children display a mix of both externalizing (aggression) and internalizing (anxiety/depression) responses. Children with emotional disturbance often display immaturity in emotional development, evidenced by poor coping skills and poor ability to regulate their emotions in response to environmental stressors.

Externalizing Behaviors Children who act out display behaviors that may be disruptive in the classroom and that may result in social problems such as rejection by peers. Some children may bully and intimidate their more vulnerable peers. Their impulsivity may cause them to act before they think about the consequences of their actions. Researchers suggest that many aggressive children interpret ambivalent cues as intentionally aggressive and respond with an aggressively defensive response. Social skills training on how to interpret social cues more accurately can be of benefit to these children.

DIDYOUKNOW

Although it was once thought that girls were less aggressive than boys, we are now aware that girls may not be physically aggressive, but they do engage in *relational aggression* by circulating damaging rumors about a victim, who is often unaware of why her peers are turning against her.

Internalizing Behaviors Children who are anxious may often withdraw or avoid situations that are stressful. Physical complaints and discomfort (headaches, stomach aches) may result in visits to the school nurse or family doctor, but often no physical reason for the complaints can be determined. For some children, anxiety may increase as exams or standardized testing sessions approach. Although fears are common in children, some children may experience debilitating fears or phobias and arrange their lives around rituals (for example, repeated counting, checking, or hand washing). A list of symptoms associated with anxiety and depressive disorders can be found in Appendix B. Other anxious responses might manifest in *school refusals* (a child refusing to attend school) after a lengthy illness or in times of stress about separating from a parent, especially after an accident or an event that triggers fear of loss.

Childhood depression is often difficult to detect because young children do not have the ability to understand or express the nature of the complex feelings that are involved. Children who are depressed may appear more irritable than sad and may act out their depressed feelings aggressively. Some children exhibit rapid mood swings that are characterized by heightened emotional reactivity and irritability—a condition known as *bipolar disorder*.

DIDYOUKNOW

Children who experience bipolar disorder have rapid mood swings; they can be irritable one minute and giddy and goofy the next. Symptoms of bipolar disorder are often confused with ADHD; however, if ADHD medication is given to a child with bipolar disorder, the symptoms may increase and the child may become very aggressive.

Severe Emotional Disturbance   Some children may experience emotional disturbance that is significantly more severe than their peers who have mild to moderate emotional problems. If emotional disturbance results in fears about the safety of either the child (self-destructive behaviors) or the child's peers (threats to others), an alternative educational placement may be required, either on a temporary basis (for example, a forty-five-day program) or on a more permanent basis (for example, residential placement).

DIDYOUKNOW

IDEA 2004 has changed the time of an alternative placement from forty-five calendar days to forty-five school days. Although such an educational placement may be changed, the burden is now on the parent to appeal the decision. Detailed information concerning alternative educational placements and parents' rights can be found in Appendix E.

Educational Planning   Educational planning for children with emotional disturbance will need to incorporate emotional and behavioral support systems into the IEP. An FBA and BIP such as those presented in Table 3.1 may need to be implemented before it will be possible to address specific learning goals. Positive behavioral interventions may be written into the IEP to assist the child in a regular or special class program. Related services such as individual or group counseling, self-esteem and anger management programs, or social skills programs might also be recommended to assist in developing more positive and appropriate behavioral patterns. Programs may be accessed through the school or in the community. Specific interventions to improve self-esteem, social competence, and social skills can be found in Chapter Thirteen. Often, a multi-agency support system can be developed to provide comprehensive support services for families in need.

> REMEMBER that educational performance can be adversely affected by an inability to learn or to establish positive interpersonal relationships. Medical management may be necessary to stabilize a child's mood swings or aggressive impulses.

Parents and teachers who have children with emotional disturbance may find helpful information about additional resources in Appendix H and in Wilens's (2003) book on medications.

Intellectual Disability

Although IDEA 2004 provides federal guidelines, each state may have slightly different ways of determining who is eligible for classification under certain categories of disability, and intellectual disability (ID) is a good example of this. While all states require evidence of subaverage IQ and impaired adaptive functioning as part of the eligibility criteria for ID, the actual scores used to determine whether a child qualifies for the program vary from state to state. Parents and teachers are often frustrated to learn that even though a child may qualify for ID status based on IQ and adaptive functioning, the child may not qualify for services under this category if academic skills do not also fall within this specified range. It may also be frustrating if the child moves to a different state and no longer qualifies because the eligibility requirements are different.

In Chapter Seven, we discuss how learning potential or intelligence is calculated based on ability scores relative to age expectations. The majority of classification systems consider an IQ below 70 to be within the ID range. Remember that approximately 2 percent of the population has an IQ score below 70. (You will see in Chapter Seven that

> REMEMBER: In order to establish eligibility for those functioning within the range of intellectual disability (ID), it is necessary to determine not only an IQ significantly below the average range, but also provide evidence of adaptive functioning deficits in at least two areas.

68 percent of the population has an IQ score between 85 and 115; the average IQ score is 100.)

The Range of Intellectual Disability   The IQ scores of individuals who are classified as intellectually disabled can range from an IQ of about 70 (plus or minus 5 points of measurement error) to an IQ below 20. There is great variability in the characteristics of children whose scores fall within this wide range. Although the range is large, the vast majority (85 percent) of children with ID fall within the mild range (IQ range from 55 to 75). Children who fall in the lower ranges (IQ less than 40) often have multiple disabilities. IDEA 2004 does not specify different levels of ID, but the *DSM-IV-TR* (APA, 2000) provides four categories. The percentages of individuals who score in different ranges and the expectations associated with each of the levels of ID (mild, moderate, severe, and profound) are shown in Table 3.3.

TABLE 3.3   RANGES OF INTELLECTUAL DISABILITY

Range of Intellectual Disability	Percentage of ID Population	Expectations
Mild (IQ Range 50/55 to 70)	85	May appear to be delayed, but prior to school entrance may be similar to peers with respect to social skills, motor skills, and communication Overall academic levels up to Grade 6 level Vocational success with minimal support and supervision
Moderate (IQ Range 35/40 to 50/55)	10	Academic expectations about a Grade 2 level Vocational success in sheltered workshops, highly structured tasks supported with behavioral methods and training
Severe (IQ Range 20/25 to 35/40)	3–4	Increased medical, motor, and neurological problems Basic pre-academic skills, limited sight vocabulary Success in group homes where they can be monitored closely
Profound (IQ Range Below 20 to 25)	1–2	Often multiple, motor, and neurological problems Augmentative communication systems (picture boards) can help communicate basic needs Long-term placement in sheltered settings to allow for close monitoring

Generally, *intellectual disability* refers to limitations in mental ability that may influence daily living and adaptation to the environment in several areas of functioning, such as daily living skills, communication skills, academic skills, social skills, self-help skills, health and safety, community use (leisure and recreation) and vocational potential.

Associated Characteristics Children with ID often have trouble learning at the same rate and depth of understanding as their nondisabled peers. They may require many repetitions to acquire a concept and may be unable to grasp abstract concepts. Developmental milestones such as talking, crawling, sitting, walking, or toilet training may be delayed. Some children with ID have a specific syndrome, such as Down syndrome (caused by a chromosomal defect) or fetal alcohol syndrome (caused by maternal alcohol consumption during pregnancy). Children with ID due to specific syndromes often have associated physical characteristics (for example, poor muscle tone and slanted eyes associated with Down syndrome or a flattened nose and widely spaced eyes associated with fetal alcohol syndrome).

Educational Planning A comprehensive psychological assessment is recommended to provide adequate insight into a child's strengths and weaknesses prior to determining special education eligibility and, if necessary, developing an IEP. Some children may require minimal accommodations in their educational program, while others may require educational programs that address significant concerns in behavioral, social, emotional, or adaptive areas.

In working with children with ID, it is important to break down goals into smaller steps in order to ensure understanding. It is also important to allow increased time for repetition and consolidation of skills. Parents and teachers can increase a child's chances of success by working together to provide a consistent home and school program that allows the child to generalize skills across different environments. Helpful links are listed in Appendix H.

Specific Learning Disabilities (SLD)

Students with specific learning disabilities (SLD) differ from students with ID because children with SLD have average to above-average intelligence, while children with ID have intelligence that is significantly below average. Although students with ID often experience academic difficulties, these difficulties often result from weaknesses in general problem-solving ability. However, children with SLD have a neurological disorder that has an impact on how they process information in specific areas, such as receiving information, classifying or sorting information, storing information, retrieving information from storage, or expressing information. These children show a significant gap between their learning potential (intelligence) and their actual academic performance. Children with specific learning disabilities are not a homogenous group because difficulties can exist in one area or a unique combination of two or more of the areas listed previously. Table 3.4 shows how problems in information processing can interfere with learning for children with SLD. Children with SLD may experience mild to severe difficulties in some or all stages of learning.

Prevalence and Types of Learning Disabilities   According to the U.S. Department of Education (2006), approximately 5 percent of children enrolled in public schools have some form of SLD. Although it was once thought that males were more likely to demonstrate SLD than females, recent studies have questioned this finding. Learning disabilities can be inherited, or they may result from problems during pregnancy or birth (for example, lack of oxygen or prematurity) or result from environmental accidents (for example, brain injury) or toxins (for example, exposure to lead-based paint). The more common types of SLD and the areas that these disabilities affect are listed in Table 3.5.

Educational Planning   Although some of the more severe learning disabilities can be detected at an early age, in most cases SLD will likely not be identified prior to the second or third grade because up to this point, many children experience processing problems due to immaturity. For example, letter and number confusions and reversals are quite common prior to eight years of age and often correct themselves with increasing maturity. Also, lags in reading, writing, and math often do not surface until about third grade because children are mastering foundation skills until this time. However, parents or teachers can request a psychological assessment if they are concerned that a child has an SLD. Because many children with SLD encounter academic problems, they may feel inadequate, resulting in lowered self-esteem, or they may act out their frustrations, resulting in behavioral problems. It is important for the child's support team to discuss how to help the child develop a more positive self-image or more appropriate ways of relieving frustration, both at home and at school.

Children with SLD often experience difficulties in their social relationships due to difficulties in transferring information from situation to situation, a failure to recognize social cues, a poor sense of timing in social circles, or other problems caused by their neurological processing difficulties. Social skills training

TABLE 3.4 HOW INFORMATION PROCESSING PROBLEMS CAN INTERFERE WITH LEARNING

Area of Learning Interference	Associated Processing Difficulties
Input of Information: Recognition of information; receptive skills	**Recognition of Information:** Sensory input (vision, hearing, touch, smell) *Requires the ability to* selectively attend to information and discriminate sights (letter orientation, spatial cues) and sounds (auditory discrimination, phonetic awareness)
Integration of Information: Coding, storage, integration, and making sense of the information received; retrieval of information	**Interpretation of Information:** Making sense of the information received: *Organizing information* (sorting, sequencing, linking to previous learning) *Storing information* (having a mental filing cabinet) *Retrieving information* (being able to remember how the information was stored, e.g., file names) *Requires the ability to* concentrate; organize and sequence information; perform mental manipulations (working memory) and retrieve information from long-term memory; understand cause-and-effect relationships; and associate visual with auditory and motor information (linking sounds to symbols and recalling how to graphically execute a letter)
Output of Information: Responding to Information: Executing appropriate responses to information based on the input and integration of information	**Expression:** Communicating through oral, written, or motor responses *Requires the ability to* inhibit inappropriate responses while initiating more appropriate responses ("stop and think"), and recognize appropriate *tempo* (too slow or too quick to respond), *spatial* (too close/too far: personal space), and *intensity* (inflated reactions or minimal reaction).

TABLE 3.5 DIFFERENT TYPES OF SPECIFIC LEARNING DISABILITIES (SLD)

Specific Learning Disability	Problem Subject	Areas of Difficulty	Examples of Difficulty
Dyscalculia	Math	Recall of math facts. Mathematical word problems; math concepts; concepts of time and money.	Inability to count by twos or threes. Not knowing what information is irrelevant in word problems.
Dysgraphia	Written expression	Handwriting; spelling; organization of written expression.	Illegible handwriting due to poor letter and number formation and poor letter spacing. Written output is poorly organized. Difficulty in beginning written tasks.
Dyslexia	Reading, spelling	Sequencing letters, sounds, and words. Confusion in directions and spatial orientation (left and right).	Letter and number reversals (*b/d*); inversions (*p/d, 6/9*); transpositions (*gril/girl*); word reversals (*saw/was*).
Dyspraxia	Fine motor skills	Manual dexterity; coordination.	Fine motor tasks such as drawing, using scissors, and tying shoes.
Nonverbal learning disorder	Visual-spatial organization, motor coordination, math skills	Poor sense of spatial awareness; poor social skills.	Poor social skills due to lack of awareness of subtle visual-spatial social cues, facial expressions, and personal space. Poor number sense.

programs can be an effective way of helping a child to understand and respond to social cues in a more appropriate way. Increased communication between family members at home and educators at school can help improve a child's success in transferring information across situations. Parents and teachers will find information on social skills interventions in Chapter Thirteen and links to additional resources in Appendix H.

Attention Deficit Hyperactivity Disorder (ADHD)

Although ADHD is one of the most commonly diagnosed disorders, affecting approximately 3 to 7 percent of school-age children, its causes are not yet clearly understood. However, recent research has discovered that children with ADHD have less activity in areas of the brain devoted to planning, sustained attention, and impulse control and that certain chemicals in their brain are not performing adequately (the neurotransmitters dopamine and norepinephrine). As a result, children with ADHD demonstrate a combination of brain-based behaviors noted in these symptoms: inattention, impulsivity, and hyperactivity.

Types of ADHD   Although many are aware of the hyperactive-impulsive type of ADHD, fewer realize that there are actually three different forms of ADHD based on how the inattentive, impulsive, and hyperactive symptoms are expressed.

> *ADHD, predominantly hyperactive-impulsive type.* A diagnosis of ADHD, predominantly hyperactive-impulsive type, applies if the child demonstrates six out of nine possible hyperactive and impulsive symptoms. A complete list of the symptoms can be found in Appendix B. Children with this form of ADHD often encounter academic difficulties when they sacrifice accuracy for speed and social problems because their impulsive and invasive behaviors tend to infringe on others' territories. Their impulsive, loud, and hyperactive behaviors often can be disruptive to classroom routines. These children often cannot control their behaviors sufficiently to allow time to think through a problem and use appropriate resources to help in their problem-solving process. As a result, they often find themselves in problem situations that they have unintentionally caused. It is not uncommon for children with this type of ADHD to also have a diagnosis of oppositional defiant disorder (ODD), exhibiting oppositional and defiant behaviors that start at home and may eventually find their way into the school environment.

> *ADHD, predominantly inattentive type.* Less is known about the inattentive type of ADHD. Children with the inattentive type of ADHD present with a host of more subtle, less obvious behaviors. These children are often undiagnosed and therefore are misunderstood because they appear lazy or unmotivated to an untrained eye. Children with the predominantly inattentive type of ADHD, sometimes referred to as attention deficit disorder

(ADD), exhibit six out of nine possible symptoms, which are listed in Appendix B. The inability to tune in to the environmental demands of the moment has caused significant frustration for these children, their teachers, and their parents, who may consider the children to be underachievers, unmotivated, or lazy.

ADHD, combined type. Children who meet the criteria for both the hyperactive-impulsive type and the inattentive type are designated as the combined type of ADHD, and as might be anticipated, these children experience significant difficulties in their academics and in their peer relationships. Similar to their peers with the hyperactive-impulsive type of ADHD, these children experience significant difficulties due to deficits in areas of the brain that control executive functions. Executive functions will be discussed in depth in Chapters Ten and Twelve.

DIDYOUKNOW

Many adults who seek counseling for depression are later diagnosed with ADHD. Their depression is a result of years of feeling that they have not accomplished their goals, despite being at or well above the intellectual level of their peers.

Educational Planning There is no single test that can be used to diagnose ADHD. However, the family physician is usually a good resource for parents who are concerned that their child might have ADHD. Most physicians will ask that someone at the child's school fill out a checklist, such as the checklist that is presented in Appendix B, that lists ADHD symptoms. A school psychologist may also observe the child in the classroom and distribute checklists or behavioral rating scales to parents and teachers, given that the symptoms of ADHD should be evident (to a lesser or greater extent) across all situations. A major difficulty in diagnosing ADHD is that many of the symptoms of ADHD are similar to symptoms of other problems, such as anxiety, child abuse, depression, bipolar disorder, or post-traumatic stress disorder. Often, children with ADHD also have learning disabilities. A comprehensive assessment conducted by a licensed professional can rule out other reasons for the symptoms or identify additional contributing factors. Parents should be asked to provide a developmental and family history. If medication is prescribed by a physician, rating scales can provide an excellent way of monitoring the effectiveness of the medication.

504 Plans and the IDEA 2004 Category of "Other Health Impairment"
Under Section 504, children with ADHD can qualify for accommodations to their program that will help them to be more successful academically. Possible accommodations might include extended time to complete assignments, reducing the length of assignments, or extended time for taking tests. Under IDEA 2004, children with ADHD may qualify for special education and related services under the category "Other Health Impairment" (OHI) if they have an impairment in "vitality or alertness, including heightened alertness to environmental stimuli that results in limited alertness with respect to the educational environment" (Individuals with Disabilities Education Act, 2004). Specific eligibility criteria differ according to the policies of the different states.

DIDYOUKNOW

States differ on eligibility criteria for special education services for children with ADHD under OHI. For example, in Florida, children can qualify for special education and related services under OHI only after an exhaustive assessment has ruled out all other potential contributing factors, including intellectual disability, emotional disturbance, and SLD. Furthermore, children must have had a 504 Plan for at least six months that has not been successful in meeting their needs. A medical statement of their ADHD condition is also required.

An extensive multi-site research project (MTA Cooperative Group, 2004) sponsored by the National Institute of Mental Health (NIMH) and the Office of Special Education in the U.S. Department of Education has listed four core interventions for ADHD:

1. Education of parents and teachers about ADHD and the types of accommodations required

2. Medical management of the disorder, recognizing the neuro-biochemical nature of ADHD

3. Behavior intervention and strategies to manage problems in areas of compliance, impulse control, delay of gratification, and task completion

4. Educational interventions to target weak academic progress due to difficulties in the following areas:
    - Task initiation (getting started)
    - Task completion
    - On-task behavior
    - Successful transitions between classes or programs
    - Organizational skills (use of a school planner)
    - Interactions with others
    - Communication between home and school
    - Note taking, study skills, time management, and prioritizing demands

Parents and teachers can find helpful links to additional resources on ADHD in Appendix H.

CHAPTER

4

SPECIFIC LEARNING DISABILITIES AND A RESPONSE-TO-INTERVENTION APPROACH

Elsewhere in this book, we will talk about the ways in which some school districts determine whether a student meets eligibility criteria for special education services. Some districts continue to use a mathematical formula to make this decision; after a child receives a comprehensive psychoeducational assessment, educators would look for a mathematical difference between his scores on intelligence measures and his scores on achievement measures. Many districts, however, are following a national movement toward using what is called a *response-to-intervention* (RTI) approach to identify whether a student has a learning disability. We've included sample RTI forms in Appendix F.

WHAT IS RTI?

Response to intervention is an approach that schools can use to help students who are struggling academically. Students' progress is monitored at each of the three stages (tiers) of intervention, which we'll discuss later. Monitoring helps schools to understand whether the interventions are working or whether they need to implement additional interventions that may have a positive impact on a student's progress. RTI allows schools to implement research-based interventions with increasing levels of intensity.

Research-Based Interventions

Teachers often implement interventions in the classroom that can be used by the entire class, a group of students, or individual students. Teachers often know from experience that the interventions they are using have been helpful to other students. In an RTI approach, however, the focus is on *research-based interventions*—that is, research must have demonstrated the effectiveness of the interventions in helping to decrease students' deficits and improve their academic performance.

Just how do teachers find research-based interventions? Larger school districts may review research literature to see which interventions are most helpful. For example, if a student does not have good recognition of letter sounds, she likely will have difficulty with the reading process. Scientific, peer-reviewed journals that focus on reading, among other sources, may have lists of reading programs that are effective in helping students with this type of problem.

At the end of this chapter, we list some resources that parents and teachers have found helpful as they move through the RTI process.

The Three Tiers

When you read about RTI, you'll often see it described as a multi-tiered approach to interventions or depicted as a pyramid of interventions (see Figure 4.1). Most states use the common three-tier approach, but some use a four- or five-tier pyramid.

In a three-tier pyramid, Tier 1 is at the bottom and Tier 3 is at the top. Envision that the area of each tier represents the number of students. When we move to a higher tier, there are fewer students in that tier. The expectation is that the research-based interventions implemented in the lower tiers will be helpful and therefore students will not need more intensive instruction and interventions.

We will discuss RTI in the context of three tiers, given that you are likely to read about this approach. Let's focus on each of the tiers, what goes on during the process, and why we move from one tier to the next.

Tier 1: Classwide Interventions   Tier 1 interventions are for students who are found to be at risk on the basis of their performance on certain tests. These

FIGURE 4.1   *Three-Tier RTI Approach*

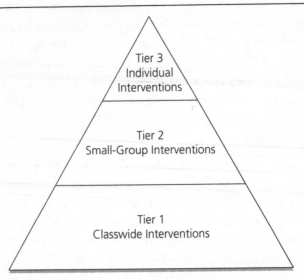

Tier 3
Individual
Interventions

Tier 2
Small-Group Interventions

Tier 1
Classwide Interventions

interventions are implemented in the general education classroom. School districts may use state tests or their own test to identify students who are at risk. Students are monitored on a regular basis (weekly is typical) to see how they respond to these interventions. Each grade level has certain goals or benchmarks that a student must meet in order to be considered to be making adequate progress. Schools collect data on students' performance and then compare the data with the benchmark. Students who are making good progress may continue with Tier 1 interventions, or they may be deemed no longer part of the RTI process. Students who continue to struggle and who are not meeting the goals for adequate progress may move to Tier 2 interventions.

Tier 2: Small-Group Interventions   Tier 2 interventions are more targeted and more intensive and are based on a student's areas of weakness and the progress that she made toward the benchmark. Like Tier 1 interventions, they are implemented in the general education classroom. Students receive more focused assistance because the interventions are administered in a small-group setting. Teachers continue to collect data and monitor student progress. Interventions that do not seem to be helping a student are replaced with new ones in an effort to find one that is effective. Many students respond well to the more individualized instruction, but those who do not may move on to Tier 3.

Tier 3: Individual Interventions In most states, Tier 3 interventions are considered special education instruction; therefore, students must meet state eligibility criteria in order to receive these services. Interventions may be provided individually or in small groups. The instruction is much more intensive, and students may be pulled out of the general education classroom for part of the day, depending on the severity of their academic problems. Tier 3 students usually work with special education personnel such as certified teachers or paraprofessionals.

Progress Monitoring

Monitoring progress is an important component of the RTI process. Data are gathered in order to assess a student's classroom performance and evaluate the instruction provided by a teacher. The initial data are called *baseline data* and are used as a starting point in evaluating the effectiveness of an intervention. Once goals are established, a student's progress toward these goals can be monitored on a regular basis. The idea is to compare a student's expected rate of learning with his actual rate of learning. Monitoring data are often documented and displayed on graphs.

Curriculum-based measurement (CBM) is a method used by teachers to see how students are progressing in areas such as reading, math, or writing. CBM can be used to track and record a student's progress in her areas of weakness. CBM can be a quick way to collect data and assess student performance. Teachers use the information to make modifications to their instruction.

Programs are available to assist teachers in making appropriate instructional decisions. The Dynamic Indicators of Basic Early Literacy Skills (DIBELS) (http://dibels.uoregon.edu) and AIMSweb (http://www.aimsweb.com) are two examples of free or low-cost programs. AIMSweb is particularly powerful and includes reproducible assessment probes for reading, language arts, math, and early literacy skills, and all data can be managed online, which is helpful if multiple teachers are engaged in monitoring progress.

DID YOU KNOW

The National Center on Student Progress Monitoring offers a great deal of progress-monitoring information for teachers and parents. This free information is available from their Web site at http://www.studentprogress.org.

ADVANTAGES OF RTI

The RTI approach has several advantages. First, it can help reduce the time a student must wait before he receives assistance in his areas of weakness. RTI is a proactive approach; students are identified early as needing assistance. Second, the goal is to provide as much assistance to students as possible in their regular education classroom. If the research-based interventions are helpful, special education services may not be needed. Third, how a student responds to the intervention may provide information about her strengths and weaknesses. Understanding what works best can help teachers provide appropriate instruction to students.

A MISCONCEPTION ABOUT RTI

We find that there is one major misconception about RTI—a belief held by some parents and teachers. Some argue that RTI is simply a way for school districts to delay providing special education services.

The goal of RTI is to implement research-based interventions as soon as a problem is identified. Many of these interventions are likely being used with students who have already qualified for special education services. Some believe that schools are holding back on certain interventions and using them only for students receiving special education services; this is untrue. The goal of RTI is to find and implement interventions that work for a student without having to label him as a special education student. If a student does not respond well to the interventions at the two lower tiers and it is believed that he needs the more intensive and more individualized instruction and interventions found in Tier 3, the Student Support Team can find him eligible for special education services. Eligibility is a team decision, and special education laws vary from state to state. To locate the laws for your state, contact your state's department of special education. Contact information can be found in Appendix G.

PARENTS' ROLE IN RTI

Parents play an active role in the RTI process. They may be asked to implement interventions in the home so that students experience consistency between what goes on at home and what goes on at school. Or parents may be asked to monitor a child to see whether she improves in specific areas. Parents may keep data on their child's progress and report it to the school during the next RTI meeting.

Such parental feedback on a child's progress can provide information that is very helpful to her teachers. We'll talk more about parent-teacher collaboration in Chapter Sixteen.

TEACHERS' ROLE IN RTI

Teachers often have primary responsibility for gathering RTI data. They may work with other teachers or the school psychologist to collect data that will be used to monitor a child's progress. This information is often shared in visual form such as charts that show where the child began (his weaknesses), where he is now (the progress he's made), and where he should be at a specific future point (the target goal). Teachers may use software programs and other resources to help them choose appropriate research-based interventions and monitor a child's progress. Microsoft Excel spreadsheets can also be used to display a child's progress.

DIDYOUKNOW

Teachers, reading teachers, teacher assistants, school administrators, and school psychologists may help implement interventions.

WHY A PSYCHOLOGICAL EVALUATION IS STILL HELPFUL

Parents have the right to request a psychological evaluation for their child at any time during the RTI process. According to some state special education regulations, however, the entire RTI process must be completed before a determination can be made about whether a child is eligible for special education services. As school psychologists, we recognize the importance of evaluation test results and how they can be used to better understand a student's needs.

An evaluation may uncover processing weaknesses that could be having an impact on a student's academic progress. These weaknesses may occur in areas such as working memory, short-term memory, long-term retrieval, auditory processing, attention, language, executive functioning, or visual-motor integration, to name a few. Without this information, educators may implement interventions blindly, without regard for how a student processes information. For example, a particular intervention may rely heavily on a student's memory; if memory is her weak area, that intervention is not likely to have a positive impact.

Consequently, we are in favor of including a psychological assessment as part of the RTI process. The evaluation does not have to be comprehensive at this stage; it can focus solely on how a student processes information. With this information in hand, a teacher can choose interventions that are most likely to be helpful, given a student's processing and academic weaknesses.

We'll discuss psychological assessments in more detail in Part Two of this book.

DIDYOUKNOW

You should meet with the school psychologist who conducted a child's assessment and ask him or her to review the psychological report in detail. This gives you an opportunity to ask questions about the test results. If possible, you should read the report before this meeting and devise a list of questions.

RTI RESOURCES

Many RTI resources are available to parents and teachers. Following is a list of some of our favorite online resources:

Intervention Central

http://www.interventioncentral.org/

This site was created by Jim Wright, who has experience as a school psychologist, school administrator, and RTI consultant. Just about everything you might want to know about interventions to help students with academic or behavior problems can be found here The site is very comprehensive, and it lists research-based interventions that have demonstrated their effectiveness in improving students' academic progress. Excellent manuals and forms are included. We have also found Jim Wright's book, *RTI Toolkit: A Practical Guide for Schools*, to be very helpful.

National Association of School Psychologists

http://www.nasponline.org/resources/resourcesbytopic.aspx?topic=Response
+to+Intervention

This national association offers more than thirty documents that address all
aspects of the RTI process. Information for both parents and teachers is
available.

National Center on Response to Intervention

http://www.rti4success.org/

What we find most helpful on this site is a chart that is designed to help schools
select the best screening tools. For each tool, the chart discusses characteristics such as classification accuracy (how accurately the tool can classify
students as either "at risk for reading disability" or "not at risk for reading disability"), generalizability (whether results from one population
can be generalized to another population), reliability (how consistently
a tool classifies students from one administration to the next), and valid-
ity (whether a tool measures what it is intended to measure). The site was
created by the American Institutes for Research.

New Roles in Response to Intervention: Creating Success for Schools and Children

http://www.nasponline.org/advocacy/New%20Roles%20in%20RTI.pdf

This fifty-five-page document was a collaborative project of the American
Speech-Language-Hearing Association, Council of Administrators
of Special Education, Council for Exceptional Children, Council for
Learning Disabilities, Division for Learning Disabilities, International
Dyslexia Association, International Reading Association, Learning
Disabilities Association of America, National Association of State
Directors of Special Education, National Association of School Psychol-
ogists, National Center for Learning Disabilities, National Education
Association, and School Social Work Association of America. This
document includes different viewpoints on RTI from these organizations
and offers parents and teachers a wealth of information about RTI and the
RTI process.

RTI Action Network

http://www.rtinetwork.org/

This site was created by the National Center for Learning Disabilities. While it does not include a comprehensive list of interventions such as the one found on the Intervention Central site, it does provide a general framework for understanding RTI. What is unique about the site is that it includes discussion boards and a blog on RTI issues, and gives you an opportunity to submit a question on an RTI-related topic or find answers to questions submitted by others.

Two

Psychological Assessments

CHAPTER

5

EVALUATING CHILDREN'S DIFFICULTIES

What, Why, and How?

Part Two is devoted to topics related to the assessment of intelligence, learning and achievement, emotion and behavior, and the executive functions. We will begin with a general discussion of the nature of "assessments" within school systems, including who might be involved, the types of assessments that might be conducted, and why assessments can be important in discovering the nature of the difficulties some children may be experiencing. In this chapter, we will answer some frequently asked questions and dispel some myths about testing. In Part Two, we will focus on psychological assessments in particular. In Chapter Six, we describe the assessment process and the typical stages that are involved. The following chapters focus on specific types of psychological assessments that can provide in-depth information about potential problem areas, including the assessment of intelligence (Chapter Seven); learning and academic achievement

(Chapter Eight); emotional difficulties or behavioral problems (Chapter Nine), and the executive functions (Chapter Ten). In the final chapter of Part Two (Chapter Eleven), we provide a summary and overview of all the information on assessment that we have presented in the form of a sample psychological report. This will be a very important chapter, because we walk readers through the report, explaining what the report says and what the results mean.

THE NATURE OF ASSESSMENT

When most people think about an assessment or evaluation conducted within a school setting, the first thing that comes to mind is testing, whether that means a pop quiz, a midterm test, or statewide or nationwide proficiency exams. Just the thought of being tested can make us cringe or bring a wide range of negative thoughts to mind, regardless of whether the tests are related to a school system, a job, a medical procedure, or something mundane like getting a driver's license. Testing often produces a sense of anxiety and fear in us because when we are tested, we are fearful that we may fail the test.

However, the process of assessment can also be viewed in a different way. If something is not performing in the way that we expect it to perform, we can conduct an assessment or evaluation in order to find out what the problem is so that we can correct it. Computer programs do this kind of troubleshooting on a regular basis. If you are working on a project and your computer system suddenly gives you an error message, it often asks you to send a message so that the system can figure out what is causing the problem. You go through the same process when your car breaks down; you take the car to the mechanic, who performs a series of tests or diagnostics to find out what is causing the problem, so that it can be fixed.

Closer to our case in point, when a child experiences a medical problem, the family physician or pediatrician is often consulted to provide information about what is causing the problem. The physician begins the evaluation by asking a series of questions about specific symptoms (for example, fever, chills, or pain) to assist in determining the nature and severity of the problem. Often, the physician performs some routine tests (taking the child's temperature; listening to the heart and lungs) to find out how the child's bodily system is functioning in comparison with how a normal, healthy child would be functioning. For example, the physician knows that average body temperature should be about 98.6 degrees Fahrenheit. The physician compares the child's temperature with this normal standard to determine whether the child has a fever. If the child has a fever, the physician attempts to diagnose what is causing the high temperature (a virus, an infection, or some other medical cause). After assessing the child's symptoms, the physician might be able to diagnose the problem and provide appropriate treatment (for example, medication). However, if the doctor is unsure of the cause of the problem based on the information available, more tests may be ordered (for example, X rays or blood work-up) to rule out some possible explanations and confirm others; this process is called *hypothesis testing* or *differential diagnosis*.

THE ASSESSMENT PROCESS: DETERMINING SPECIAL NEEDS

When children or adolescents are not performing well in school, it is very important to determine why this is the case in order to recommend solutions to the problem. Several steps are often initiated prior to a referral for a comprehensive assessment, which will be discussed shortly.

Stage 1. Initially, a number of school-based interventions are attempted to assist children who are experiencing school difficulties. Often, these interventions (such as a change in seating or peer tutoring) are effective in increasing academic performance.

Stage 2. Further school-based evaluations and informal assessments, such as educational tests or classroom observations, may be undertaken to obtain more information about a child's performance.

Stage 3. If a child continues to experience school problems despite interventions, more specific information may be required in order to determine why the child is having problems. A referral for a number of different types of assessments may be initiated, depending on the problems the child is experiencing. At this stage, a comprehensive assessment would likely be recommended because the duration, intensity, and frequency of the problem signal the need for increased concern,. The problem has been resistant to the interventions that have been attempted and is ongoing (duration); the problem is more serious than expected, given the child's age (intensity); and the problem is occurring on a regular basis (frequency).

Comprehensive Assessment

A comprehensive assessment may consist of assessments and evaluations conducted by a number of possible members of the student's support team, including mental health professionals, service providers, and educators working within the school system, and may be augmented by input from community professionals outside the school system, if necessary (for example, medical reports). Parental permission is required for assessments that are not part of routine educational screening. Assessment of hearing and vision are conducted prior to other assessments to ensure that there is no physical reason (for example, a need for glasses) for the child's academic difficulties. Each professional report provides valuable information to assist in determining whether the child's needs fall within a category that would warrant eligibility for special education and, if so, whether related services (such as speech therapy or physical therapy) may also be required to enhance the child's opportunity for academic success.

MEMBERS OF THE STUDENT'S SCHOOL AND COMMUNITY SUPPORT TEAM

This section provides a brief overview of potential members of a child's support team, the nature of their expertise, the focus of their assessments, and their roles in remediation or intervention. Finally, we describe the crucial role of parents on a student's support team.

Mental Health Service Providers

Mental health service providers may or may not be located in the school on a regular basis.

School Psychologist   Although the degree of post-graduate training varies from state to state, school psychologists at a minimum must have at least a master's degree or a specialist degree. which they receive after a bachelor's degree. Some school psychologists hold a doctoral degree (Ph.D., Ed.D., or Psy.D.). The role of the school psychologist is discussed at greater length in the next chapters. A psychological assessment must be part of the comprehensive assessment, and as a result, school psychologists play a vital role in conducting assessments to provide information about children's functioning in a number of areas, including intelligence, academic achievement and learning, executive functions, social and emotional development, behavioral problems, and conducting observations regarding performance within (classroom observations) and outside (playground observations) of the classroom. (All the areas that might be assessed and that could be part of the comprehensive psychological report are discussed in detail, in Chapters Six through Ten.).

School psychologists also assist teachers and parents in developing strategies to manage learning and behavioral problems in the classroom and at home.

School Social Worker Most school social workers have a master's degree in social work (MSW), although some have completed a baccalaureate social work program. The National Association of Social Workers (http://www.socialworkers.org/) identifies four primary areas of practice for social workers: early intervention to alleviate stress between individuals or groups; problem solving that involves students, parents, school personnel, or community agencies; early identification of students at risk for problems; and working with groups in the schools to increase skills in coping, social competence, or decision making. A school social worker often acts as a liaison between a student's home and school or between the home and community agencies. In addition, a school social worker monitors factors such as student attendance or family hardship that may be affecting a student's success. A school social worker can bring valuable information to a student's support team by conducting assessments of developmental histories to obtain information from parents about the child's development that identify the student's strengths and problem areas.

Speech-Language Pathologist Most speech-language pathologists have a master's degree. As in most professions, licensing or certification varies by state. Speech-language pathologists, sometimes called *speech therapists,* perform a variety of valuable services in the schools. They assess speech functions; diagnose speech disorders; and treat problems related to speech (expressive and receptive language), communication, voice, swallowing, fluency, as well as pragmatics (the social context of communication). Speech-language pathologists can assist in the use of alternative systems of communication, called *augmentative communication*. Speech-language pathologists work with children to develop speech and language skills individually and in small groups. The speech-language pathologist's report is a common component of the child's initial comprehensive assessment profile.

Physical Therapist Practicing physical therapists usually need a master's degree from an accredited physical therapy program and a state license. The American Physical Therapy Association (APTA, http://www.apta.org) states that physical therapists provide services for individuals with "medical problems or other health-related conditions that limit their abilities to move and perform functional activities in their daily lives." Within the school system, children who qualify for special education services might be assessed by a physical therapist, who would provide input on whether they may require additional services to increase their mobility so that they can move as independently as possible within the school environment and participate in classroom activities (for example, manage stairs, restrooms, and the cafeteria). In this case, the physical therapy report would become part of the comprehensive assessment package submitted to the team for consideration to determine whether a student is eligible for special education and related services. Physical therapists focus on the development of strength, mobility, and fitness.

Occupational Therapist Occupational therapists have a master's degree or higher, and occupational therapy is a regulated profession in all states. Within the school system, occupational therapists evaluate children's capabilities, recommend and provide therapy, modify classroom equipment, and help children participate in school activities. A therapist may work with children individually or in small groups. Occupational therapists focus on enhancing and facilitating performance in daily activities such as writing, cutting, and other fine motor skills, as well as daily life skills, such as self-care skills required for children to feed, dress, and otherwise care for themselves. Like other service providers, an occupational therapist would conduct an assessment, if requested, and the report would also become part of the student's comprehensive assessment profile.

PEOPLE OFTEN ASK

What is the difference between physical therapy and occupational therapy? Occupational therapists and physical therapists have similar roles and share an interest in helping others with the development of physical skills and daily living skills and in adapting environments to meet individual needs; however, their area of focus for pursuing these goals differs:

- Physical therapists have additional knowledge in the areas of gross motor skills, mobility, and positioning (balance, walking, and general movement).

- Occupational therapists have specialized knowledge of fine motor and sensory skills.

Service Providers Involved with Hearing, Vision, or Other Sensory Functions
Children and adolescents who experience problems with hearing, vision, or other sensory deficits may obtain services from qualified professionals who specialize in providing adaptive and assisted technology to improve students' ability to succeed in school. For example, children who are deaf-blind (have concurrent hearing and visual problems) would likely require extensive screening, including audiological and ophthalmological or optometric evaluations, medical evaluations, and psychological and communication evaluations in addition to specific assessments of the need for assistive technology.

Educators Commonly Part of the Team

Compared to community and school team members who are not permanently located in the child's school, a number of educators are affiliated with the child's specific school who are also integral members of the child's team.

School Counselor or School Guidance Counselor A school counselor or guidance counselor is an educator who is trained in counseling and advising. Although school counseling degree requirements and certification differ among states, according to the American School Counselor Association (ASCA) "professional school counselors are certified/licensed educators with a minimum of a master's degree in school counseling."

The ASCA National Model for the role of the school counselor (http://www.schoolcounselor.org/) includes some of the following areas: working with students directly on a group, individual, and classroom level to assist in the development of student competencies and achievement in a variety of areas, and conducting ongoing program outcome evaluations. The role of the school counselor can vary depending on the needs of the particular school district and the level of education in the school (for example, elementary, middle, or high school); however, some of the major tasks that the counselor can be responsible for include providing advice and guidance for students regarding: academic concerns, college readiness, and personal or social development. Some counselors also provide group and individual counseling sessions for students, depending on student needs.

Exceptional Child Chairperson, Special Services Coordinator, or Special Education Lead Teacher Many schools have one person who is designated as the primary person responsible for helping school administrators plan programming for exceptional children. The title of the person in this role varies widely among different school districts; however, the primary function of the individual is to coordinate case management and paperwork for the Student Support Team (SST) or Student Assistance Team (SAT) (again, the name varies from district to district). In some districts, the school counselor will have this responsibility.

The individual in this role, regardless of the title, will often meet with regular teachers, resource teachers, students, and parents to discuss and monitor students' academic progress and any social, emotional, or behavioral concerns. This type of meeting is usually the first level of intervention at the school. Students who continue to have problems after interventions have been attempted may be referred to the school psychologist for assessment (with parental permission).

School Resource Teacher; Special Education Teacher All states require that special education teachers, also known as *resource teachers,* be licensed or certified, which requires a bachelor's degree, at a minimum. Some teachers complete an approved training program in special education teaching, while others can complete an alternative or equivalent program or take a test to obtain their certification in special education. Some states require a master's degree. Although it varies by state, some teachers begin with credentials to teach general or regular education (kindergarten through twelfth grade) and then obtain further training in a specialty area, such as learning disabilities or behavioral disorders. Although most resource room teachers entered their profession dedicated to meet the needs of children with disabilities, it can often be a challenging task, especially given the number of meetings and the amount of paperwork that must be completed. It is our hope that the information in this book can provide a greater understanding and appreciation of the service that special education teachers provide through an increased awareness of the nature of children's disabilities, the challenges they face, and the support that is available.

Regular Education Teacher Although children with special needs who qualify for special education and related services may receive some support from the school's resource teacher, this may not mean that the child will receive all their education in the resource room. Some support services can be delivered within the regular classroom. Even if the child is removed from the classroom to receive support services in the resource room, this is likely for only a short period during the day. Therefore, the majority of children who qualify for special education services will spend the majority of their day in the regular classroom with the regular classroom teacher. This situation can be challenging for even the most dedicated and devoted teachers. In the remaining chapters, we intend to provide useful information that can help to lessen the stress, open the lines of communication, and address some of the most common problems facing regular education teachers today.

DIDYOUKNOW

Special Note to Regular Education Teachers: School psychologists often spend more time providing resources and consultation to regular education teachers than to resource room teachers. Children are often under more pressure and challenges in a regular classroom due to increased class size and demands than in a resource room and, as a result, can be more difficult to manage and support. Observing a child in two environments—the regular classroom and the resource room—can provide a psychologist with a unique perspective and result in valuable information that can assist in reducing the child's problems in the regular classroom setting.

Student Support Team Lead Teacher In some states, the Student Support Team (SST) and lead teacher submit the referral for an initial evaluation for special education eligibility. The SST lead ensures that the student is given vision and hearing screenings and collects the necessary paperwork for the referral (for example, grades, classroom performance, an observation, standardized test scores). The SST lead may also be the one who runs the initial eligibility meeting when it's time to review the psychological evaluation, while the lead special education teacher runs the eligibility meetings when it's time for re-evaluation.

Parents: Essential Members of the Team Assessment and evaluation of the nature and severity of a child's problem cannot be complete without valuable insights from information provided by the child's parents. Parents who are able to meet with professional service providers and educators to answer vital questions about their child and voice concerns they may have are providing an important contribution to their child's ultimate success in measurable ways. It is not always easy, however, to take time off from work or other obligations to meet with school personnel, and despite the best intentions, forms sent home are sometimes left unread or unanswered because of yet another crisis. Throughout this book, we will attempt to address many issues that frustrate parents and teachers and to provide helpful suggestions that may open up the channels of communication between home and school, resulting in increased success for children within the educational system.

SUMMARY

This chapter has addressed assessment and evaluation from a number of different angles. First, *why* should assessments be conducted? Assessments provide information to help understand the severity of a child's problem and determine the extent and nature of resources that might be needed based on the assessment information. The second question, about *what* will be assessed, focused our attention on the different members of the SST and the nature of the different types of assessments that are conducted to provide information about the total child. Finally, how the comprehensive assessment is used to develop a student's IEP was reviewed to demonstrate the various facets of determining eligibility for special education and related services. In the remaining chapters in Part Two, we will be devoting considerable attention to a variety of assessments that are conducted by school psychologists as part of the comprehensive assessment package to provide insight into a child's difficulties. In Part Three, we will concentrate on how these assessments can inform intervention planning for the child in the school system. Finally, in Parts Four and Five we will discuss the IEP in greater detail and the special education laws that influence it. In subsequent chapters, it will become increasingly apparent that parents are also a vital component in the assessment process and that all parts of the system need to work together to help a child achieve the highest goals possible.

CHAPTER

6

INTRODUCTION TO ASSESSMENT

What's It All About?

PSYCHOLOGISTS AND THE PRACTICE OF PSYCHOLOGY IN THE SCHOOLS

We will begin our discussion of the psychological assessment with an introduction to psychologists in general, their training and expertise, and then focus on the various roles of the school psychologist, including the administration and interpretation of psychological assessments.

Question: What Are the Different Types of Psychologists?

Whereas some psychologists work primarily with adults, other psychologists work mainly with children, adolescents, and their families. Child psychologists can provide various forms of therapy or assessments based on their training in clinical or counseling psychology, school psychology, or pediatric psychology.

Individuals are able to refer to themselves as "psychologists" only if they are licensed by the state in which they are practicing. When psychologists move from one state to another, they must qualify to practice in the new state under the state's standards. A psychologist is not permitted to practice in any state without a state-recognized license or certification; this assures that the public is protected from unlicensed and untrained individuals. Licensing requirements vary from state to state and country to country; however, all licensing bodies require evidence of continuing education to ensure that practitioners remain current in their knowledge.

In the majority of states, a psychologist licensed in clinical, school, or counseling psychology must have a Ph.D. or Psy.D. in clinical, school, or counseling psychology, satisfy pre- and post-degree internships, and pass a series of professional exams. Licensed mental health counselors may practice with a master's degree (usually requiring two additional years of study after the bachelor's degree), after satisfying a period of post-degree supervision requirements. Clinical psychologists and pediatric psychologists often practice in private practice, clinics, hospitals, and mental health centers.

Psychological assessments of child and adolescent functioning can be conducted by clinical psychologists (most likely found in private practice, clinics, or mental health facilities), pediatric psychologists (most likely located in hospitals), or school psychologists (most likely found in private practice or public school settings).

Do All Psychologists Give the Same Type of Tests?

Although psychologists are trained to administer and interpret a variety of different assessment instruments, individual preferences will result in psychologists administering different instruments to evaluate the same area of functioning. This is important to know because school districts often have a preferred list of assessment instruments for different problems.

DIDYOUKNOW

A Special Note to Parents: Parents can have an independent evaluation of their child conducted, at their own expense, by contacting an independent psychologist. Family physicians are often good sources from whom to request a referral to a psychologist in the community who works primarily with children. Under certain circumstances, which will be discussed later, a school district may pay for the cost of an independent evaluation when a parent requests an alternative assessment to the one conducted by the district's school psychologist. The majority of psychological evaluations of children and adolescents take place within the school system. Under the law, the public school system is also responsible for providing assessments free of charge to students enrolled in private schools.

If an assessment is conducted by someone other than the school psychologist assigned to the particular school district where the child is enrolled, it is important (especially if the psychologist is not local) that the psychologist be in touch with the school psychologist, or the school district, to verify the types of assessment instruments that the school district will accept in order to meet the criteria for their admission process to special education. Different school districts have different regulations about the specific assessment instruments that they will accept for different placements.

Question: What Is the Difference Between a Psychologist and a Psychiatrist?

Psychologists go to graduate school to study advanced-level courses in psychology and obtain their Ph.D. or Psy.D. (some may have an Ed.D.). Psychiatrists attend medical school and study to become physicians. Psychiatrists are physicians who take their residency in psychiatry to learn how to apply their medical knowledge to mental problems. Because psychiatrists are physicians, they are able to prescribe medications, whereas the vast majority of psychologists cannot do so, except in New Mexico and Louisiana, where, due to a shortage of psychiatrists in those states, psychologists who have the appropriate training can prescribe medications.

DIDYOUKNOW

If you have questions about whether a psychologist is registered or certified to practice in your state, you can contact the Association of State and Provincial Psychology Boards (ASPPB) at http://www.asppb.org. The ASPPB is the association of psychology licensing boards in the United States and Canada and can provide information for contacting your state psychology board.

Because our book is primarily concerned with children and adolescents who have disabilities and special needs that may require special education and related services, we will talk primarily about the role of school psychologists in the schools.

THE ROLE OF THE SCHOOL PSYCHOLOGIST

Although school psychologists may also practice in clinics, private practice, mental health facilities, and hospitals, most practice within the public education system. School psychologists have a minimum of a master's or specialist degree that they receive after their bachelor's degree, while some have a doctorate (Ph.D., Psy.D., or Ed.D.).

DIDYOUKNOW

School psychologists employed by the public school system provide assessments to children free of charge to parents. Under the law, the public school system is also responsible for providing assessments free of charge to students enrolled in private schools.

School psychologists can serve many functions in the schools, including working with students individually or within groups; however, the school psychologist must have parental permission to become involved with a child, even if it means observing a specific student in the classroom. Nonetheless, the school psychologist can provide general assistance to teachers regarding effective teaching and learning strategies, as well as classroom management techniques for children who are experiencing school problems. School psychologists often provide assistance to school personnel, parents, and the community through such services as

- Consultation and collaboration to increase communication between the home, the school, and community resources

- Conducting evaluations of student difficulties in areas of achievement and learning, social-emotional difficulties, and behavioral problems

- Providing interventions in the form of counseling, strategies to cope with adjustment problems, behavioral management strategies for the home and schools, and skills-training sessions in social skills development and anger management

- Designing and conducting prevention programs for children at risk of learning, academic, and social problems

- Researching and monitoring the effectiveness of intervention programs and strategies

The National Association of School Psychologists (http://www.nasponline .org) suggests a number of child and adolescent problems for which school psychologists are commonly asked to provide assistance, including:

- Fears (school refusal; family concerns, such as divorce or death) and anxieties

- Social anxieties or feeling isolated, problems making and keeping friends

- Developing effective organizational skills (time management, using an agenda, and so on)

- Increasing effective study skills and work habits

- Academic difficulties

- Issues of self-esteem and acceptance of weaknesses or discovery of talents

- Increasing behavioral control and anger management

- Feelings of depression and thoughts of suicide

- Experimentation with drugs and alcohol

- Coping with difficult adjustments, such as transitioning to middle school, high school, and college, job hunting, and thoughts of quitting school

- Concerns about their own abilities or aptitudes

THE PSYCHOLOGICAL ASSESSMENT: AN IMPORTANT PART OF THE COMPREHENSIVE ASSESSMENT

In order to address some of the child and adolescent concerns noted in the preceding section, the school psychologist often conducts an assessment or an evaluation to obtain valuable information about the nature and severity of the problem. This information is necessary to develop an appropriate plan to assist the student. Most school psychologists function as part of the child's school support team composed of professionals from the multiple disciplines discussed in Chapter Five. The psychological assessment often complements information obtained from assessments and evaluations performed by other members of the team. The resulting comprehensive assessment package provides an overall picture of the "total child."

Overview of the Psychological Evaluation Process

A psychological evaluation involves many of the same steps that were outlined in the example of the medical evaluation introduced in the Chapter Five. A psychologist's goal is to determine the nature of a child's learning or social-emotional problems in much the same way that a physician seeks to find the cause of medical problems. The psychologist does this through the use of interviews, tests, and observations. Results from various tests are compared with so-called normal or *standard scores*, similar to the way that the physician compares test results with what would be expected for a normally developing and healthy child. In this way, the psychologist can determine *the nature of the problem* (learning problem, emotional problem, behavioral problem, and so forth) and *the severity of the problem* (the degree to which the child's scores differ from what is expected, given the child's age and grade level).

How Will I Know When a Psychological Assessment Is Necessary?

Parents and teachers often ask when an assessment should be requested. The decision is not one that is usually made quickly, but is part of a process of ongoing monitoring and review. We introduced three stages in the assessment process in the preceding chapter; here we will discuss the stages in greater depth.

DIDYOUKNOW

Assessments can be requested by parents or teachers. Parents may request an evaluation of their child from the school or the school may recommend, and ask permission for, an evaluation. According to IDEA 2004, a parent or a state agency—including a state educational agency (SEA), such as a state department of education, or a local education agency (LEA), such as a school district—has a right to request an initial evaluation to determine whether a child qualifies for special education and related services under IDEA 2004.

Stages in the Student Evaluation Process

There are three fundamental stages in the process.

Stage One   Before the school recommends a psychological evaluation for a child, difficulties have often been evident and monitored for some time. Thus, the psychological assessment should be thought of as part of the overall *process* of problem solving to better understand the nature and extent of a child's difficulties.

In the initial stages of monitoring a child's progress, schools often conduct regular in-school meetings to generate informal interventions in an attempt to address concerns. Most children will benefit from these interventions and no further assistance may be required. Examples of early and informal types of school-based interventions include making a change in seating arrangements (seating the child closer to the teacher); teaming the child with a student who has stronger academic performance; or involving the child in small-group instruction.

Early on, progress review meetings may be informal, such as a discussion between a teacher and guidance counselor. If concerns persist despite several interventions, more formal meetings may take place, involving a variety of professionals, including the teacher, guidance counselor, special education teacher or resource, curriculum specialist, speech pathologist, school psychologist, school social worker, or school administrator. Parents are encouraged to attend these meetings and to provide any additional information or concerns that they may have. The names of these school team meetings (for example, *student assistance team, child study team, student support team*, or *student intervention team*) will vary depending on the school district; however, the meeting goals are universal and aimed at information gathering to assist the decision-making process.

DIDYOUKNOW

According to IDEA 2004, school districts may use up to 15 percent of their IDEA funds to develop and provide early intervention services for educational or behavioral supports for students at risk of being referred to special education programs and services at some later date.

Stage Two   At this stage, the special education teacher might conduct informal assessments such as the Brigance tests to evaluate academic skills, while the school psychologist might be asked to review the school file or observe the child in the classroom. As mentioned previously, parent permission is always required if the school psychologist is asked to observe a particular child. Teachers can do classroom observations or administer screening tests like the Brigance without parent permission.

DIDYOUKNOW

The Brigance tests evaluate a child's academic strengths and weaknesses, indicating whether the expected curriculum goals have been mastered for the child's given age and grade level.

Often, the school guidance counselor, school resource teacher, or assistant principal may observe the child at this stage to suggest different strategies based on their observations. Some school districts may require that several parent interviews, interventions, and observations be completed prior to initiating a request for formal psychological assessment. Ultimately, information from these assessments or observations is shared with parents during an educational meeting held to discuss whether a more formal psychological assessment may be required.

DIDYOUKNOW

If a child is experiencing academic problems, one of the first assessments that should be conducted is to have vision and hearing evaluated to rule out whether such problems are contributing to the child's school difficulties.

Stage Three   When the school team requires more specific information about a child's learning or emotional problems, or a parent requests an initial evaluation, then a referral for psychological assessment may be initiated (after parent permission is obtained). Once all the evaluations are completed by the diagnostic team (special education teachers, curriculum specialist, guidance counselor, school psychologist, speech pathologist), the various professionals meet with the parents to share the results of their individual evaluations (this can be done individually or as a group). Ultimately, the *diagnostic team* presents the evaluation results and recommendations to the staffing specialist who presides over the staffing team committee meeting where the decision is made regarding whether special education and related services are warranted. Under IDEA 2004, parents must be notified of this meeting (often called the *staffing meeting* or *eligibility meeting*) two weeks prior to the meeting date.

Steps in the Psychological Assessment

The psychological assessment itself is a process that may involve a number of steps. An overview of what to expect is provided in Table 6.1.

How to Prepare a Child for an Assessment

Parents and teachers often wonder what they can do to prepare a child for an assessment. If the assessment is taking place in a clinic or private practice, the parent should inform the child that he or she will be working with a psychologist, who is a person who has studied how children think, learn, and feel. You can share your concerns and feelings about the child's frustrations at school and reassure the child that the psychologist is there to help understand why the child is experiencing difficulties learning and can suggest ways to present information that will make it easier for the child to be successful in school.

If the child is being seen by the school psychologist, there may be a time lag between obtaining permission for an assessment and having the actual assessment take place. As you can see in Table 6.1, there are several steps that must occur before the school psychologist actually makes contact with the child. Therefore, parents and teachers should just let the child know that help is on the way, and that at some time in the future, the school psychologist will be working with him or her to find out how he or she learns so that everyone can help make learning easier.

DIDYOUKNOW

Most children actually enjoy the individual attention afforded by the assessment sessions. During the assessment, the child has the undivided attention of the school psychologist, who is positive and encouraging of the child's efforts. Most children thrive in this situation. In fact, after the assessment situation, it is not uncommon for children to approach the school psychologist and ask if they will be working together again, another day.

TABLE 6.1 POSSIBLE STEPS IN THE PSYCHOLOGICAL ASSESSMENT PROCESS

1.	Child is referred for psychological assessment.
2.	Parent gives consent for assessment.
3.	Screenings are conducted to determine that vision, hearing, and speech/language functions are normal.
4.	If limited English proficiency is suspected, language dominance testing is conducted to determine the appropriate language for assessment that would yield the most accurate picture of the child's knowledge and understanding.
5.	The referral is directed to the special services department of the school district.
6.	The referral is assigned to the school psychologist for the school or to the bilingual school psychologist, whoever is most appropriate.
7.	The school psychologist reviews the child's cumulative file (school records) to gather information concerning academic progress, interventions, absenteeism, grade retentions, previous assessments, standardized testing, and so on.
8.	The school psychologist meets with the child's teacher(s) to obtain current information.
9.	The school psychologist begins the formal assessment process, which *may* include: • Observation of the child in the classroom or on the playground • Administration of a variety of standardized assessment instruments • Parent interview
10.	Results of the assessment are documented in a written report.
11.	The report is discussed in the educational meeting and parents receive a copy of the evaluation report.

What Takes Place in the Assessment Session?

Parents and teachers are often curious about what an assessment session is like. When school psychologists begin working with the child, they initially engage the child in a rapport-building task to place the child at ease, such as asking the child about favorite movies, books, or hobbies, or asking the child to draw some pictures, if that is the child's interest. Once rapport is established, the school psychologist usually begins by describing the nature of the tasks to be introduced.

TYPES OF PSYCHOLOGICAL ASSESSMENTS AND EVALUATIONS

There are many different types of psychological assessments, depending on the nature of the problem to be evaluated, such as:

- Intellectual functioning

- Academic skills

- Executive functions, information processing, and memory

- Social-emotional or behavioral development

We will focus on each of these different areas in greater detail over the next few chapters, so the present description will be very brief.

Intelligence tests provide a broad estimate of a child's ability and a profile of strengths and weaknesses. Assessments of achievement will focus on the child's academic levels relative to his or her age and grade expectations. Often a comparison of ability and achievement can be very helpful in evaluating differences between performance and expectations. Any significant differences between ability and achievement are a signal that further assessment may be required to investigate possible barriers to success. Additional evaluation may include an investigation of potential processing problems (attention, memory, visual motor problems, organization, and so forth) or social-emotional or behavioral problems, or both.

In addition to academic concerns and processing problems, some children may demonstrate disruptive behaviors or act out in the classroom. In this case, assessment may be requested to determine the nature of the behavioral problem(s). A key question to address is: *What is causing this child to act out?*

> ## DIDYOUKNOW
>
> Some children with behavioral problems can be acting out because of academic frustration, while other children with behavior problems do not learn effectively because the behavior interferes with learning. Which came first, *the behavioral problem or the academic problem?* Often the school psychologist attempts to address this difficult question as part of the assessment process.

Other more subtle emotional problems may also be evident, such as a child's withdrawal from social contact due to poor social skills, anxiety, or depression. Although a child's externalizing behaviors (acting out, aggression, or disruptive behavior) are far more obvious and readily observable than possible internalizing problems (anxiety or depression), finding out the reason that a child is experiencing emotional or behavioral difficulties is often a daunting task for the school psychologist.

Rarely are the answers obvious, and the psychologist is often required to include several steps in the evaluation process such as meeting with the child, observing the child in the classroom (or on the playground), meeting with the child's teachers (present and past), and talking to the parents.

Different Types of Assessments and Different Assessment Instruments

Parents and teachers should become familiar with the different types of tests that professionals use and what each of these instruments measures. Increasing your knowledge in this area will not only help you to better understand the child's assessment results, but will also provide a better understanding of how the child learns compared to other children. Understanding the assessments will also help you to become more prepared and aware of what questions to ask the school psychologist. In the next few chapters, we will provide information concerning some of the more well-known assessment instruments that are frequently used by school psychologists.

Goals of the Psychological Assessment

School psychologists rely on *standardized* tests, which means that the tests have specific instructions as to how they are to be administered and have *established norms* (expected ranges of scores) based on previous administrations of the test to a wide range of children across the United States. Using these tests allows the school psychologist to compare a student's performance with a large number of children of similar ages.

> **DIDYOUKNOW**
>
> The norms for the Wechsler Intelligence Scale for Children (WISC-IV, Wechsler, 2003) were obtained based on 2,200 children aged 6 years to 16 years, 11 months, across the United States, and included children representing special groups (gifted, learning disabled, those with intellectual disabilities, and so on).

It is always advisable that more than one assessment instrument (referred to as a *battery of psychological tests*) be included as part of the assessment, and that information about the child be obtained from different sources (such as parents *and* teachers). In this way, the school psychologist can determine whether the problem is evident in more than one area (all or some academic areas, behavior, social-emotional difficulties) and whether the problem exists across situations (home and school), or only occurs in one situation, such as in school but not at home.

In addition to formal *norm-referenced tests,* school psychologists also obtain information through less formal methods, including observations (in the classroom, on the playground, or test-taking behaviors); interviews (with parents and teachers); reviewing school records; and engaging the child in activities such as asking the child to bring a classroom reader to the assessment session and read from it.

> **DIDYOUKNOW**
>
> Observing the child in the classroom is one of the most common methods used by school psychologists to obtain a firsthand look at how the child is functioning, relative to peers. Although the children are aware of a visitor in the classroom, they are unaware that anyone in particular is being observed, and as a result, it provides an opportunity to see the amount of time a child spends in on-task versus off-task behavior, and how well a child responds to classroom instruction.

Should I Meet with the School Psychologist Before the Assessment?

If parents or teachers have any concerns about the nature of the assessment, the types of assessment instruments that will be used, or if they feel that they have important information to provide before the assessment begins, they should arrange for an appointment to visit with the school psychologist prior to the assessment.

If a parent or teacher has any information that might influence the assessment (for example, recent family difficulties or a recent incident involving the child at school), it is important to share this information with the school psychologist as soon as possible, for it may affect the assessment results, or how the results are interpreted, and may even suggest the need to delay the assessment until the situation is resolved.

Can a Parent or Teacher Sit in on an Assessment?

Occasionally, parents and teachers, especially of younger children, wonder if the child might be more at ease during the assessment if a familiar adult were present. There are several arguments for prohibiting parents or teachers from sitting in on the assessment, including:

- Increased level of distraction for the child

- Increased tendencies for the child to be inhibited in his verbal responses

- Less opportunity for the school psychologist to establish rapport

- Increased sense of anxiety for the child

- Violation of test instrument confidentiality

- Increased risk of invalidating results

Test construction and copyright laws prohibit the sharing of test item content with those who are not licensed to use the products. This is true because significant amounts of time, money, and effort go into standardizing the instruments' results based on age expectations (remember that more than two thousand children were involved in obtaining norming standards for the

WISC-IV, for example). If item content were to be distributed outside of professional circles, the test would no longer have value because results can be tampered with.

DIDYOUKNOW

Psychologists cannot release item content of the test items to parents or teachers because this would be in violation of the test's privacy and confidentiality. The psychologist will discuss the results of your child's assessment in a psychological report. In the next chapters, we have provided some examples of the more technical parts of these reports, and in Chapter Thirteen, a sample report is discussed and explained.

Another reason why it is not advisable to have someone sit in during an assessment is that many of the instruments have timed portions and the addition of another person creates a natural distraction, which could affect the outcome. Having a family member in the room (mother, father, or sibling) can make a child more apprehensive in responding. From a very young age, children look to their caregiver (for example, the mother or a sibling) for nonverbal cues regarding whether they are on the right track or wrong track. This phenomenon is called *social referencing*. The process is instinctive and, although words are rarely shared, children learn to read their parent's signals for a yes or no based on subtle visual cues such as an eye blink, raised eyebrow, shift in seating position, and so forth. If a parent were allowed to sit in during the assessment, a child would instinctively look for these visual cues to monitor and gauge performance. This social referencing could also result in a child changing responses, if it is suspected from subtle cues that a response was incorrect. (See the example in the following "Slice of Life" box). Children also are very aware of their teacher's cues, as well, although through increased use of standardized testing in the classrooms, teachers are becoming more and more aware of the need to monitor and avoid giving out any subtle hints.

A SLICE OF LIFE: A TRUE STORY

A parent arrived early to pick up her seven-year-old daughter, who was seeing a psychologist in private practice. There were only a few items left to administer, so the psychologist asked the parent to please wait quietly in the adjoining room. For the next few minutes, when the child gave an incorrect response or one that was slightly off, her mother softly grunted or shifted in her chair (unfortunately, the chair had a squeak). Each time she heard the faint sounds coming from her mother, the little girl quickly changed her answers. Although the mother was not intentionally signaling the child, she was nevertheless doing so in messages that were coming through loud and clear.

CHAPTER

7

THE ASSESSMENT OF INTELLIGENCE

In this chapter, we will discuss how intelligence is defined and how it is measured. We will also talk about some of the important ways that intelligence test scores can be helpful in better understanding a child's particular strengths and weaknesses.

WHAT IS INTELLIGENCE?

Intelligence is a measure of problem-solving ability. Some common ways of describing intelligence include *the ability to learn, the ability to adapt to one's environment,* and *the ability to solve new problems*. Intelligence is often referred to as IQ, which actually stands for "intelligence quotient," or the actual score obtained on an intelligence test. The psychologist who assesses intelligence in a school setting is interested in determining a child's "learning ability" related to school-based tasks, such as academic functioning. The term *cognition* can also be used to refer to *thinking skills* or *cognitive factors* that are involved in intelligence. Cognition or *knowledge* relates to intelligence when we evaluate a child's knowledge about certain topics and how well the child applies this information to new tasks.

In school, children are taught a number of key academic skills. A child's ability to learn these skills is based on several factors, including:

- Previous exposure to information

- Problem-solving ability

- Memory

- The ability to draw on previous experiences to help find solutions to new problems

Children who score higher on intelligence tests are more likely to draw on past experiences and use that information to help them solve new problems. Psychologists and educators refer to this process as being able to *transfer* information from one context (or situation) to another. Children with lower IQ scores, or with some specific learning disabilities, may acquire enough knowledge to solve a specific problem; however, they do not readily see how this information might also relate to solving a different but similar problem. In other words, they have more difficulty transferring information from one context to another. When this happens, they have to start from scratch to solve each new problem.

SLICE OF LIFE

A kindergarten teacher was having extreme problems teaching John the letters of the alphabet. She even made a set of letters out of green construction paper (John's favorite color). Finally, after several months, John proudly identified the entire alphabet. The teacher was so excited that she marched John into the adjoining classroom so that John could demonstrate his alphabet skills to the other kindergarten teacher. In that classroom, the letters of the alphabet were written in bright red letters on a border above the white board. To the teacher's dismay, John could not recognize one letter. Returning to her classroom, John immediately identified each of the green letters correctly. The teacher realized that John had learned the alphabet in green, and he did not recognize that the letters remained the same even though their color had changed to red. As unbelievable as this may seem, *this is a true story*.

Fortunately for John, the story has a happy ending. When the school psychologist observed John in the classroom, he found that John had problems transferring information from task to task, but that he was an astute observer and would watch the child next to him for clues on what to do next. Building on this strength, the school psychologist suggested that John buddy up with the stronger student, which helped John considerably. The teacher also began using multicolored letters, and letters in different textures (wood, plastic, and felt) to help John understand that the letters remained the same, despite the different colors or textures. Together, the classroom teacher and school psychologist developed intervention strategies that had a profound influence on John's ability to apply what he had learned in one situation to another situation.

WHERE DOES INTELLIGENCE COME FROM?

Children's intelligence can be influenced at birth by heredity (genes), prenatal toxins (such as a mother consuming alcohol or drugs during pregnancy), chromosomal defects (such as Down syndrome), or birth trauma (such as lack of oxygen, which may occur for a number of reasons such as having the umbilical cord wrapped around the neck). A child's environment can also have a powerful influence on intelligence. Some children have many opportunities to learn because they are exposed to a wide variety of learning experiences. Other children may have less exposure to new situations and consequently may experience less opportunity for learning. Unfortunately, intelligence can also be lowered by exposure to brain injury (accident) or environmental toxins, including exposure to lead-based paint or drugs such as inhalants.

Although IQ scores can predict academic and later occupational success, merely having a high IQ does not ensure success. Intelligence tests do not measure motivation or other more subtle learning problems, such as difficulties with memory, that might interfere with success.

REMEMBER: IQ scores are considered more stable with increasing age, and IQ scores obtained for preschool children should be regarded cautiously because they are not as reliable. Some young children may score lower than their true ability due to a lack of experiences or fewer opportunities, whereas others may score higher because they live in an environment rich in experiences.

HOW IS THE IQ SCORE CALCULATED?

The easiest way to understand IQ scores is to relate mental age (MA) or the mental capacity based on the test score, to chronological age (CA), or the actual birth age. For example, if Donny is five years old (CA) but he has the mental age (MA) similar to that of a four-year-old (MA), we would calculate his intelligence score by dividing the MA by the CA and then multiplying the result by 100. In our example, the resulting intelligence score would be 80. Because the average IQ score is 100, then Donny's intelligence score would be below average.

CALCULATING AN IQ SCORE

$$(MA \div CA) \times 100 = IQ$$

Donny's mental age (MA) = 4 years
Donny's chronological age (CA) = 5 years

$$(4 \div 5) \times 100 = 80$$

Donny's IQ = 80

WHAT IS TED'S IQ?

Ted is very bright boy. Although Ted has a CA of 8 years (birth age), his score on the IQ test is more typical of a child with an MA of 10 (mental age). When we use the formula of $(MA \div CA) \times 100$ we find out that Ted has an IQ of 125.

Although the actual mathematical computation of IQ is more complicated, these examples should provide a general idea of what an IQ score means. It is not uncommon for some individuals to be skeptical and concerned about the use of IQ scores in the educational system and how this information might be misused (for example, if a child's IQ score is below average, does that mean the expectations for success will be lower?). Although expectations can influence behavior, the benefits of knowing a child's IQ far outweigh any potential risks. The positive side of knowing an IQ is that it helps us to understand, at a basic level, where a child's problem-solving abilities are in relation to other children at the same age level. Furthermore, as we will soon discuss, IQ is not a single score; the IQ score is actually a composite score based on a number of tests (subtests) that measure different areas of functioning. When we look at the subtest scores, we often can find patterns of strengths and weaknesses that can assist greatly in developing an individualized education program (IEP). Later, we will discuss how the child's initial IEP is developed based on results and recommendations from the initial comprehensive assessment, which often includes intelligence testing.

WHAT DO INTELLIGENCE TESTS LOOK LIKE?

The majority of intelligence tests are developed to measure problem-solving skills in two major areas: verbal ability and visual ability. Tasks that measure verbal ability are usually presented orally and require the child to provide verbal responses. Areas evaluated can include measurements of vocabulary knowledge, verbal reasoning, and practical information. Children who score high on verbal tasks usually have better-developed communication skills, good listening skills, and are likely to be avid readers. On the other hand, visually oriented tasks require hands-on performance (completing puzzles, constructing block designs) or visual reasoning (selecting one picture or design from several visual alternatives). Visual tasks require minimal verbal expression. Some visual tasks are timed (using a stopwatch), resulting in either bonus marks for speed or no points for solving the problem after the given time limit.

HOW RELIABLE ARE IQ TESTS?

Any test score can fluctuate from assessment to assessment because of many outside factors, such as illness, fatigue, lack of sufficient rapport, or performance anxiety. However, IQ tests are highly reliable and provide results within a 5 to 10 percent range of accuracy. In the psychological report, there should be a statement to the effect that:

> *There is a 90 to 95 percent chance that the scores reported are a true indicator of the child's ability, and that the child's IQ score falls within the range of _____ to _____.*

Because different IQ tests sample different types of abilities, it is possible that a child's IQ on one test can differ from that obtained on another IQ test. In addition, different environmental conditions present at the time of testing can also contribute to variation in IQ scores. Nonetheless, research has shown that individually administered IQ tests are among the most reliable measures that we have and are a strong predictor of a child's ability to learn academic subjects.

WHAT DO THE TEST SCORES MEAN?

IQ scores can be reported in several ways: standard scores, percentiles, and age equivalents. Each of these scores is obtained by comparing the child's performance with the available range of scores for his or her peer group.

DON'T STOP NOW!

Numbers can be intimidating. When some of us see math, we just want to run the other way. But, if you walk through this section one step at a time, we promise that you will have a better understanding not only of IQ scores but of what the whole psychological report has to say about your child.

Here Come the Numbers: Put on Your Safety Belts—We Are in for a Numbers Ride!

In this section, we will talk about how scores from IQ tests can help us understand a child's ability in terms of strengths and weaknesses, and help us form possible expectations for performance. Standard scores are a common measurement that allow us to compare scores across a number of different types of assessment instruments.

Standard Scores

IQ tests report their scores as *standard scores*. In our initial example, we discussed how measuring a child's temperature provides a comparison with the normal standard score, which for temperature is 98.6 degrees on the Fahrenheit scale. So regardless of which thermometer you use, the numbers will represent the same scale. Similarly, scores on different tests (for example, achievement tests and IQ tests) can be compared if the scores are all using the same scale. Standard scores are based on the normal distribution of scores that look like the bell-shaped curve presented in Figure 7.1. In this distribution, the majority of scores fall in the middle or the average range. The average score (called the mean) is 100, which falls in the exact middle of the bell. If we were to test

FIGURE 7.1   *Normal Standard Distribution and Standard Scores*

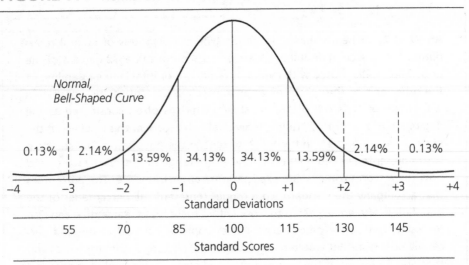

2,000 people, we would find that that 50 percent of the people would score above 100 and 50 percent would score below 100. However, we would also find that the majority of people who took the IQ test had scores that deviated from the mean (called the *standard deviation*) by 15 points on either side. Roughly 68 percent of the population would score within *one standard deviation of the mean:*

- 34 percent would obtain an IQ score between 85 and 100 (100 − 15);
- 34 percent would obtain an IQ score between 100 and 115 (100 + 15).

What about 2 standard deviations above or below the mean? How many would score in that area? Well, if we look again at our bell shape, we see that the biggest concentration of population is in the center within one standard deviation on either side. However, as we move toward the ends of the bell on either side, we are losing more and more people. If we looked at these narrow portions under the bell, representing 2 standard deviations (15 + 15) or 30 points from the middle on either side, we would find about 2 percent of the population would score *within two standard deviations of the mean:*

- 2 percent would obtain an IQ score at or below an IQ of 70
- 2 percent would obtain an IQ score at or above an IQ of 130.

DIDYOUKNOW

An IQ of 70 or below marks the range where a diagnosis of mental retardation or intellectual disability is considered. Approximately 2 percent of the population is diagnosed with mental retardation, or intellectual disability. At the other end of the spectrum, approximately 2 percent of the population will obtain an IQ score of 130 or above, which is often considered as the beginning of the "gifted" range. Individuals who score at this level are at the 98th percentile and are in the top 2 percent of the population. The standard scores presented in Table 7.1 reveal the entire range of possible IQ scores and how these scores can provide expectations for performance. The percentiles that accompany the standard score ranges represent the percentages of the population who are expected to score within these levels. Percentiles can also represent cumulative percentages. For example, if I scored at the 2nd percentile on a test, that would mean I was at the bottom of the test scores and that only 2 percent of the population would score at this level. If, however, I scored at the 98th percentile, that would mean that I was at the top of the scores, as only 2 percent of the population would score above me.

DIDYOUKNOW

Two out of three people who take an IQ test will obtain an IQ score somewhere between 85 and 115.

A Description of IQ Ranges

Extremely Low Range   Children who score in the extremely low range are in the bottom 2 percent of the population. Children who are within this range would be expected to find academic skills very challenging and would most likely require special education services to master basic academic concepts. When a child scores within this range, or *the borderline range*, the school psychologist (or social worker) will require additional information about *adaptive functioning levels* (daily living skills).

Adaptive Functioning: It is always helpful to obtain information about adaptive behavior from the child's teacher and parents, because each can provide a different perspective on adaptive skills evident at home and at school.

TABLE 7.1 IQ RANGES, STANDARD SCORES, AND DESCRIPTIONS

IQ Ranges	Standard Score Range	Percentile Ranges	Description
Extremely Low Range	Below 70	.02 to 2nd percentile	Children in this range will find academic tasks very challenging and will likely require special education services.
Borderline Range	70 to 79	2nd to 8th percentile	Children in this range will experience increasing academic difficulties, especially in the upper grades.
Average Ranges			68 percent of the population score within the average ranges. The majority of children at the lower end will likely experience more academic challenges. The majority of children at the upper end will likely solve tasks with relative ease.
Low Average Range	80 to 89	9th to 24th percentile	
Average Range	90 to 109	25th to 74th percentile	
High Average Range	110 to 119	75th to 90th percentile	
Superior Range	120 to 129	91st to 97th percentile	Children in this range will likely need additional challenges and enriched programming.
Very Superior Range (Gifted)	130 and above	98th percentile or higher	Children in this range often qualify for gifted programs to accommodate their advanced learning needs.

Interviewing the parent can often provide valuable information about the child's developmental history (when the child started walking, talking, and so forth) and medical history. There are also adaptive rating scales that parents and teachers can complete, such as the Adaptive Behavior Assessment System, Second Edition (ABAS-II) or the Vineland Adaptive Behavior Scales, Second Edition (Vineland-II). These scales assess daily adaptive functioning or living skills in areas such as self-care, independence, communication skills, social skills, leisure activities, health and safety, and so forth. An example of some of the questions that may be asked about past development can be seen in Table 7.2, along with other thoughts to consider in preparing for an education meeting. Information that teachers may want to bring to the meeting, as well as questions and considerations they may have for the parent, are presented in Table 7.3.

TABLE 7.2   QUESTIONS AND CONCERNS FOR PARENTS

A. Information That Parents Can Bring to an Educational Meeting	
Information to Consider	**Questions to Ask the Teacher**
How long is your child spending on homework each evening?	What is a reasonable amount of time my child should be spending on homework?
Does your child play well with children in the neighborhood?	Does my child have friends at school?
Is there anyone your child is frightened of at school?	Is my child is fearful of any of his classmates?
What subject does your child like best?	Which subject(s) is my child doing best in, and in which subject(s) is he having problems?
Are you getting everything that the teacher sends home for you to read?	Are there any parent groups or parent information sessions that I can attend?
Does your child have an agenda (a school planner)?	Do teachers write assignments in students' planners or check if the assignments are written down by students?

B. Questions the School Psychologist or Social Worker Might Ask		
Developmental History	**Family History and Family Context**	**Child's Current Health and Mental Status**
At what age did your child first, sit, stand, walk, say a first word, or talk in sentences?	Is there a family history of mental illness, ADHD, or learning disabilities?	How is your child's health? Is he frequently ill or relatively healthy?

TABLE 7.2 *(Continued)*

B. Questions the School Psychologist or Social Worker Might Ask		
Developmental History	**Family History and Family Context**	**Child's Current Health and Mental Status**
Was your child easy or difficult to manage as a baby?	How many children are in the family and do they all live at home?	Does your child often complain of aches and pains?
Did your child have any major illnesses or injuries as an infant, toddler, or child?	How well does the child get along with his siblings?	Is your child currently taking any medications?
Was your child overactive as a toddler?	Is this a single-parent or two-parent family? If a single parent, who has custody of the child and what are the visitation arrangements?	Does your child look forward to going to school, or would he prefer to stay home?
Is your child a good sleeper? How is your child's appetite?	Does your child have certain chores that he or she is responsible for at home?	Does your child have friends in the neighborhood? Is he invited to other children's homes?
	What is the main method of discipline? Who is the disciplinarian?	Does your child bring work home for you to see, or does he lose it or hide it?
	How does your child respond to being disciplined?	Does your child belong to any groups or clubs outside of school?
		What does your child like to do best when he is at home?

Scores for adaptive functioning can also be reported as standard scores, and comparisons can be made between IQ level and adaptive levels in several areas. Informed decision making for children who score within the extremely low IQ range requires consideration of several factors, including intellectual level, academic performance, and adaptive functioning (strengths and weaknesses in adaptive skills). Interventions would be expected to target skill development in the adaptive as well as academic areas.

TABLE 7.3 QUESTIONS AND CONCERNS FOR TEACHERS

A. Information That Teachers Can Bring to an Educational Meeting	
Information to Consider	*Questions to Ask the Parent*
Is the child completing homework and bringing the homework back to school?	Does the child do his homework in the same place and time each night? How long is your child spending on homework each evening?
Does the child have friends in the classroom? Does the child eat lunch with a group of children or alone? Are there any particular children the child avoids?	Are there children in the neighborhood, and does your child play well with children in the neighborhood?
Does the child complain of others not liking him or threatening him?	Has your child mentioned anyone that frightens him at school?
What are the child's strengths? Are there subjects the child does very well in?	Does the child talk about school subjects or activities that he really likes?
What are the child's weaknesses? Are there any subject(s) the child is having particular problems with?	Does the child mention parts of the school program that he really dislikes or feels that he is doing poorly in?
Are you sure that the parent is getting information that is sent home with the child?	Does the parent want to start a homework assignment book that is signed each night, and can be checked to see if the assignments are done?

B. Questions the School Psychologist or Social Worker Might Ask the Teacher		
School History—Daily Functioning	Current Academic/Learning Concerns	Child's Current Health and Mental Status
Has the child experienced...	**Is the child able to . . .**	**Is the child . . .**
• problems all along, or is the problem recent?	• follow directions as well as peers?	• frequently ill, or does she complain about not feeling well?
• frequent school moves?	• work independently on seatwork?	• currently taking any medications?

TABLE 7.3   *(Continued)*

B. Questions the School Psychologist or Social Worker Might Ask the Teacher		
School History—Daily Functioning	**Current Academic/ Learning Concerns**	**Child's Current Health and Mental Status**
Does the child have . . .	**Is the child able to . . .**	**Is the child . . .**
• regular attendance?	• make transitions appropriately?	• in frequent fights with classmates?
• tardy arrivals?	• express himself adequately?	• a loner? Or does the child have a few close friends?
Does the child usually . . .	• tolerate frustration?	
• come to school prepared to work (bringing books, pencils, homework)?	• problem solve effectively?	
• have an organized desk and book bag?	• remember facts and details?	
• arrive well rested?	• ask for help when he needs it?	
• arrive dressed appropriately, given the weather?	• read and comprehend at grade level?	
• complain of being hungry, tired, or having problems at home?	• solve math problems at grade level?	
	• complete written assignments at grade level?	
	• focus on work without being distracted?	

Borderline Range   Children who obtain scores in the borderline range are midway between the average ranges and the extremely low range; because they fall on the borderline, the term *Borderline Range* is used. These children pose the most difficult challenges for decision-making teams because they may or may not qualify for special education assistance, depending on specific criteria that vary from state to state.

Children within this range often experience significant difficulty in transferring information from situation to situation. For example, what they learn one day might not be transferred to the next day's lesson. What they learn in reading may not generalize to their written work. Therefore, rather than building on prior skills to construct a cumulative learning curve based on an increasing body of knowledge, their learning may be based on individual pieces of information that do not connect into a bigger picture. The story of John at the beginning of this chapter is a very good example of how deficits in transferring information can have a negative impact on learning.

However, some children in the Borderline Range may do relatively well, especially in the earlier grades, if they have strengths in long-term memory. If this is the case, they may amass a good sight vocabulary and spell or decode words with relative ease. As work becomes more complex, however, these children may begin to struggle with reading comprehension and the more challenging aspects of written work. They may also experience difficulties solving math problems that involve a lot of information, especially if they must figure out what information or numbers to ignore in the problem. Children in this range perform best in situations of high structure, clear directions, and consistent limit setting. Frequent repetition may be required to consolidate learning.

Average Ranges Children in the average ranges should not experience significant academic difficulties unless they have other contributing problems, such as a specific learning disability, attention problems, emotional or behavioral problems, or motivational problems. There are three broad ranges that fall within the "average range": lower average, average to high average, and superior range.

Lower Average Range (IQ: 80 to 89) As would be expected, depending on the particular pattern of strengths and weaknesses, children within the Lower Average Range may experience problems with comprehension, or they may require more time and more repetitions of a concept before they can consolidate the information. Children in this range may seem to be one step behind the pace of the majority of children in the class and are in danger of falling further behind if not given time or practice to consolidate foundation skills. Parents will need to be in touch with teachers and monitor progress to ensure academic success. Teachers may need to provide more time and repetition to ensure success.

Average to High Average Ranges (IQ: 90–109; 110–119)   Children who score in these ranges demonstrate normal to above-normal capacity to learn and should not be experiencing significant academic difficulties. If significant academic concerns are evident, further assessment should be conducted in different areas (processing, behavior, emotion, and observation) to help pinpoint and clarify the nature of the difficulty.

Superior and Very Superior Ranges (IQ: 120–129; 130+)   Children who score in these ranges are in the top 10 percent of the population intellectually and may require more-challenging academic tasks and enhanced learning environments. If academic concerns are evident, there is serious need to investigate why the child is not performing to potential. These children are not immune from problems such as a learning disability, attention problems, and emotional or behavioral problems that can be barriers to success. Children who score at the 135 level or above are in the top 2 percent of the population. This IQ score is often set as the admission criteria for most gifted programs.

COMMON INSTRUMENTS THAT MEASURE INTELLIGENCE

A discussion of all possible IQ tests is beyond the scope of this book, so we will focus on the three most commonly used measures. The selection of which measure to use will be based on the psychologist's preference and the circumstances surrounding the assessment. If a child has a language deficit, for example, the psychologist may want to use the Differential Ability Scale, as it contains a special nonverbal scale. The Universal Nonverbal Intelligence Test may also be used because this instrument requires only motor responses (for example, point to an answer or construct a design).

DIDYOUKNOW

Some school districts have a list of acceptable psychological instruments, including IQ tests, that may be used as part of the initial assessment. Psychologists in private practice may not be familiar with the district's specific requirements, or with child assessments conducted in another school district or state, and may need additional testing to match the district's requirements. This information is available from the school psychologist or by contacting the student services department of your local school district.

Wechsler Scales

Depending on the child's age, one of three scales can be administered: Wechsler Preschool and Primary Scale of Intelligence—Third Edition (WPPSI-III: ages 2 years, 6 months to 7 years, 3 months); Wechsler Intelligence Scale for Children—Fourth Edition (WISC-IV: ages 6 years to 16 years, 11 months); and Wechsler Adult Intelligence Scale—Fourth Edition (WAIS-IV: ages 16 to 90 years). Because the WISC-IV is the alternative that would apply to the majority of school-age children, we will focus on this particular test.

WISC-IV

The WISC-IV (2003) is the fourth revision of the Wechsler scales for this age range. The test provides an overall Full Scale IQ, as well as four index scores: Verbal Comprehension Index, Perceptual Reasoning Index, Working Memory Index, and Processing Speed Index. Full Scale IQ and index scores are reported as standard scores (mean of 100, standard deviation of 15). Information about the different subtests, examples of items, and descriptions of what the tests measure are presented in Table 7.4.

The **Verbal Comprehension Index** is a measure of a child's verbal reasoning, verbal concept formation, word knowledge, and practical or social judgment.

The **Perceptual Reasoning Index** involves tasks of perceptual reasoning that require minimal or no verbal response and measure nonverbal concept formation and visual problem-solving ability. Visual motor performance (speed) can earn bonus points in constructing block designs.

The **Working Memory Index** is a measure of a child's ability to mentally hold information in short-term memory while manipulating (performing an operation on) the information in some way, such as when doing mental math problems.

The **Processing Speed Index** measures a child's speed of copying or scanning visual information, or both.

The following case study of Jason will help to illustrate how intelligence test scores can assist in better understanding learning difficulties.

INTRODUCING JASON

Jason, who is eight years of age, has a history of academic difficulties. He repeated the kindergarten program to allow for consolidation of core skills. He has been recently diagnosed with ADHD and takes 15 mg of Adderall each morning at the beginning of the school day. Despite retention and Title I assistance (a federally funded program to assist children with reading, mathematics, and writing), Jason continues to struggle academically, especially in reading. Jason has just turned eight, and the class is more than halfway through the first-grade curriculum; however, Jason's parents and teacher are concerned that he has not yet mastered pre-reading skills. Jason's scores on the WISC-IV are presented in Table 7.5.

TABLE 7.4 WECHSLER INTELLIGENCE SCALE FOR CHILDREN (WISC-IV)

Index and Subtests	Example of Items (Items Increase in Difficulty)	What the Tests Measure
Verbal Comprehension Index		
Similarities	*"How are a table and a chair alike?"*	Verbal reasoning and concept formation, auditory comprehension, and memory
Vocabulary	*"What is a fountain?"*	Word knowledge and verbal concepts; verbal expression and language development
Comprehension	*"Why should we take vitamins?*	Conventional standards, social judgment, maturity, and common sense
Perceptual Reasoning Index		
Block Design	*Can you make your blocks look like mine?*	Analysis and synthesis of visual information, ability to work from a visual model, visual organization

(continued overleaf)

TABLE 7.4 WECHSLER INTELLIGENCE SCALE FOR CHILDREN (WISC-IV) *(Continued)*

Index and Subtests	Example of Items; Items Increase in Difficulty	What the Tests Measure
Picture Concepts	*Which pictures go together?*	Visual concepts and visual reasoning
Matrix Reasoning	*Which design comes next?*	Sequential reasoning, pattern completion; classification and serial reasoning
Working Memory Index		
Digit Span	*"Repeat these digits after me: 7–5–8–3–1"*	Attention, auditory perception, concentration, short-term memory
Letter-Number Sequences	*"Listen to these numbers and letters and repeat the numbers and then letters in the right order: A-3-J-9"*	Focused attention, recall for sequences, executive functions, and working memory
Processing Speed Index		
Coding	*"Copy the symbols for the correct numbers in the boxes under the numbers."*	Perceptual and graphomotor speed; timed task allowing two minutes
Symbol Search	*"If this symbol is in that row, check yes, if not check no"*	Scanning speed and accuracy; two minutes allotted, wrong are subtracted from the right

Jason's Full Scale IQ on the WISC-IV was 87 (Range 82–92), which is at the upper limits of the Low Average range. Based on Jason's overall IQ score, his learning potential would not predict serious academic difficulties. However, the index scores reveal a pattern of strengths and weaknesses that can help us in understanding why he is having problems. Jason's index scores ranged from a high of 102 (Average) for Perceptual Reasoning to a low of 78 (Borderline) for Processing Speed; a discrepancy of this magnitude (24 points) is highly significant, occurring in less than 1 in 20 students.

TABLE 7.5   JASON'S IQ SCORES

Index Scores	Standard Score	Range	Percentile	Description of Range
Verbal Comprehension Index (VCI)	85	79 to 93	16	Low Average
Perceptual Reasoning Index (PRI)	102	94 to 109	25	Average
Working Memory Index (WMI)	88	81 to 97	21	Low Average
Processing Speed Index (PSI)	78	72 to 90	7	Borderline
Full Scale IQ	87	82 to 92	19	Low Average

Index	Subscales Included Under This Index	Subscale Score	Strength/ Weakness
Verbal Comprehension Index (VCI)	Similarities	5	Weakness
	Vocabulary	9	
	Comprehension	9	
Perceptual Reasoning Index (PRI)	Block Design	12	Relative Strength
	Picture Concepts	8	
	Matrix Reasoning	12	Relative Strength
Working Memory Index (WMI)	Digit Span	8	
	Letter-Number Sequence	8	
Processing Speed Index (PSI)	Coding	6	Weakness
	Symbol Search	6	Weakness

Although Jason demonstrates an obvious strength in Visual/Perceptual Reasoning, he takes a significant amount of time to copy and scan information (Processing Speed Index).

DIDYOUKNOW

The IQ scores of children with ADHD often appear similar to other "normal" children for several reasons: the testing situation is novel and therefore helps sustain interest or attention; the IQ test is organized by the administrator; and the testing situation is usually relatively free of distractions. The two areas in which children with ADHD are most likely to show weaker performance are Processing Speed and Working Memory.

The individual subtests that make up the four index scores (see the lower portion of Table 7.5) are presented as scaled scores with a mean (average) score of 10 and standard deviation (unit of comparison) of 3. Therefore, average scale scores range from 8 to 12. Any scores below 8 or above 12 deserve extra consideration. Jason has significant problems seeing how verbal concepts and ideas are related (Similarities) and, to a lesser extent, how several visual pictures might share a common theme (Picture Concepts). Based on these scores, we would anticipate that Jason would have problems using examples from life experiences to help make concepts more meaningful to him, unless directed to do so.

Another area of weakness would be the actual time it takes Jason to complete tasks (Processing Speed) compared with other children in the classroom. His strengths in visual/perceptual reasoning suggest that the use of visual symbols is one method that could assist Jason in better understanding the relationships that exist between concepts. Based on the results of Jason's performance on the IQ test, the school psychologist can now assess academic performance to determine how closely these scores match what would be predicted given his Full Scale IQ.

Other Intellectual Assessment Instruments

Although we have focused primarily on the Wechsler Scales, there are several other instruments that also measure intelligence. The following is a list of the most common alternative assessment measures that are used.

Stanford-Binet Intelligence Scales, Fifth Edition (SB5: 2003)   The SB5 is also commonly used to assess intelligence in children but, unlike the Wechsler Scales, the SB5 uses a single instrument for all age levels (2 years, 0 months to adults age 80 years and over). In addition to the Full Scale IQ, the SB5 provides standard scores for Verbal and Nonverbal IQ, based on composite scores obtained for five verbal and five nonverbal scales. The five scales on the SB5 include Fluid Reasoning (*problem solving in novel situations*), Knowledge (*acquired information*), Quantitative Reasoning (*reasoning with numbers*), Visual/Spatial Processing (*spatial analysis*), and Working Memory (*mental manipulation*).

The Differential Ability Scale—Second Edition (DAS-2: 2007) The DAS-2 provides a General Conceptual Ability Score (GCA) for very young children (2 years, 6 months to 3 years, 5 months), and two additional cluster scores for children between 3 years, 6 months and 5 years, 11 months: Verbal Ability and Nonverbal Ability. One other additional cluster, Spatial Ability, is added for children over 6 years of age, resulting in three clusters in addition to the GCA. One benefit of using the DAS-2 is the Special Nonverbal Composite score, which can be substituted for Verbal Ability, if the examiner believes that administration of the verbal tasks is not appropriate (for example, language problems, speech or hearing impairment).

Other Measures of Intelligence and Cognitive Ability There are several other measures of intelligence, including: Reynolds Intellectual Assessment Scales (RIAS), Universal Nonverbal Intelligence Test (UNIT), Wechsler Nonverbal Scale of Ability (WNV), Kaufman Assessment Battery for Children, Second Edition (KABC-II), Cognitive Assessment System (CAS), and the Woodcock-Johnson III Tests of Cognitive Abilities (WJ III). The WJ III will be discussed further in Chapter Eight, when we discuss the use of this instrument to probe potential information-processing difficulties.

CHAPTER

8

EVALUATION OF ACADEMIC AND PROCESSING PROBLEMS

The assessment of intelligence is usually only one component of the assessment process. Psychologists often administer a battery of tests to pinpoint the nature and extent of a child's learning problems.

ACHIEVEMENT TESTING

Academic assessment is often an integral part of the comprehensive assessment. Children are often referred for assessment because they are experiencing academic problems. Recall that although IDEA 2004 does recognize thirteen categories of disabilities, special education assistance would only be warranted if the disability was found to interfere significantly with the child's learning. Therefore, assessment of achievement is vital to determining whether a child qualifies for special education assistance based on his or her current level of academic performance. Furthermore, the psychologist has access to a wide variety of norm-referenced instruments that measure achievement and provide a profile of the child's achievement in core areas (reading, math, and written expression) relative to peers of a similar age and grade level. These norms are based on administrations of the test to large samples of children from different geographical locations and social-economic backgrounds across the United States.

How Do Psychologists Measure Achievement?

REINTRODUCING JASON

Recall that Jason, the eight-year-old boy we introduced in Chapter Seven, was struggling with the first-grade language arts program. Last week, Jason got only three words correct on his spelling list of ten words. Compared with other children in his class, Jason can recognize only about half of the sight words and, even then, he is inconsistent in his attempts. On the other hand, Jason has no problems in math. The question is: how far behind is Jason, actually?

Standardized Achievement Tests When the psychologist administered an intelligence test, he was able to determine that relative to similarly aged peers, Jason's ability level was roughly within the average range (upper Low Average). Jason's profile revealed weaknesses in abstract verbal reasoning, and his slow speed of copying could contribute to academic concerns; however, all things being equal, his learning ability does not explain why Jason is experiencing academic difficulties. The next likely step in the process would be to compare Jason's achievement scores with academic scores of other children of similar ages or grade level to determine where Jason's academic functioning levels are in three core areas of academic performance: reading, written expression, and mathematics. The psychologist would be interested in obtaining answers to the following questions:

- Given Jason's age, where should he be functioning academically?

- Given Jason's IQ, is he functioning at the predicted academic levels?

- Is Jason's academic performance consistent across the three major academic areas of reading, written expression, and mathematics?

In order to answer these questions, the psychologist administers a *norm-referenced* achievement test, which allows him to compare Jason's academic performance with the academic skills expected of other children Jason's age, and additionally, to compare academic levels to levels expected, given his IQ level.

How Can the Psychologist Determine What Is "Normal" Academic Functioning for Jason?

Remember that IQ scores were reported as *standard scores* with a mean (average) of 100 and a standard deviation of 15. There are a number of individual achievement tests available, such as the Wechsler Individual Achievement Test, Third Edition (WIAT-III), the Kaufman Test of Educational Achievement, Second Edition (KTEA-II), Diagnostic Achievement Battery, Third Edition (DAB-3), and the Woodcock-Johnson III Tests of Achievement, that report results of achievement as standard scores, allowing for a direct comparison between expectations (IQ scores) and academic performance.

Jason's scores on the WJ III Achievement Test are presented in Table 8.1; they indicate that both reading and written expression are in the extremely low range based on age expectations.

Comparison of Academic Scores Based on Age Expectations (Age Norms)

When Jason's academic responses on the WJ III Achievement Test are compared with the expected responses based on norms available for eight-year-old boys, Jason performs well below the expected levels for reading and written expression. In fact, Jason's responses are more typical of an average child between 6 years, 1 month of age (written expression) and 6 years, 4 months of age (reading).

In considering grade equivalents, although the majority of the class has passed the midway point of the first-grade program, Jason is at a late-kindergarten (written expression) to beginning first-grade (reading) level in language arts. However, because Jason is already one year behind his classmates (remember, he repeated kindergarten), these lags are even more pronounced than they appear on the surface. In reporting test scores, it is more important to base comparisons on age rather than grade-based comparisons for this and other reasons that are beyond the scope of this book.

TABLE 8.1   JASON'S SCORES ON THE WJ III TESTS OF ACHIEVEMENT: AGE, GRADE EQUIVALENTS, PERCENTILES, AND STANDARD SCORES

Academic Cluster	Age Equivalent Years/Months	Grade Equivalent	Percentile	Standard Score	Description
Broad Reading	6/4	1.1	1	65	Extremely Low
Broad Mathematics	7/1	1.7	23	89	Low Average
Broad Written Expression	6/1	K.8	1	63	Extremely Low

Comparison of Achievement Scores Based on Intellectual Expectations
Remember that IQ scores are presented as standard scores with a mean of 100 and standard deviation of 15. A child's standard score for achievement should be within one standard deviation (15 points) of his IQ score.

WHAT ARE THE EXPECTATIONS?

Because Jason has an IQ score of 87, we would expect his academic standard scores to range between a low of 72 (87−15) and a high of 102 (87+15). Scores within the range of 72 to 102 would be within one standard deviation above and one standard deviation below the score predicted by his IQ of 87.

A comparison of Jason's achievement scores and IQ scores is presented in Table 8.2. When we compare Jason's standard scores for reading (65) and written expression (63) to his expected level of performance suggested by his IQ (87), we find that Jason is well in excess (22- to 24-point differences) of this 15-point discrepancy in both areas. However, when we compare his mathematics score (89) to his predicted level (87), we find that the difference between these two scores is very small. Jason is just about where we would predict he would be in math. The relationship between standard scores obtained for academic performance relative to Jason's Full Scale IQ score is shown in Figure 8.1.

TABLE 8.2 WJ III TESTS OF ACHIEVEMENT STANDARD SCORES AND EXPECTED PERFORMANCE BASED ON IQ.

Academic Cluster	Age Equivalent	Percentile	Standard Score	WISC-IV IQ	Discrepancy
Broad Reading	6/4	1.1	1	87	−22
Broad Mathematics	7/1	1.7	23	87	+2
Broad Written Expression	6/1	K.8	1	87	−24

FIGURE 8.1 *A Comparison of Standard Scores in IQ and Academic Achievement*

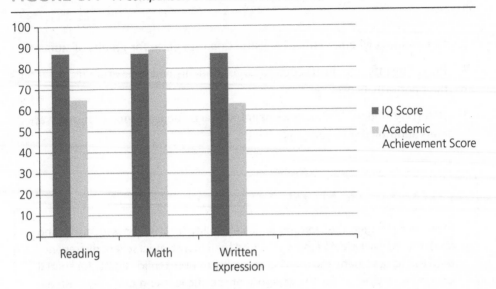

Is the Discrepancy Formula Used by All Districts, and Is It Universal?

Comparing standard score differences between ability and achievement scores is referred to as a *discrepancy model* or using a *discrepancy criterion.* This model has met with great controversy. Some people feel that this method penalizes children at the lower extreme. For example, if a child has an IQ of 85, he would need to score below 70 to demonstrate a significant discrepancy between ability and achievement. However, if a child has an IQ of 115, he could obtain a standard score of 100 academically, which is in the average range, and still be considered to have a significant discrepancy between ability and achievement.

Some districts consider a 15-point discrepancy between ability and achievement significant for younger children (under eleven years of age), but then require a 22-point difference (one and a half standard deviations) for children above eleven years of age. Other school districts may require as much as a two standard deviation difference, which would mean a 30-point difference between achievement and IQ. The rationale is that it is more difficult to have a large gap between achievement and ability at younger age levels. Despite the inherent flaws in the discrepancy model noted previously, many districts will continue to use this model, while others may follow a response-to-intervention (RTI) approach, as allowed by IDEA 2004. The RTI model was discussed at length in Chapter Four but, to review, the three-tiered model includes the following phases:

1. Determining whether effective instruction is in place for groups of students

2. Providing effective instruction to target students and measuring its effect on their performance

3. Referring students for an assessment whose response-to-intervention warrants additional interventions

DIDYOUKNOW

IDEA 2004 changed the wording about eligibility for children with a learning disability. Schools are *no longer required* to demonstrate a severe discrepancy between achievement and intellectual ability to find a child eligible for special education services under the category of specific learning disability. Instead, the school district *may use* an evaluation of the child's failure to respond to scientific, research-based interventions to document a specific learning disability.

What Are the Academic Skills That Achievement Tests Measure?

As outlined in the previous example, most standardized achievement tests provide a composite score for reading based on a number of subtests, which may include tasks of single-word decoding, reading fluency, and comprehension. A composite mathematics score would likely involve tasks of calculation, fluency, and problem solving. Written expression is often measured through spelling tests and tasks designed to measure sentence and paragraph construction. It is important that whatever instrument is used to measure these core academic areas, that measures include more than just decoding, spelling, and math calculation skills, but also include assessment of a child's reading comprehension, math problem solving, and written expression (beyond spelling).

ASSESSMENT OF PROCESSING SKILLS

In our case study, the psychologist has found that Jason has a significant discrepancy between the performance that would be predicted by his intelligence score and his actual academic performance in the areas of reading and written expression. The next step might be to administer additional tests to determine whether learning difficulties result from problems that Jason might have in processing auditory or verbal information.

What Is a Processing Assessment?

A significant discrepancy between ability and achievement suggests that there is some factor other than learning ability that is undermining a child's academic success. There are several possible reasons why a child may encounter academic difficulties, including a lack of motivation, lack of interest, frequent absenteeism, emotional or behavioral difficulties, family or adjustment difficulties, and processing problems. Children whose academic success is compromised by processing difficulties often can be diagnosed with a specific learning disability that describes the nature of their specific processing problem.

What Kinds of Processing Problems Exist?

Children with specific learning disabilities likely have no physical vision or hearing problems, and the majority of these children have average to above-average intelligence. However, their ability to be successful academically, and sometimes socially, can be compromised by unique deficits in how information is processed. An overview and in-depth discussion of the various types of specific learning disabilities can be found in Chapters Two and Three. At this point, the focus will be on the role of assessment in determining the nature of processing difficulties.

Information processing can break down as information is received at the *input stage* (auditory, visual, or motor recognition problems), at the *integration stage* (interpretation, short- and long-term memory, or organization of information), or the *output stage* (oral, written communication, or motor responses). Children who have problems with attention and concentration often experience difficulty receiving information and sustaining attention long enough to allow for sufficient interpretation. Impulsive children may jump to the expression stage and virtually bypass the interpretive process.

Weaknesses in processing information can occur at several different levels and can result in specific learning problems. Some of the more common types of processing skills and deficits are listed in Table 8.3. Possessing difficulties in any of these areas can result in poor academic performance despite good intellectual ability and motivation. Children with these types of processing problems are often very frustrated, painfully aware of their poor academic progress, and may suffer from low self-esteem.

TABLE 8.3 INFORMATION PROCESSING: TYPES OF PROCESSING AND THE IMPACT ON LEARNING

Information Processing	Description
Attention and Concentration	Ability to attend to auditory and/or visual information Ability to selectively attend to important versus extraneous information Ability to sustain attention over time Ease of distractibility
Memory	Auditory and visual memory Short-term memory (use within a few seconds, for example, use for task instructions) Working memory (ability to hold information in a state of mental awareness, while mentally manipulating information or performing some operation on the information) Longer-term storage and retrieval of information
Executive Functions	Planning and organization
Cognitive Fluency	Ease of ability to retrieve information from storage and apply that information to current problem-solving tasks; decision-making speed
Processing Speed	Ability to perform simple cognitive and motor tasks that are automatic, repetitive, and require sustained attention over the course of time

How Are Processing Deficits Assessed?

The psychologist may use one or more of the several available instruments for measuring processing skills and deficits. Some of the more common instruments used include

- Woodcock-Johnson III Tests of Cognitive Abilities (WJ III)

- Children's Memory Scale (CMS)

- Wechsler Memory Scale, Fourth Edition (WMS-IV)

- Test of Memory and Learning, Second Edition (TOMAL-2)

- Wide Range Assessment of Memory and Learning, Second Edition (WRAML2)

- Comprehensive Test of Phonological Processing (CTOPP)

TABLE 8.4   JASON'S RESPONSES TO SUBTESTS OF THE WOODCOCK-JOHNSON III TESTS OF COGNITIVE ABILITIES ASSESSMENT

Processing Area	Age Equivalent	Percentile	Standard Score	Description
Visual-Spatial Thinking	10–3	77	111	High Average
Short-Term Memory	7–4	22	89	Low Average
Long-Term Memory/Retrieval	4–8	0.1	54	Extremely Low
Working Memory	6–0	9	80	Low Average
Cognitive Fluency	5–9	4	72	Borderline
Processing Speed	6–4	5	76	Borderline
Auditory Processing	6–0	16	85	Low Average
Phonemic Awareness	5–8	12	82	Low Average

As might be expected, these instruments also present results as standard scores, and they allow for a direct comparison of how processing skills align with intellectual ability. As a case in point, let's look at how our eight-year-old, first-grade student Jason scored on his processing assessment. The psychologist administered the WJ III Tests of Cognitive Abilities battery, and a summary of Jason's processing scores is presented in Table 8.4.

By now, the standard scores should begin to take on a more meaningful role, as we look at a third set of scores. Although Jason's scores suggest a significant strength, there are also several areas of processing deficits. On the extreme positive end, Jason has an obvious strength in Visual-Spatial Thinking. This result is consistent with previous scores obtained on his IQ test. Strengths noted on Block Design and Matrix Reasoning of the WISC-IV also measure visual-spatial reasoning. Remember that these were two of Jason's strongest subscale scores on the IQ test. Children with strengths in these areas often do well with mathematics.

However, at the other end of the spectrum, Jason is slow to get information down onto paper (Processing Speed), which would likely result in problems finishing written work or paper-and-pencil tasks on time. Jason's ability to retrieve information from long-term memory is very poor (Extremely Low range score in Long-Term Memory/Retrieval), and may result in the frustration of information being "here today and gone tomorrow." In addition, Jason is not an efficient thinker (which may result from poor organizational skills or may be influenced by his poor ability to retrieve information). Basically, it takes Jason longer to solve problems because he does not use the most efficient ways to sort, retrieve, and respond to information.

DIDYOUKNOW

Retrieving information from long-term storage is similar to trying to locate a file in a filing cabinet or trying to locate a file on your computer. If you can't remember how the information was stored (file name, and so on), you can experience significant problems trying to access that information.

As you might anticipate, it is now time to compare these processing scores to expected levels that would be predicted given Jason's IQ or ability levels. A quick glance at the scores presented in Table 8.5 tells the story. When we compare standard scores obtained on the processing assessment with Jason's IQ score, it becomes evident that Long-Term Memory/Retrieval is well in excess of the 15-point difference (standard deviation) needed to suggest a significant

TABLE 8.5   A COMPARISON OF STANDARD SCORES AND EXPECTED PERFORMANCE BASED ON IQ

Processing Area	Standard Score	WISC-IV IQ Score	Discrepancy
Visual-Spatial Thinking	111	87	+24
Short-Term Memory	89	87	+2
Long-Term Memory/Retrieval	54	87	−33
Working Memory	80	87	−7
Cognitive Fluency	72	87	−15
Processing Speed	76	87	−11
Auditory Processing	85	87	−2
Phonemic Awareness	82	87	−5

difference between ability and processing skill in this area. Cognitive Fluency is also significantly below what would be anticipated (–15), while Processing Speed also approaches significance (–11).

Although the majority of assessment of processing skills or deficits would involve the psychologist working directly with the child, it is also possible to obtain information concerning processing skills through other techniques, such as classroom observation, teacher-parent interviews, and parent-teacher completion of standardized questionnaires.

In Jason's case, there are no complicating emotional, behavioral, or social problems, so the assessment ends at this point, because assessment of IQ, academic ability, and processing all present a consistent picture. If Jason had not been already diagnosed with ADHD, further assessment would have likely included rating scales for ADHD. An example of some rating scales for ADHD will be discussed in the next chapter.

Jason has a specific learning disability that is impeding his progress in reading and written expression. Jason's learning disability is manifested in significant difficulties retrieving information stored in long-term memory. Jason is also slow to generate solutions to problems. This sluggish tempo has an impact on his learning to the extent that Jason will often be "one step behind" his fellow classmates. The danger in this type of processing deficit is the cumulative impact of always playing catch-up in an academic world that is most likely full speed ahead. By the time Jason has come up with the correct solution, or retrieved the information from his memory bank, the class has probably moved on to another topic. As a result of the assessment information, Jason's educational team can now begin working on an intervention plan to help him develop more efficient memory strategies and to increase his fluency in thinking, reading, and writing.

CHAPTER

9

ASSESSMENT OF EMOTIONAL DIFFICULTIES AND BEHAVIORAL PROBLEMS

In the preceding four chapters, we have discussed the nature of assessment and psychological assessment in particular. We have discussed the assessment of intelligence, learning and information processing, and achievement, all of which have involved the psychologist working one-on-one with the individual child using a variety of psychological tests. In this chapter, we will cover a number of topics related to assessment that have not yet been covered, including

- How psychologists investigate concerns about a child's possible attention problems, emotional difficulties, or behavioral problems

- The use of parent and teacher rating scales to assess a variety of child problems

- Techniques that psychologists use to observe children in the classroom

DIDYOUKNOW

According to a Surgeon General's report issued in 1999, 20 percent of all children (one in five children) have a diagnosable mental disorder.

In Chapter Six, we discussed a number of common problems that children experience that often come to the attention of the school psychologist. We also briefly mentioned that children who act out or whose behavior is disruptive often stand out. These are the first types of children that the school psychologist usually hears about; however, there are many reasons why children can behave poorly. Sometimes, there are things going on in the child's life, at home or at school, that the child does not understand. Children may act out when they are frustrated, either emotionally, mentally, or academically. Children who act out (for example, with disruptive behaviors or aggression) are said to demonstrate *externalizing behaviors*.

Not all children respond to stress and frustration by acting out. Some children may withdraw, become sad or anxious, or have a wide variety of physical (somatic) complaints. Children who respond to stressful events by bringing the problem inside them are said to have *internalizing behaviors*. Unfortunately, internalizing behaviors, such as depression, anxiety, or physical complaints, are often difficult to detect and may go unnoticed for some time. Once these internalizing problems are detected, it can be difficult to determine why the child has these feelings. One reason that the assessment of emotional and behavioral difficulties can be so challenging is that children often do not fully understand their emotions. Unlike adults, children often are not able to verbalize what is causing them to be unhappy, sad, or worried. Adults may be unaware that children may blame themselves for things going on in the home or at school that are not within their control.

Another difficulty in determining the nature of a child's emotional or behavioral problems is that children often have problems in more than one area at the same time, a condition that is called *comorbidity,* which basically acts as a *double whammy*. Some of the common problem areas that often go together are children who may have ADHD and another set of behavioral problems called oppositional defiant disorder (ODD). Children who have ODD can be very negative and refuse to comply with requests or choose to ignore requests completely. What a lot of people do not know is that some disorders can appear very different from what people expect them to look like. For example, when most people think of ADHD, they think of the child who is hyperactive and impulsive, a child who is impatient, can't wait his turn, and acts out. This form of ADHD often occurs with ODD, which can cause significant problems at home and at school, as the two externalizing behaviors have an increased negative effect when combined.

However, there is another form of ADHD, the inattentive type. Children with this kind of ADHD are not impulsive or hyperactive, but rather are easily distracted, have problems concentrating, lose necessary materials, and are forgetful. These children tend to develop more of the internalizing problems, such as anxiety and depression. However, it is also common for children to have more than one internalizing disorder at the same time. For instance, a child may have symptoms of both depression and anxiety, or may express feelings of anxiety through many physical (somatic) complaints.

DIDYOUKNOW

In Appendix B, we have provided a number of "Checklists for Child Problems" that can be a very helpful tool for teachers and parents in screening children for problems. The checklists include some common symptoms and indicators for a variety of child problems, such as: ADHD, ODD, anxiety, depression, and behavioral issues. These checklists can help parents and teachers decide whether a problem is a potentially serious concern.

WHAT ARE THE TOOLS FOR EVALUATING EMOTIONAL AND BEHAVIORAL CONCERNS?

There are several types of instruments available to assist in evaluating the degree to which children may be suffering from attention problems, emotional difficulties, or behavioral difficulties. In addition to observing children either in the classroom or on the playground (which we will explain in a minute), the psychologist may also want to interview teachers and parents to determine whether concerns are consistent across situations. Interviews can be either informal or very structured.

Behavior Rating Scales

Often, psychologists will ask teachers and parents to complete behavior rating scales. Individuals completing the scale are asked to rate the degree to which each item is true for the child. The rating scale will provide statements about a number of different potential problem areas, such as those shown in the example rating scale in Table 9.1. Based on the responses, profiles are generated that indicate how the child was rated relative to similar-aged peers who do not experience the same problems.

TABLE 9.1 EXAMPLE OF A BEHAVIOR RATING SCALE

Rating Scale for Children and Youth	Parent Form ☐		Teacher Form ☐	
Please indicate the degree to which each of the following statements describes the child's behavior in the past few months:	**Never**	**Sometimes**	**Often**	**Always**
1. Is upset if routines are changed				
2. Has problems paying attention				
3. Is nervous				
4. Complained of headaches				
5. Got into a fight				
6. Refused to obey				
7. Had a friend over to play				
8. Completes homework				
9. Plays alone				
10. Cries easily				
11. Shares with others				
12. Fidgets				
13. Says "Nobody loves me"				
14. Is constantly on the go				
15. Doesn't seem to listen				

Jason's parent and teacher both completed a standard rating scale that evaluates problems in a number of areas. The resulting profiles are available in Figure 9.1. As we can see, Jason's teacher rated his anxious and attention behaviors higher than Jason's mother did, although both placed these two areas within the at-risk to clinically significant range.

T-Scores and Behavior Rating Scales

We spent a lot of time discussing the use of standard scores in the comparison of scores for IQ, achievement, and information processing. Now we are going to

FIGURE 9.1 *Teacher and Parent Profiles for Jason*

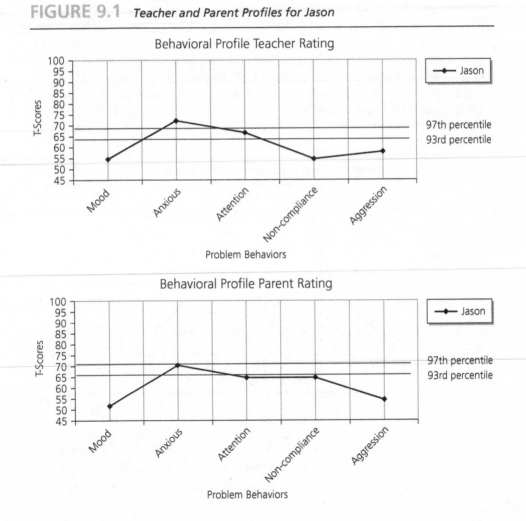

introduce a different type of scale. When we are using rating scales, the scores are represented by T-scores, which have an average score of 50 and a standard deviation of 10. You can see how the T-scores compare with the standard scores in Figure 9.2. Scores on this scale that are one standard deviation below or above the mean would range from 40 to 60. Once we start to go above this level, behaviors are becoming more atypical and have more serious consequences. A T-scores of 60 places the functioning at the 90th percentile (only 10 percent of the population score at this level); a T-score of 65 represents functioning at the 95th percentile, which is in the top 5 percent of the population; and a T-score of 70 is at the 98th percentile (top 2 percent of the population).

A VERY IMPORTANT DISTINCTION

Whereas higher scores on tests of achievement and IQ represent higher functioning, higher T-scores represent higher ratings for problems, such as problems with emotion, behavior, or attention, and therefore represent higher scores for dysfunction.

FIGURE 9.2 *Standard Normal Distribution and T-Scores*

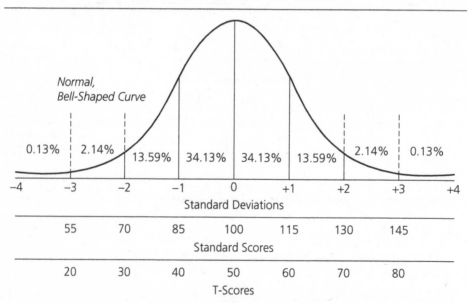

Some of the more common broad behavior rating scales are listed below:

- Child Behavior Checklist (CBCL)
- Teacher's Report Form (TRF)
- Youth Self-Report Form (YSR)
- Behavior Assessment System for Children, Second Edition (BASC-2) (parent and teacher forms)
- Conners Third Edition (Conners 3) (parent, teacher, and student forms)
- Devereux Behavior Rating Scale–School Form (parent and teacher forms)

Parents may be surprised at the number and range of questions sampled by these rating scales. The CBCL, TRF, and the BASC-2, for example, include more than one hundred questions. The reason there are so many questions is that the scales evaluate behaviors across several different domains (depression, anxiety, attention, acting out, and so on), and several questions are required to provide an adequate picture of whether the child is experiencing significant problems in any given area. However, completing the questionnaire can be quick, because respondents are required only to indicate the degree to which a behavior occurs (never, sometimes, often, and so forth).

Do Parents and Teachers Agree or Disagree in Their Ratings?

As might be expected, differences between raters are common. Not only do parents and teachers often differ in their ratings of a child, differences also exist between different teachers (different classes) and between different parents (mother and father). However, it is important to collect as much information as possible to obtain a better understanding of where the behaviors are taking place in order to develop the most appropriate plan for assisting the child. A child may have few problems in a math class because he excels in this area, but he may exhibit more inappropriate behaviors in an intensive reading class because he is a poor reader and is lost in the program. Or a child may have few problems in the morning classes, but get progressively worse as the day wears on and the child's frustration mounts. A child may not experience any problems at home because the focus is less structured and the child can relax. The child may also experience many problems at home because he is able to vent his frustration in this setting and not at school.

INDIVIDUAL ASSESSMENT OF EMOTIONAL AND BEHAVIORAL DIFFICULTIES

In addition to asking parents and teachers to complete rating scales, the psychologist will likely want to talk with the child and have the child complete a number of different tasks to help evaluate his emotional and behavioral responses, relative to similar-aged peers. There are many types of instruments and techniques available, ranging from unstructured requests for the child to draw pictures, to having the child complete personality inventories, or having him or her rate his or her own emotional responses on rating scales similar to those given to parents and teachers.

If a psychologist is concerned that a child may be depressed or anxious, the psychologist may ask the child to complete one of many available depression or anxiety scales that ask children to rate whether they feel sad or anxious (a lot, a little, or not at all) in different situations. The psychologist can then compare the child's pattern of responses with responses of other "normal" children and "depressed or anxious" children of similar ages to determine whether the child is more depressed or anxious than would be expected. Of course, evaluations of emotional and behavioral responses are more difficult with younger children because they often do not understand the nature of their own feelings and have limited expressive vocabulary. For younger children, observations of behavior and obtaining parent and teacher information are likely to yield the most accurate picture of problems.

As children grow older, there are more assessment instruments available to assist the psychologist in evaluating the nature and extent of a child's emotional or behavioral problems. However, the value of these instruments is only as valid as the child's honesty in providing the responses. Some children, despite significant behavioral or emotional difficulties, will respond as if they are having no problems whatsoever. Other children may exaggerate their difficulties in an attempt to obtain increased attention. Regardless, psychologists are trained to read between the lines and evaluate a child's emotional and behavioral status based on how the total picture evolves from information obtained from a variety of methods and sources (observations or interviews with the child, rating scales completed by the child, and information obtained from parents and teachers).

Classroom Observations

Throughout this section on assessment, we have often referred to classroom or playground observations as providing a wealth of information for school psychologists. Although teachers are able to observe the child's behaviors daily, classrooms are busy with ongoing activities and many highly active children. As a result, teachers cannot focus exclusively on one child in the same way as the school psychologist who has come to observe that specific child. In this way, we become a second set of eyes, like an invisible camera that can observe and record behavior patterns because we are totally focused on the child that we are there to observe. But what exactly is involved in the observation itself? Psychologists are trained to be observers of behavior, and there are several types of observational techniques that can be used, depending on the problem to be observed, where the observation is taking place, and what information we are trying to collect. The following is a description of some different observational methods that may be used.

Running Record   This method is often used when the psychologist is informally looking at how the child is responding in the classroom or playground setting. In this type of observation, the goal is to look for different patterns of behavior that can point to strengths or weaknesses in meeting academic (classroom) or social (playground) demands. The psychologist will take notes on important behaviors that can be shared with the child's teacher or parents and recommend strategies to improve the child's success in the classroom and on the playground. For example, the psychologist might find that the child's seating arrangement (close to the water fountain) is an additional point of distraction, and recommend that the child be moved closer to the center of the room, or closer to the teacher. On the playground, the child may not be interacting with others, and may be hanging on the sidelines, not knowing how to gain entry into the group (very common problem). In this case, the psychologist might suggest team activities that link the child with others automatically.

Time Recording or Event Recording   In this case, the psychologist has a very specific agenda. A potential problem has been flagged (off-task behavior, speaking out of turn, not remaining seated, and so on) and the psychologist observes the child to get a handle on the severity of the problem. For example, the teacher is concerned because Janice is not completing independent seatwork. For this observation, the psychologist uses a method that will allow him or her to determine the percentage of time that the student is doing seatwork (writing when required). By the end of the half hour, the psychologist has only recorded ten times that Janice was actually writing in the workbook during the time observed. The psychologist concludes that Janice was working (on-task) for less than a third of the time given to work on the task.

But What Is the Expectation for a Child at Janice's Grade Level for This Task?   In order to determine what should be a reasonable amount of time on task for Janice's grade level, the next time the psychologist observes Janice, she also observes a child that the teacher has suggested has excellent seatwork performance. This time, when the psychologist observes Janice, she does so for the first thirty seconds of every minute, and then observes the model student for the next thirty seconds. That way, she will be able to compare on-task behavior for both students. The psychologist finds that during this observation session, Janice used only 25 percent of her time completing seatwork, but that the model student was writing on the response sheet 70 percent of the time observed. As a result of this observation, the psychologist recommends that they establish a goal of having Janice work on independent seatwork for 50 percent of the time assigned. This goal is midway between the model student's and Janice's current seatwork productivity.

Behaviors and Outcomes   When the psychologist observed Mark, he noted that every time Mark was uncooperative, the new teacher's assistant went over to him and tried to engage him in completing the task. However, Mark's uncooperative behavior began to increase. Mark was enjoying the attention that he was getting from the teaching assistant and became more uncooperative as a result. The psychologist recommended that Mark's uncooperative behavior be responded to by removal of free activity time at the end of the class and that the teacher's assistant ignore his uncooperative behaviors. By the end of the week, Mark was more cooperative and enjoying his free-time activities.

In the preceding example, classroom observation has provided a "second set of eyes" to observe why a student's problem behavior might increase despite adding an intervention to reduce it (teaching assistant is monitoring behavior). In this case, the attention provided by the teaching assistant was actually reinforcing or rewarding Mark's inappropriate behaviors. Although, once flagged, this seems like an obvious observation, it is the case that these types of connections can often go undetected.

CHAPTER

10

EXECUTIVE FUNCTIONS

What They Are, Why They're Important, and How They're Assessed

WHAT ARE EXECUTIVE FUNCTIONS?

Executive functions (EF) refer to the many tasks that our brains perform when we are engaged in thinking and acting—specifically, in the process of solving problems. Executive functions are called into action when we are attempting to learn new information, recalling information from the past, or retrieving information from our memory. Executive functions also guide individuals in using information from past experiences to solve problems on a daily basis. EF includes such activities as planning, organization, attention to relevant details, and managing time and space. Because EF refers to a cluster of abilities, there are a number of theories about how EF should be conceptualized. EF has been likened to the chief executive officer (CEO) of a corporation because it is responsible for mobilizing, organizing, and sustaining the basic cognitive, emotional, and behavioral processes so that problem solving can be effective in achieving the goals. If one or more of the processes is not functioning properly, then there is increased likelihood that the goals will not be achieved adequately.

Researchers have identified several processes that are integral to successful problem solving for goal-oriented behaviors. According to Gerard Gioia (2005), there are two major types of executive functions: functions that are important in regulating behaviors and emotions, and functions that are related to cognitive processes.

Executive functions responsible for *behavioral or emotional regulation* allow an individual to

- Inhibit or defer ongoing responses that are not relevant to goal attainment in favor of engaging in more appropriate goal-oriented responses

- Shift from one task or situation to another that is more relevant to attaining the goal

- Control and regulate emotional responses to avoid interference from attaining a goal

Executive functions involved in *metacognitive problem-solving processes* allow an individual to

- Initiate a task or activity and effectively attend to the task

- Hold information in the mind while actively manipulating it mentally (working memory)

- Engage in effective planning strategies, including anticipation of future events and outlining important steps that may exist in the process

- Organize oneself in a purposeful and goal-directed manner

- Monitor behaviors (awareness) and adjust or revise when necessary (flexibility)

We will return shortly to a more in-depth discussion of the components outlined here, but first, let's look at an example of how a deficit in one of these areas might serve to block successful goal-directed behavior. Several models have been used to describe EF. Perhaps one of the most common and readily understood models is the one that was proposed by Russell Barkley (1997), who developed a model of EF to describe the problems that children with the impulsive type of attention deficit hyperactivity disorder (ADHD) experience when faced with the challenge of sustaining goal-directed behavior. At the top of Barkley's model is *the ability to inhibit or defer ongoing responses,* which Barkley refers to as *behavioral inhibition.* Children who have the hyperactive-impulsive type of ADHD often have very poorly developed behavioral inhibition. Based on Barkley's model,

FIGURE 10.1 *Executive Functions and the Role of Behavioral Inhibition*

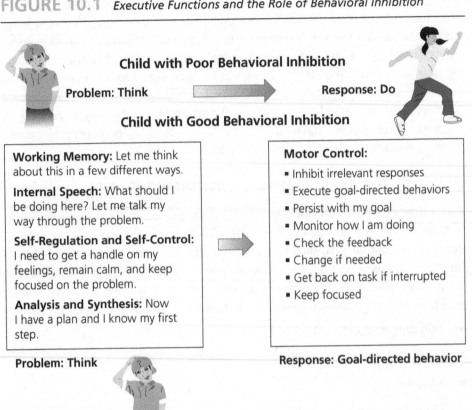

Child with Poor Behavioral Inhibition

Problem: Think → Response: Do

Child with Good Behavioral Inhibition

> **Working Memory:** Let me think about this in a few different ways.
>
> **Internal Speech:** What should I be doing here? Let me talk my way through the problem.
>
> **Self-Regulation and Self-Control:** I need to get a handle on my feelings, remain calm, and keep focused on the problem.
>
> **Analysis and Synthesis:** Now I have a plan and I know my first step.

> **Motor Control:**
> - Inhibit irrelevant responses
> - Execute goal-directed behaviors
> - Persist with my goal
> - Monitor how I am doing
> - Check the feedback
> - Change if needed
> - Get back on task if interrupted
> - Keep focused

Problem: Think

Response: Goal-directed behavior

Images drawn by Rachel Wilmshurst.

children with poor behavioral inhibition will not be successful in problem solving for several reasons. Figure 10.1 illustrates the differences between children with and without good ability in the area of behavioral inhibition.

In the example, the child with poor behavioral inhibition sees a problem and then acts, without taking the time to effectively process the information. This child is not able to stop engaging in a behavior that is not relevant to the task at hand or is distracted by irrelevant circumstances and, as a result, does not think the problem through adequately. Often, children with poor behavioral inhibition are unaware that they have completely missed the point or the target goal.

On the other hand, a child who has good behavioral inhibition is able to stop and think his way through a problem by using four key executive functions: working memory, internal speech, self-regulation and control, and analysis and synthesis of the information relevant to the problem-solving task. These four executive tasks provide the child with a much better response to problem solving: a response that has been well thought-out, organized, and removed from as much emotional turmoil as possible since this could also influence poor decision making. For the second child, the final response is well suited to the problem at hand because the child has taken the necessary intermediary steps to guard against poor decisions and impulsive responses. We will return to Barkley's model later, when we discuss how impaired EF can be responsible for poor performance across a number of different disabilities, such as ADHD.

WHY ARE THE EXECUTIVE FUNCTIONS IMPORTANT?

Each of the executive functions introduced so far has a very important role to play in decision making and problem solving. While some of the functions serve to direct the course of goal-directed responses and are very action-oriented, other functions act more to coordinate the responses into the total response pattern. Gioia (2005) refers to these two types of executive functions as the *conductor functions* and the *orchestra functions*. Examples of **conductor** functions include

- Initiating goal-directed actions
- Working memory
- Planning
- Organization
- Self-monitoring
- Inhibiting responses
- Flexibility
- Emotional regulation

The **orchestra** side of the EF function serves to process:

- Inputs from sensory perceptual processes
- Motor outputs
- Emotion
- Visual-spatial processes
- Memory
- Knowledge and skills required to integrate information and provide feedback

In the learning environment, the conductor and the orchestra work together to create a seamless product based on our abilities to

- Develop plans

- Track timelines

- Multi-task

- Use past information to guide present responses

- Seek assistance, as needed

- Effectively engage in group work

- Evaluate our ideas and those of others

- Seek more information, if required

- Monitor and reflect on our own performance

- Edit our work and make changes, corrections, and modifications

- Complete work on schedule (NCLD, 2009)

In summary, EF represents a set of related but distinct skills in areas of control, management, and self-regulation that are responsible for organizing and directing our behaviors, thoughts, and feelings. Given the wide range of skills involved in EF, it is not difficult to understand how impairment in EF can have a substantial impact on a child's cognitive, behavioral, and social-emotional development and functioning both academically and socially, on a daily basis.

Individuals who are able to engage in effective goal-directed problem solving can do so because they have strengths in the areas of EF that provide the foundations for success. These individuals set goals that are realistic (attainable rather than impossible); plan and organize their responses in a way that is logical and leads to goal attainment; initiate responses (rather than procrastinate) in pursuit of their goal; block distractions or inhibit behaviors that are not compatible with their goal; monitor their performance and if need be, are flexible enough to be able to shift their behavior in a direction that is more in tune with achieving their goal. Individuals who are lacking in these EF skills will experience challenges in meeting their goals, the seriousness of which will be determined by the number of skills that are lacking. For example, if the only difficulty you have is in monitoring your performance, you may still be successful in the majority of tasks but then fail on the tasks where monitoring is essential. However, someone who has deficits in developing realistic goals and in planning and organizing would be expected to have more significant problems in successfully attaining their goals.

Although EF affects us on virtually every level, there are some situations where EF is more crucial than others. For example, in a highly structured and predictable situation, the need for EF is minimized. However, in novel situations, when we have no previous experience to refer to, EF becomes increasingly important. Similarly, we would require more EF support for problem solving in high-stress situations versus situations in which we feel more calm and relaxed. Finally, making decisions and solving problems regarding future events also places more emphasis on EF than problem solving regarding current situations.

Given the numerous possible areas where EF can break down, there is no single definition of executive dysfunction. Instead, the goal is to develop a profile of an individual's strengths and weaknesses in EF that underscores problems with successful goal attainment. In the next section, we discuss how these individual profiles can be determined.

HOW ARE THE EXECUTIVE FUNCTIONS ASSESSED?

Given the complex nature of EF, it is not surprising that there is no single assessment that can measure all aspects of EF. In addition, there are problems associated with assessing EF through performance-based measures because in these situations, the examiner often performs the majority of tasks that are related to EF (for example, tasks are initiated by the examiner; the test situation is planned and well organized; the goals of the test are pre-established; the assessment room is quiet and free from distractions; and tasks for the most part are time-limited and novel).

There are a number of different neuropsychological assessments that attempt to tap into parts of the executive functions. The Wisconsin Card Sorting Test and the Category Test are two tests that attempt to measure how an individual responds to finding the rule for solving a set of problems and then how the individual responds when given a new set of problems that cannot be solved by using the old rule. The theory is that those who experience problems have deficits in their ability to shift strategies between tasks, which is one component of EF. However, specific test responses may not capture the complex nature of how an individual solves problems about life on a daily basis. Also, problem solving in reality is far more complex and requires an individual to take many more factors into consideration. Currently, the *test batteries* (a test that includes several different components) that are available to evaluate executive functions in children, such as the Delis-Kaplan Executive Function System, often require considerable time to administer and expertise in neuropsychology. Procedures that can assist in determining brain scan activity, such as a magnetic resonance imaging (MRI), are cost prohibitive for most clinicians.

However, rating scales have been developed to rate a number of behaviors that are associated with EF. One of the most popular rating scales is the Behavior Rating Inventory of Executive Function (BRIEF), which has rating forms for parents and teachers of children aged two to eighteen and a self-report form for children aged eleven to eighteen (Gioia, Isquith, Guy, & Kenworthy, 2000). The BRIEF provides scores for Behavioral Regulation (Inhibit, Shift, and Emotional Control scales) and Metacognition (Initiate, Working Memory, Plan/Organize, Organization of Materials, and Monitor scales), as well as an overall score for EF. The higher the scores on the BRIEF scales, the more serious the problem is. The instrument is reliable and has been used in a number of research studies.

EXECUTIVE FUNCTIONS: A COMMON THREAD AMONG DISABILITIES

As was previously mentioned, given the number of abilities that are subsumed under EF, it is possible to anticipate a number of different profiles that could result, based on the specific types of strengths and weaknesses that may be involved. Not only are there differences in profiles between individuals, but students with different disabilities also may demonstrate different patterns of strengths and weaknesses in EF, which we will discuss in this section.

The National Center for Learning Disabilities (NCLD) identifies some of the general barriers to learning that are common to many of the disabilities, including problems with

- Developing a plan

- Initiating tasks and generating ideas

- Estimating the amount of time required to complete a project

- Communicating information in an organized, logical, and sequential manner

- Retrieving information from long-term memory and manipulating information in short-term memory

The NCLD also notes a number of typical comments made by parents and educators about children with disabilities who have deficits in EF:

- Forgetful, problems planning ahead, trouble with setting goals to plan ahead

- Problems with organizing and prioritizing information

- Engage in all-or-nothing thinking: either focus on details or on the big picture, but not both

- Difficulty disengaging from one task and shifting to another

- Have problems with shifting between time periods (for example from the past to the present) or types of information (from concrete to abstract)

- Become increasingly overwhelmed as workload increases

- Have problems with applying what has been learned to a task in order to demonstrate knowledge

Profiles of EF Among Different Groups

Gerard Gioia and his colleagues (Gioia, Isquith, Kenworthy, & Barton, 2002) conducted a study in which they administered the BRIEF to children who had various disabilities, including ADHD, reading disorders (RD), autistic spectrum disorders (ASD), and traumatic brain injury (TBI). The results of their study are summarized here.

Attention Deficit Hyperactivity Disorder (ADHD) Children with ADHD-Combined type (ADHD-C children demonstrate both inattention and hyperactivity-impulsivity) exhibit more overall problems in EF than those with ADHD-Inattentive type (ADHD-I), and significantly more severe problems on the BRIEF Inhibit Scale than children with ADHD-I, children with RD, children with ASD, or children with TBI. The Inhibit Scale measures a child's ability to "inhibit, resist or not act on an impulse, and the ability to stop one's behavior at the appropriate time."

This is the behavioral inhibition function that was described by Barkley earlier. One of the problems that individuals with ADHD-C exhibit is an inability to sustain goal-directed behaviors in situations that are mentally challenging and not immediately rewarding (for example, homework or studying). People often ask why children with ADHD are able to sustain attention for video games and not homework. The answer is that video games are self-rewarding, while homework is not. Other scales that were clinically significant for the ADHD-C group include Shift (flexibility to shift from one activity to another) and Emotional Control (regulation of emotional responses).

Children with ADHD-I have higher scores than children with other disabilities in Working Memory (capacity to hold information in mind while mentally manipulating it), Plan/Organize (ability to manage current and future-oriented tasks), and Monitor (self-appraisal during and after task completion). Children with ADHD-I exhibit more problems with tasks associated with the metacognitive aspects of EF (working memory, planning, organization, self-monitoring), while those with ADHD-C experience problems with EF in areas of metacognition and behavior regulation (inhibitory control, emotional modulation).

Reading Disabilities or Disorders (RD)

Children with a reading disability (RD) score significantly lower than those with ADHD-I on the scales of Working Memory and Plan/Organize; however, they are not lower than those with ADHD-I on the Self-Monitoring scale. Compared with individuals who do not have reading disorders, those with RD score higher on all scales of the BRIEF, with significant differences noted in Working Memory and Plan/Organize. Similar to children with ADHD-I, those with RD also scored higher on EF scales related to metacognition rather than EF scales associated with behavior regulation.

REMEMBER: Scores on the BRIEF indicate worse performance the higher the scores are on the different scales. So when comparing children with RD to those with ADHD-I, children with RD do better in areas of Working Memory and Plan/ Organize, but perform as poorly as those with ADHD-I in areas of Self-Monitoring.

Autistic Spectrum Disorders (ASD)   Children with autistic spectrum disorders (ASD) score significantly higher than children with no disabilities on all the EF scales, and they score significantly higher than any disability group on the Shift scale of the BRIEF. This is not surprising, given that symptoms of ASD often include a rigid adherence to nonfunctional routines in their daily life and highly stereotypical and repetitive behaviors (for example, hand flapping, lining up objects) that they resist being disengaged from. In addition, for children with ASD, scores on Emotional Control were among the highest overall, only slightly lower than the scores of children with ADHD-C, suggesting very poor ability to manage their emotional responses, which may result in exaggerated reactions to even minor events. Significant weaknesses in self-monitoring (high scores on the Monitor scale) were also noted for children with ASD, who typically have difficulty understanding how their behavior may affect others.

Traumatic Brain Injury (TBI)   Results concerning EF for children with traumatic brain injury (TBI) were directly related to the extent of injury. Children with severe TBI were at greater risk for dysfunction in EF related to behavior regulation and metacognitive problem solving. Even children with moderate levels of TBI demonstrated significant problems in metacognitive skills related to planning, organization, and self-monitoring.

Behavioral Disorders   Although Gioia and his colleagues (2002) did not include children with behavioral disorders in their study, many children with behavioral disorders also have ADHD-C and learning disabilities, which would result in EF deficits in areas found for children with disabilities in these areas. Children who have behavioral problems often exhibit significant difficulties in the EF areas related to behavioral regulation, including Inhibit (ability to control impulses and stop an ongoing behavior) and Emotional Control (appropriate modulation of emotional responses). If metacognitive deficits also exist, it is important to address issues in behavior regulation prior to interventions for metacognitive functions.

CHAPTER

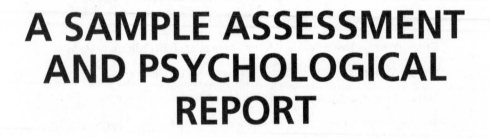

A SAMPLE ASSESSMENT AND PSYCHOLOGICAL REPORT

After completing a psychological assessment, a school psychologist will write a report that summarizes the test scores. This report may be mailed to the student's home so that parents can see the results before the meeting that will be held to discuss the test results. This meeting gives parents and teachers the opportunity to learn about a child's strengths and weaknesses and what can be done to help maximize his learning.

Psychological reports vary widely. They may be as short as three pages or as long as twenty pages or even more. Many reports include tables of scores, which may be integrated in the report or attached at the end. Despite the many variations in psychologists' reports, most of them include the following essential information:

- Assessment procedures

- Referral and background information

- General observations and impressions

- Test results and interpretations

- Summary and recommendations

ASSESSMENT PROCEDURES

In most psychological reports, there is a section in which the school psychologist lists the tests and other assessment measures that were used in the evaluation, which may include cognitive, processing, or achievement tests; behavioral rating scales completed by parents, teachers, or the child; or classroom observations. The section might look like this:

Assessment Procedures

Woodcock-Johnson III NU Tests of Cognitive Abilities (WJ III NU Cog.)

Reynolds Intellectual Assessment Scales (RIAS)

Developmental Test of Visual-Motor Integration, Fifth Edition (VMI-5)

Woodcock-Johnson III NU Tests of Achievement (WJ III Ach. NU)

Test of Written Language, Fourth Edition (TOWL-4)

Behavior Assessment System for Children, Second Edition: Teacher Rating Scales (BASC-2: TRS)

Behavior Assessment System for Children, Second Edition: Parent Rating Scales (BASC-2: PRS)

Children's Depression Inventory (CDI)

Piers-Harris Children's Self-Concept Scale, Second Edition (Piers-Harris 2)

Revised Children's Manifest Anxiety Scale, Second Edition (RCMAS-2)

Records review

REFERRAL AND BACKGROUND INFORMATION

A psychological report includes a section that describes the reasons for the referral and relevant background information. If a child is having behavior problems and her parents have recently divorced, for example, this information will be included. It is important to know about any environmental factors that might explain a child's unusual behaviors or sudden drop in grades. A school will list the number of absences, tardies, office referrals, and days suspended, if applicable, as well as current grades.

School districts may use their own background information form to collect data on developmental milestones, behavior at home, hobbies, others who live in the home, and so on. Often, this form does not provide a comprehensive assessment of a child's background, so a school psychologist may supplement it with a form such as the Behavior Assessment System for Children, Second Edition: Structured Developmental History (BASC-2: SDH). The BASC-2: SDH is a twelve-page history and background questionnaire that is completed by parents or other caregivers. It provides a thorough review of a child's developmental, educational, medical, psychological, and social history. While it may take parents some time to fill it out, it is an excellent source of information. On many occasions, by including this questionnaire, we have obtained helpful information that parents forgot to provide in other paperwork or even in an interview. Some parents do not wish to share certain information; we understand that. We offer parents the opportunity to share personal information via telephone rather than including it on a form that many people may see.

Here is an example of how background information might be presented in a psychological report:

Mary was referred for a psychological evaluation because she made little academic progress during this past school year. She also appears sad at times and does not interact much with her friends at school.

Information concerning Mary's developmental progress, birth history, school history, and behavior at home was provided by her parents on the Student Support Team's background form. No problems during Mary's birth were reported. Major developmental milestones were reported to have been reached within normal time ranges. Her parents indicated that she broke her femur at age four and had to wear a body cast for fourteen weeks. They also indicated on a brief behavior checklist that Mary can be trusted, acts younger than other children her age, is overly dependent on others, is restless, and is easily frustrated.

School records indicate that Mary had two excused absences because of illnesses this school year, as well as two unexcused tardies. She has no office referrals or suspensions. Mary attended preschool and repeated kindergarten. Her grades for the last marking period were all C's except for a B in art. Mary's written work is poorly developed, and she has difficulty with sequencing a story. When Mary works with her teacher and is prompted, her story is quite a bit better and more consistent with appropriate grade-level work.

Mary passed her vision and hearing screenings on 05/04/10. The screenings were completed by the school nurse.

GENERAL OBSERVATIONS AND IMPRESSIONS

Observations of the child during the assessment period are reported in the psychological report. A school psychologist may conduct a classroom observation or multiple observations in different settings (perhaps the classroom, lunchroom, and playground) to get a broad picture of a child's behavior. The psychologist's notes on the child's behavior toward others, attention level, activity level, on-task behavior, response to teacher redirection, and other behaviors will be recorded and reported as part of the evaluation.

Observations during psychological testing are helpful in order to assess whether the child's behavior had a negative impact on the test results. If it did, the evaluation may be invalid, and additional testing may need to be completed.

General observations in a psychological report might look like this:

> Mary was evaluated in the conference room at the front of her school. Testing conditions were good; the ambient temperature was comfortable, the lighting was appropriate, and the noise level was very minimal. Rapport was readily established, and she was cooperative during the testing session. During the evaluation, Mary appeared to be in good health. She was dressed appropriately for the weather and displayed adequate grooming skills. She related well to the examiner, used language appropriate for her age level, maintained good attention and a normal activity level, and used good interpersonal and communication skills. The test results are believed to be valid.

TEST RESULTS AND INTERPRETATIONS

The section that reports test results will be the longest part of a psychological report. The results of all the tests that were administered will be analyzed and reported. Some school psychologists report all test results individually, while others may integrate some test results. For example, if two different achievement tests were administered, they may be summarized together because they measure similar things. We discussed in previous chapters what the scores mean. Rather than repeat that information here, we'll simply provide an example of part of a psychological report that summarizes different test results:

> The **Woodcock-Johnson III NU Tests of Cognitive Abilities (WJ III NU Cog.)** is a norm-referenced measure of cognitive ability that is designed to assess the

various skills that an individual uses to learn new information. The WJ III NU Cog. includes tasks that measure different aspects of cognitive ability. Clusters of tests provide the primary basis for test interpretation.

Results indicate that Mary's General Intellectual Ability, or her overall level of intelligence, falls in the low average range.

The Verbal Ability cluster is a measure of language development that includes the comprehension of individual words and the comprehension of relationships among words. Verbal Ability is an important predictor of cognitive performance. Mary's performance falls in the low average range.

The Thinking Ability cluster represents an aggregate of the abilities that allow a child to process information that has been placed in short-term memory but cannot be processed automatically. Mary's performance falls in the low average range.

The Cognitive Efficiency cluster represents the capacity of the cognitive system to process information automatically. Mary's performance falls in the average range.

The Long-Term Retrieval cluster represents the ability to store information and fluently retrieve it later in the process of thinking. Mary's performance falls in the very low range. This is her weakest area.

Working Memory refers to the ability to hold information in immediate awareness while performing a mental operation on the information. (Simple memory span tests are not tests of working memory.) Mary's performance falls in the low average range.

The Short-Term Memory cluster represents the ability to apprehend and hold information in immediate awareness and then use it within a few seconds. Mary's performance falls in the low average range.

The **Reynolds Intellectual Assessment Scales (RIAS)** is an individually administered test of intelligence.

On the Verbal Index, Mary demonstrated low average skills. The Verbal Index involves tasks such as using verbal clues to identify objects and solving verbal analogies. Tasks in this area require verbal comprehension, expression, and reasoning skills.

On the Nonverbal Index, Mary demonstrated low average skills. The Nonverbal Index involves tasks such as identifying the object that is different within a group of objects and identifying the missing item in a picture. Tasks in this area require abstract and concrete reasoning as well as visual discrimination skills.

On the Memory Index, Mary demonstrated low average skills. The Memory Index involves tasks such as reciting facts from a story read orally by the examiner as well as identifying a previously viewed object from a group of similar objects. Tasks in this area require auditory and visual short-term memory skills.

The **Developmental Test of Visual-Motor Integration, Fifth Edition (VMI-5)** requires a student to copy geometric forms on printed pages within restricted areas, without any erasures. These drawings are scored very strictly, and neatness is an important factor in scoring a figure. Mary attained a standard score of 79, which falls in the low range. This score suggests a weak ability in complex visual-motor integration, and this weakness may negatively affect Mary's ability to efficiently complete written assignments.

The **Woodcock-Johnson III NU Tests of Achievement (WJ III NU Ach.)** and **Test of Written Language, Fourth Edition (TOWL-4)** are norm-referenced measures of academic achievement.

Oral Expression is a measure of linguistic competency and expressive vocabulary. Mary's performance falls in the average range.

Listening Comprehension is a measure of listening ability and verbal comprehension. Mary's performance falls in the low average range.

Written Expression is a measure of a student's overall ability to express herself in writing. Mary's performance falls in the low and very low ranges.

Basic Reading is a measure of reading decoding. Mary's performance falls in the low average range.

Reading Comprehension is a measure of the ability to comprehend what is being read. Mary's performance falls in the low average range.

Reading Fluency is a measure of the speed of reading sentences and answering yes-no questions. Mary's performance falls in the low average range.

Math Calculation is a measure of problem solving. Mary's performance falls in the average range.

Math Reasoning is a measure of the ability to solve math problems by using reasoning skills. Mary's performance falls in the low average range.

The **Behavior Assessment System for Children, Second Edition (BASC-2)** is an integrated system designed to facilitate the differential diagnosis and classification of a variety of emotional and behavioral disorders of children and to aid in the design of treatment plans. This measure was completed separately by Mary's classroom teacher and her mother. Scores in the clinically significant range suggest a high level of maladjustment. Scores in the at-risk range may identify a significant problem that might not be severe enough to require formal treatment or may identify the potential to develop a problem that needs careful monitoring. According to both respondents, Mary is not exhibiting significant problems with internalizing, externalizing, or adaptive behaviors.

The **Children's Depression Inventory (CDI)** is a self-report checklist consisting of questions that are designed to evaluate the presence of depressive ideation. Based on Mary's responses, it does not appear that she is experiencing higher levels of depression than other girls her age.

The **Piers-Harris Children's Self-Concept Scale, Second Edition (Piers-Harris 2)** is a self-report instrument that assesses self-concept in children and adolescents. The scale presents a number of statements about the way some children feel about themselves. Children respond to each statement by deciding whether or not it describes the way they feel. Based on her responses, Mary does not appear to be experiencing significant problems with self-concept.

The **Revised Children's Manifest Anxiety Scale, Second Edition (RCMAS-2)** is a self-report instrument designed to assess the level and nature of anxiety in children and adolescents. Based on her responses, Mary does not appear to be experiencing significant problems with anxiety. However, it is important to note that her pattern of responses suggests she may be "faking good." Thus, there is a chance that she is experiencing problems with anxiety and is attempting to cover them up.

SUMMARY AND RECOMMENDATIONS

The final section of a psychological report summarizes the test results. It will likely be a brief summary that doesn't include individual scores. The school psychologist will include a list of recommendations that may help mitigate any weaknesses the child may have. Here is an example of a summary:

Mary is a nine-year-old female student in the third grade who was referred for a psychological evaluation because she made little academic progress during this past school year. She also appears sad at times and does not interact much with her friends at school.

Current test results indicate that Mary's intelligence is low average. Her cognitive efficiency skills are average; her verbal ability, thinking ability, working memory, and short-term memory skills are low average; and her long-term retrieval skills are very low.

Mary's visual-motor integration skills are very weak.

Achievement test data indicate that Mary's performance is average in oral expression and math calculation; low average in listening comprehension, basic reading, reading comprehension, reading fluency, and math reasoning; and low to very low in written expression.

Behavior rating scales completed by Mary's classroom teacher and her mother do not indicate that she is experiencing significant problems with internalizing, externalizing, or adaptive behaviors. Self-report rating scales completed by Mary do not indicate significant problems with self-concept, depression, or anxiety.

Mary's eligibility for special education services will be determined by an interdisciplinary team. The team should consider all available information in making this determination.

Mary's test results indicate that she has three problems: poor long-term retrieval, visual-motor integration, and written expression skills. Recommendations should be made to address these three main areas. It is possible that Mary's problems with writing can be attributed to difficulties with the creative process of writing. Writing tasks may require that she retrieve stored memories, which may be difficult for her because she has trouble with long-term retrieval. Mary would benefit from techniques to help her recall information. Because she has handwriting issues, Mary may try to get away with writing as little as possible if the task is difficult. Consequently, an evaluation by an occupational therapist may be warranted to see whether Mary has a problem with fine motor skills and how they can be improved.

Three

Guidelines for Successful Interventions

CHAPTER

12

INTERVENTIONS AND SUPPORTS TO ADDRESS EXECUTIVE FUNCTION PROBLEMS

In Chapter Ten, we introduced the many types of skills and abilities that are part of the executive functions in areas of metacognition (thinking and problem solving) and the regulation of behavior. Typically, EF skills such as planning ability start to emerge as young as two years of age, while more mature aspects of EF are evident by ten to twelve years of age. However, children with deficits in EF may not develop the skills needed to interact appropriately with their environment, resulting in a variety of cognitive, social, and academic problems.

TARGETING GOALS FOR INTERVENTION

Children with EF deficits may demonstrate problems in a number of areas that can affect academic and social functioning, including problems with initiating, organizing, monitoring, and evaluating task performance as well as regulating behavior and emotions. Given the range of possible difficulties, it is important to isolate which of the problems listed are part of the child's dysfunction and then effectively target those areas to help the child improve. The majority of skills can be taught by direct instruction through increasing the child's awareness and then systematically teaching the child how to develop the necessary skill set. In general, the most important aspect of intervention for EF deficits will be to introduce the child to strategies that can be used to effectively apply problem-solving skills to goal-directed activities.

Teaching a child to break a task down into smaller steps will allow the child to develop a set of routines for problem solving and a repertoire of problem-solving skills that are familiar and successful. Initially, the coach guides the child by asking relevant and leading questions, which the child will eventually learn to ask independently. With practice, the child will begin to internalize these steps, and ultimately, the coach should be able to step aside and cue the child to draw on his own set of questions when that is appropriate.

DIDYOUKNOW

Parents, teachers, and peers can all serve as coaches for children who have difficulties with problem solving by modeling appropriate problem-solving strategies. They can also teach children to monitor the results as they attempt to apply the skills they have learned to new situations in their daily activities.

A STEP-BY-STEP INTERVENTION FOR GOAL-ORIENTED PROBLEM SOLVING

Interventions for problem solving involve four basic steps: Goal, Plan, Do, Review (Gioia, 2005). This four-word strategy provides a reminder that is easily stored in a child's memory. When asked what to do to solve the problem, the child should be able to respond, "Goal, Plan, Do, Review." As we will discuss, more steps can be added to the problem-solving formula (for example, prediction), depending on the child's age and the nature of the task (simple or complex). A model for building a step-by-step intervention plan to develop problem-solving skills is presented in Table 12.1.

REMEMBER to have the child learn this simple phrase:

Goal → Plan → Do → Review

The intervention program can be introduced to the child by explaining that people use problem solving every day to help them think, plan, and do what they need to get done. Next, let the child know that there is a way to problem solve that can be used for a variety of different types of problems and that these steps can help him to plan and finish activities every day. Once the child

TABLE 12.1 STEPS TO GOAL SETTING AND PROBLEM SOLVING

Stage	Steps	Questions
GOAL	Step 1	What do I want to do/accomplish?
PLAN	Step 2	What materials do I need? List the materials needed. If I don't have them, where can I get them?
	Step 3	What tasks need to be done? Which should be done first, second, next, etc.? List the tasks that need to be accomplished, in the proper sequence.
PREDICTION	Step 4	How well do I think I will do? (Self-Rating: Scale 1–10)
	Step 5	How well does the coach think I will do? (Coach-Rating: Scale 1–10).
DO	Step 6	Checklist 1: Did I get all the materials? If no, why not? How can I solve this?
	Step 7	Checklist 2: Have I done all activities on my list? If no, why not? How can I solve this?
REVIEW (self)	Step 8	How did I do? (Self-Rating: Scale 1–10)
	Step 9	How well does the coach think I will do? (Coach-Rating: Scale 1–10).
REVIEW (project)	Step 10	What worked?
	Step 11	What didn't work?
	Step 12	What will I try next time, to make it work better?

Source: Adapted from Ylvisaker, M., Szekeres, S., & Feeney, T. (1998). Cognitive rehabilitation: Executive functions (p. 244). In M. Ylvisaker (Ed.), *Traumatic brain injury rehabilitation: Children and adolescents* (2nd Ed.). Boston: Butterworth-Heinemann.

understands that problem solving can be taught the same way that other academic subjects can, the child is ready to begin.

Problem solving can be overwhelming, but by using a step-by-step procedure, the child can learn to identify parts of the process and gain confidence practicing each of the steps. The overall goal is to teach the child how to work through a problem, using a planned approach instead of acting impulsively. By learning how to identify the steps that are part of the task demands, the child can learn to identify the goal (or problem), identify the required steps for accomplishing the task, and provide questions and labels that will guide the process in a systematic way. For example, let's look at the task of completing homework. Using Table 12.1 as a guide, we begin with the Goal stage of the process. When asked to identify the goal, the child responds, "I need to do my homework." The coach assists the child by asking for the goal in more specific terms—for example, "Exactly what homework do you have due tomorrow?" In step 2, the child is asked to identify the assignments that are due (Plan stage). The coach continues to guide the child by asking more specific questions. In step 3, the child is asked to list the materials needed to do the homework (for example, school agenda, the paper on which homework assignments are recorded, any take-home sheets to be completed, papers, pencils and any other materials necessary to do the task). In the initial stages of guiding the child, it is important to have the child make actual lists of the assignments and all materials needed. This way, the child can compare the actual list with what was needed in his review (steps 6 and 7). With a list of assignments and the necessary materials to perform the tasks at hand, the child is almost ready to enter the Do phase, but before he does, let's get him to predict how he thinks he will do on the task.

The prediction stage can help children with EF deficits to improve their concept of space, time, and future-oriented activities. Asking children to predict how well they will do and even asking how long they think it will take to complete the task can provide very interesting information for future coaching sessions based on the child's responses. Later in this chapter, we will discuss how *prediction* can be a helpful intervention for improving self-monitoring, self-evaluation, and self-awareness.

A WORD OF CAUTION ABOUT SUCCESS PREDICTIONS

Younger children and those with a limited success record may be prone to overestimating their success and may be frustrated or discouraged when they do not achieve their goals. For this reason, it may be best to postpone this phase until the child has gained a greater sense of confidence in his problem-solving skills or to replace the competence question ("How well do you think you will do?") with a time-based question (for example, "How long do you think it will take you to finish all your homework correctly?"). It is important to add the word *correctly* to a time-based question, to discourage a child from rushing against the clock at the expense of accuracy.

Steps 6 and 7 represent the actual Do stage of the task—in our example, completing homework. Here the child learns to self-monitor as he or she is working on the homework and to record any problems that occur. Did he have all the required materials? If not, did he have to start hunting for them before he started his assignments, or did he find out part way through that some materials were missing? Similarly, did he complete all the homework assignments? Possible reasons for not completing homework in specific areas might include running out of time, not understanding the questions, not bringing home the right books, and not writing down the correct information (for example, not writing down correct page numbers for the assignment). Each of these errors when discovered can provide a valuable lesson for future planning—that is, what the child can do in the future to ensure that the error does not recur.

In steps 8 and 9, children should rate themselves on their success for the assignment (in this example, homework) and compare it to the coach's rating to assist the children to improve self-monitoring in the future. It is very important for children to understand how they can do better next time, if they remember the lesson learned from what they did today.

Finally, steps 10 and 11 set the stage for incorporating flexibility and the ability to shift strategies when the current strategy is not working. For example, if the reason for not finishing math homework was because the child did not copy down the text pages, how could he or she have solved that problem? Could the child have called a friend to get the correct pages? Next time, the child will want to take more care in copying down assignment information, so that he or she can do a better job. A Homework Planning and Review Sheet is available in Table 12.2 to help the child in the initial stages of organizing the problem-solving approach. This sheet can be photocopied and used to help guide the child through the process.

We have devoted significant time in this chapter to the EF skills involved in problem solving because problem solving is complex and draws on so many different EF abilities. However, it is also important to be able to help a child who is struggling with a particular type of EF function and to that end, we provide interventions in a number of different areas that can be used at home and at school, as well as suggestions for how IEP or 504 Plans can incorporate these goals into a child's educational plan (Gioia, 2005)

In the next section, we will discuss a number of intervention plans that can be used to address specific tasks, including goal setting, planning, organization, and self-oriented tasks of monitoring, self-awareness, and self-initiating. Following a discussion of intervention strategies for each of these areas, we will provide

TABLE 12.2 HOMEWORK PLANNING AND REVIEW SHEET

GOAL	To complete homework for: (Date)_____		
PLAN	**Subject** 1._____	**Assignment** 1._____ _____ _____	**Material Needed** 1._____ _____ _____
	Subject 2._____	**Assignment** 2._____ _____ _____	**Material Needed** 2._____ _____ _____
	Subject 3._____	**Assignment** 3._____ _____ _____	**Material Needed** 3._____ _____ _____
	Subject 4._____	**Assignment** 4._____ _____ _____	**Material Needed** 4._____ _____ _____
REVIEW	How I did (my rating): Self-Rating: 1 2 3 4 5 6 7 8 9 10 Coach Rating (Parent, Teacher, or both): Parent: 1 2 3 4 5 6 7 8 9 10 Teacher: 1 2 3 4 5 6 7 8 9 10		
	What helped, what worked? _____ _____ _____ _____ _____	What was wrong or missing? _____ _____ _____ _____ _____	
FUTURE SUGGESTIONS	Next time I should: _____ _____		

Source: Adapted from Ylvisaker, Szekeres, & Feeney, 1998, p. 244.

examples of potential goals and objectives from these interventions, which can become part of the child's IEP or 504 Plan.

Goal Setting

In this section we will provide interventions that can assist children to improve their abilities to set reasonable goals, which includes increasing their awareness of the time needed to accomplish tasks and drawing their attention to how their day is organized around predictable routines.

Interventions You can provide a number of time and task estimation exercises to help a child develop an awareness of time and how it relates to workload and routine functions. Show the child a number of activities (for younger children, use an actual concrete object; for older children, describe the situation verbally), and ask the child to estimate how long it will take to complete tasks, such as these estimates:

Academically Based Estimates

- Read a ten-page story (adjust the pages to age; show younger children the book)
- Read a paragraph (with comprehension)
- Write a paragraph about dogs (sentence for young children)
- Answer ten addition questions (increase difficulty for older children)
- Write out the weekly spelling list five times

Environmentally and Home-Based Estimates

- Walk to the playground from his classroom
- Walk to the library from his classroom
- Walk home
- Eat breakfast
- Complete homework
- Complete a puzzle of _____ pieces (with younger children actually show the puzzle)
- Clean his room

One of the major lessons of goal setting is to set *reasonable* goals that are obtainable. The preceding exercises can provide learning experiences that help children to see that their estimates may not be realistic and draw more attention to what is possible. For time estimation exercises, a stopwatch can be an effective tool for measuring the actual time that a task takes, which can then be compared with a child's predicted time.

Both at home and at school, one of the first tasks of goal setting might be to set up an overall routine that is predictable and clear. Many children with EF deficits are not consciously aware of routines that are going on around them, and asking a simple question—for example, "What will be the next thing that we do this morning?"—may be very informative. If the child is unaware, it will be important to draw attention to the predictable nature of routines in that setting. At home, a list of routines may be placed in a prominent place, such as on the refrigerator door. These reminders might list daily goals in the order that they are most likely to occur during the day:

Morning

- Wash and dress

- Eat breakfast

- Get to school on time

Afternoon

- Snack

- Free time (30 minutes)

- Finish goal/plan parts of homework sheet

Evening

- Set the table for dinner

- Eat dinner and help with dishes

- DO homework/ REVIEW (how did I do?)

- Free time

- Ready for bed/ story

The child should participate in developing the list, which will help reinforce a predictable and organized environment and draw attention to the time and function (goal) of certain activities. When events occur that disrupt the normal course of events (for example, the child has baseball practice on Tuesday and

Thursday nights), the list can serve as a reference for discussions about what changes should be made.

In addition to providing practice in time-based estimates, it is also important to engage a child in determining what his or her academic goals are in the short term and the long term. For example, if a child is in a reading series that has four levels, ask the child how many books he or she thinks will be read at that level by the end of the week or month, or have the child predict what level he or she will get to by the end of the year. Or ask the child to predict how many spelling words the child knows now, and how many words he or she would like to add to the list each week, each month, and so on.

Goal Setting: IEP or 504 Plan Examples

Goal: Stuart will be involved in helping to establish instructional goals for reading and math.

Objective: Stuart will be able to predict with 80 percent accuracy whether or not he can appropriately complete the task (reading or math) regarding:

- the number of books read on a daily and monthly basis
- the number of math questions he will complete daily

Planning

One of the major goals for children who experience EF deficits is to engage them in learning how to plan activities in a purposeful way. The following interventions are aimed at increasing children's awareness of thinking about their world in a way that is structured and predictable. The tasks target the sequential nature of events and focus on the order in which events occur.

Interventions   Often, children with EF deficits do not know how to plan their activities in a meaningful way. There are many tasks at school and at home that can be used to increase a child's awareness of the steps involved in developing a plan. A number of suggestions are provided to reinforce a child's attention to the steps involved in developing a plan and to increase planning ability. Be sure to adjust the difficulty level to match the age of the child.

- Give the child a cartoon strip that is cut up and mixed up. Ask the child to put the comic strip together in the correct order.

- Develop a shopping list and then draw a map showing where the stores are located. Ask the student to figure out the best way to get all the items on the list in the fastest time. Ask the student to find the best route.

- Cut up a list of directions for making candy, a toy plane, or something else. Mix up the directions, and have the child sort out the right sequence.

- Give the child a grocery list and a diagram that shows which items are kept in each aisle in the store. Ask the child to suggest the fastest way to get all the items.

- Have the child plan a birthday party for a friend. What needs to happen? What materials are needed? What tasks need to be completed, and in what order?

- Give the child three pictures, and have him create a story that has a beginning, middle, and end.

Planning: IEP or 504 Plan Examples

Goal: Stuart will be able to identify the sequence of events that leads to a given conclusion.

Objectives:

- Stuart will be able to list three things that he needs in order to complete his homework in math.

- Stuart will be able to identify three steps that he uses to study his spelling list.

- Stuart will be able to make a plan for improving his scores on weekly spelling tests.

Organization

Children with executive function deficits often appear to be very disorganized. They seem to have no sense of how similar items might be clustered together to make them more accessible. As a result, they often spend a lot of time searching for materials that they have misplaced (for example, lessons, notebooks, pens). At home, their bedroom is often in disarray, and at school, their backpack and desk often overflow with important and irrelevant materials jammed together.

Interventions   When faced with the challenges of middle school or secondary school arising from an increased workload and multiple teachers and classrooms, organizational problems can increase dramatically for children who have deficits in EF. For older students, a planner or agenda is necessary for academic survival.

- Depending on the child's age, a daily timetable, record book, planner, or agenda is an important tool for helping the child to record all information in the same place. The book should be used to record all homework and project assignments.

- For a student who is new to using a planner, the teacher and parent can work together to get the child started on the successful use of a planner. The teacher can check the planner before the child goes home to make sure it is correct, and the parent can initial the planner page to let the teacher know that the child used the planner to do the homework assignments.

- Many classroom teachers reserve a consistent place in which to list the assignments for each subject (for example, the upper right-hand corner of the board). This consistency is excellent training for a child who is expected to copy the assignments into the planner.

- Some teachers of younger students schedule a biweekly or monthly cleanup time when everyone in the class organizes their desks and book bags. This routine can be very helpful for students with EF deficits because it encourages them to organize and observe how successful peers organize, and it also allows them to avoid being admonished in front of their classmates.

- Encourage students to have a home binder and a school binder, each with a divider for each subject. A student can take the school binder to class each day and then transfer papers to the home binder at night. Binders are preferable to notebooks because handouts can be punched and placed in the binder along with notes taken in class. Keeping the majority of information in the home binder is beneficial because if the child loses notes or the school binder, all the major information is backed up and safely stored at home.

- Students with organizational problems often find major tasks overwhelming. A child with executive function deficits who is told, "Clean your room" or "Write an essay" may feel that she has been given an insurmountable task. Teach a child to break tasks down into their component parts. For example, rather than telling a child to clean the entire bedroom, discuss the various possibilities for approaching the problem. Divide the room into four or five sections (such as closet, desk, shelves, toy box) to be cleaned over four or five days. Rather than trying to write an entire essay at once, a student can work on parts of the project (such as selecting a topic, deciding on the major question to focus on, searching for research findings, writing an introduction, summarizing major findings, and creating a conclusion). This way the child can receive feedback on each part before going to the next section.

Organization: IEP or 504 Plan Examples

Goal: Stuart will develop an orderly and systematic way of organizing his personal items and academic assignments.

Objectives:

- Stuart will organize his desk and book bag on a biweekly basis.
- Stuart will come to class prepared with pens, pencils, homework, and school binder 95 percent of the time.
- Stuart will be able to outline the necessary steps for writing a paragraph in response to a prompt.
- Stuart will submit new material from his home binder to his teacher for biweekly review.

Self-Monitoring, Self-Evaluation, Self-Awareness, and Self-Initiating

Children with EF deficits often do not evaluate themselves or monitor how they are doing. Interventions to improve this characteristic focus on increasing a child's awareness of the need to review his or her current status relative to where he or she desires to be (future goal). Equally important is establishing a sense of *self-efficacy,* which is our ability to realistically appraise our strengths and weaknesses. This ability is important in defining realistic outcomes when faced with challenging tasks.

Interventions   When we evaluate our own performance, we may feel very vulnerable and as a result, we may become overly critical of ourselves or others. When we believe that what happens to us is primarily a result of our own actions (a concept referred to as *internal locus of control*), we may be critical of ourselves and tend to blame ourselves for any poor results, errors, or misgivings. On the other hand, if we believe that what happens to us is primarily a result of others' actions (a concept referred to as *external locus of control*), we may be critical of those around us and tend to blame others for our difficulties. Individuals who have an internal locus of control may be overly hard on themselves but tend to feel that they can control the outcome of situations. Those who have an external locus of control tend to blame others for their difficulties and, as a result, may never develop appropriate skills in self-monitoring, self-evaluation, and self-awareness. Our confidence in our ability to succeed (self-efficacy) and our understanding of the nature of the task will predict our ability to self-initiate a task.

The self-reflective components of EF are probably the most difficult aspects of successful problem solving and goal attainment faced by individuals of any age. Some individuals constantly strive to overachieve; others who are less confident may characteristically underachieve. Ideally, overconfidence or lack of confidence would be replaced by realistic appraisal of what is possible and how to meet those goals. Some of the strategies that can be used to help children monitor their progress, evaluate their goal attainment, and recognize their strengths and weaknesses are these:

- Using the "Predict" portion of the "Steps to Goal Setting and Problem Solving" in Table 12.1 provides important feedback for children who are learning how to monitor their performance and evaluate their results realistically. The question posed ("How well do I think I will do?") can be applied to any situation, event, or problem and can be used as a starting point to encourage self-reflection and increase the accuracy of appraisals.

- Successful prediction requires a more mature understanding that everyone has strengths and weaknesses (self-awareness/self-efficacy). Given the nature of a task, an individual should be able to predict within a reasonable degree of accuracy how well he will do. For example, if I am poor at math, then an expectation that I will score 100 percent on my math exam is unreasonable; however, if someone asks me how well I will likely do on the math exam (given my past experience, current knowledge, and aptitude), I might say 70 percent. Can that percentage be improved? It is quite likely that it can, if I accept tutoring, but first, I must recognize my weakness. Having children predict their performance and then compare it to an actual grade can be devastating for some, but appropriate prediction exercises can help to open the door to discussion, realistic appraisals, and positive interventions. For example, a teacher or parent might ask a child, "Given that you didn't do as well as you predicted, how can we help you improve?"

- Teachers and parents can encourage children to self-monitor in several ways. While correcting errors always has the potential to increase feelings of self-doubt, if presented in the appropriate context, it can be used as a lesson to enhance future performance. At school, having children self-correct their own work, (for example, a spelling test) can often help them increase their awareness of their own errors. At home, a parent can point out a poorly made bed and ask what could be done to make it better. In this way, the child learns to self-correct without loss of self-esteem.

- Lessons in self-awareness are possible on a daily basis. Teachers and parents can assure children that everyone is better at some things and not as good at others. Having a child draw up lists of his best and not-so-good abilities can provide a forum for self-reflection and future discussions. At home, parents can praise children for their strengths, encourage them to acknowledge areas where they may not be as strong, and talk about possible ways to improve.

Self-Monitoring, Self-Awareness, Self-Initiation: IEP or 504 Plan Examples

Goal: Stuart will be able to predict his academic performance with greater accuracy by recording his predicted grade and actual grade for each test this term, and identify which subjects are easy and which are difficult for him.

Objectives:

- Stuart will be able to predict his grades relative to obtained grades with 70 percent accuracy.

- Stuart will be able to identify which subjects are easy and which are difficult for him on the basis of his actual grades.

Goal: Stuart will initiate dialogue when he does not understand.

Objectives:

- Stuart will ask the teacher for assistance whenever he does not understand a question.

- Stuart will begin each assigned task once the necessary questions have been asked.

CHAPTER

13

INTERVENTIONS TO BOOST SELF-ESTEEM, SOCIAL COMPETENCE, AND SOCIAL SKILLS

In this chapter, we will focus on how a person's self-concept changes over time and the importance of social competence in the formation of a healthy self-concept. Our *self-concept* is a complex system of beliefs about ourselves. We develop our self-concepts based on judgments or evaluations of how we are doing when we compare ourselves with others or our own ideal self. It is possible to have a good self-concept in one area (such as sports) and a poor self-concept in another area (such as mathematics).

The self-concept (also known as *self-esteem, self-image,* or *self-worth*) is formed from three major sources of information that we obtain from others: words, feelings, and behaviors. What I think about myself is often based on others' comments about me; what I feel about myself often comes from others' emotional reactions to me; and how I behave is often in response to others' reactions to me.

Another source of information that helps build or reduce self-concept is the set of internal standards used to judge one's performance. If these standards of ideal performance are too high, a person may feel that he or she does not measure up. Consequently, the person develops feelings that devalue a sense of worth, resulting in a low self-concept or self-image in that area. Children often learn these internal standards from watching how their parents, teachers, and peers judge their performance at school and at home.

CHANGES IN SELF-CONCEPT AT DIFFERENT AGES

Very young children (three to five years of age) think in all-or-nothing terms. Therefore, a young child's self-concept often fluctuates between extremes such as happy and sad or good and bad. The child often over-generalizes and reasons, *If I'm good at coloring, then I'm good at everything. If I'm bad because I spilled the milk, then I'm bad, period!*

By the time a child enters the first grade (approximately six years of age), reasoning allows the child to sequence emotions and behaviors. At this stage of development, the child begins to develop a greater understanding that a person can be happy and then sad, thereby allowing some flexibility and continuity in the emotional repertoire. However, it is not until approximately the third grade (eight years of age) that children can begin to accept and understand the concept of experiencing two coexisting emotions such as being both happy *and* sad. However, at this stage, a child can only attach the two emotions to two separate people. A child might reason, *Johnny and Stuart may have two separate feelings about me. Johnny may describe me as good, but Stuart may say I'm bad.* The child is not yet capable of understanding how both feelings could come from the same person. At this stage, children are also capable of understanding that they can be good in one area (math), but poor in another (art).

It is not until approximately ten years of age that a child begins to understand the concept of ambivalent feelings (one person having conflicting emotions). At this point, children are capable of understanding how someone can continue to love them despite being very angry with their behavior. It is also at this stage that the self-concept becomes further influenced by how children evaluate themselves and their achievements compared with their peers. Self-descriptions and comparisons also shift from the more absolute terms used earlier (for example, good or bad, nice or mean) toward descriptors that emphasize the social or more interactive aspects of this developmental period (for example, shy or friendly).

Young adolescents often maintain an idealistic and naïve view of what should be that has not yet been tempered by experience. Adolescents' awareness that others are capable of thinking about other people results from the self-conscious fear that others are often thinking about and evaluating them. It is through the process of comparisons with peers and peer acceptance that an adolescent's fears are alleviated and he or she begins once again to grow in self-confidence.

THE THREE COMPETENCIES

In addition to the evolution of the self-concept based on our growing understanding and increased perceptions of ourselves and the world around us, our self-concept is also influenced by our perceptions of self-competence in three specific areas: *cognitive* (academic/school/career), *physical* (athletic/artistic), and *social* (peer groups) domains (see Figure 13.1).

Self-Esteem Based on Cognitive/Achievement Performance

Children can measure their success relative to their peers in several different areas. For children in special education, learning and achievement can be two areas that cause significant frustration and challenge. These children may work very hard to master tasks, but their efforts may not result in success for many reasons, such as poor memory, processing problems, or difficulties in problem

FIGURE 13.1 *The Three Competencies of Self-Concept*

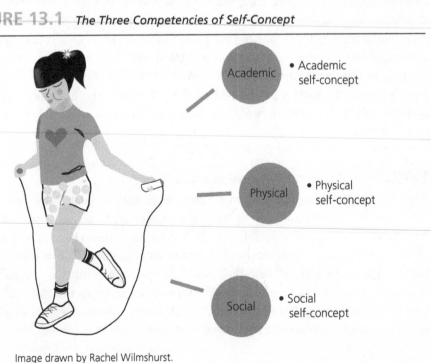

Image drawn by Rachel Wilmshurst.

solving. Some children may feel dumb and may begin to avoid academic work because of the frustration and their lack of success. For many children, small-group work centers or resource room assistance can provide a safer environment and a slower pace, allowing them to attempt and acquire new skills.

Children should always be praised for their efforts, and tasks should be presented at levels that are neither too challenging nor too easy. Challenges that are too steep will frustrate a child, who may then develop feelings of helplessness about future efforts to master tasks. Tasks that are too easy may provide a sense of false competence and not prepare a child to take on greater challenges. Breaking down complex tasks into smaller segments can help a child to master more difficult tasks in stages that build on earlier successes.

A number of children who receive special education assistance may have a recognizable physical disability (such as a vision, hearing, or orthopedic problem). These children obtain accommodations for their disability in ways that will enhance their ability to learn (for example, wearing glasses or a hearing aid, or using crutches or a wheelchair). However, children with less obvious disabilities (such as ADHD, learning disabilities, or emotional disturbance) may be misunderstood by their teachers, parents, or peers, who may believe that these children are not achieving adequately because of a lack of effort. Such children may be described as lazy or unmotivated or not caring about school. For these children, it is important to praise their efforts and to understand that having a learning problem is a significant burden that they must carry with them throughout their academic years. The more that parents and teachers understand exactly where the child's disability lies, the more they can help the child cope academically and develop a healthy self-concept based on success in areas other than academics.

Self-Esteem Based on Physical Competencies

Although competence in academic areas might be evaluated by our actual achievement in certain subject areas, our competence in physical pursuits may be a function of our athletic abilities, or fine motor skills. These different areas of mastery can assist children in discovering an area other than academics that they can excel in and increase their self-concept, as a result. As the next box discusses, often parents will remove children from extracurricular activities because of their lack of academic success. However, children who are receiving special education assistance have been determined eligible for special services because of a legitimate learning problem that falls within one of the major categories recognized by IDEA.

DIDYOUKNOW

When children are having academic difficulties, many parents feel that the first thing to go should be extracurricular activities. They reason that because Johnny is failing his spelling tests, he should lose the privilege of playing on the baseball team. However, for many children, not passing spelling tests may be a legitimate result of their learning disability. For some of these children with learning disabilities, athletics may be the only area in which they are capable of excelling. If these children lose the activities, they also lose the opportunity to feel successful compared with their peers. .

For children with disabilities, developing a healthy self-concept will often require stretching outside the academic system to include activities that can increase self-confidence and feelings of success. It is important to find opportunities in the community that are available for these children because involvement in these activities might contribute to the development of potential competence and skills, in areas such as sports, art, dance, theater, music, agricultural or horticultural groups, gymnastics, baton, and so on.

Having addressed the need to expand rather than restrict extracurricular activities for children in special education, it is also important to realize that there is a limit to the number of extracurricular activities that should be scheduled. Recently, there has been increased recognition that some parents over-schedule their children in far too many activities, which can increase stress for many family members. We are not advocating this situation by any means; we simply want to impress upon readers that extracurricular activities can be a very important component in building self-esteem for children in special education.

Self-Esteem Based on Social Competence and Social Skills

Although very young children often engage in solitary play or parallel play with peers, as they mature, there is an increased emphasis on the need to develop skills that emphasize interactive and cooperative play with others. Therefore, the third competency—social competence—gains increasing importance as a factor in the development of self-esteem as a child matures.

Developing social competence involves four prerequisite skills:

1. The ability to recognize and respond to both nonverbal and verbal information

2. Sensitivity to the needs and feelings of others

3. The ability to engage in interpersonal problem solving

4. Awareness of peer group norms

Children who lack social competence are said to have poor social skills. Children who have special needs, especially those who find it difficult to learn because of a learning disability or attention problems, are likely to experience social difficulties as well. The reason for the overlap is that social learning requires much the same skills as learning in any other subject. If children have trouble with problem solving in academic situations, they are likely to also encounter problem-solving difficulties in social situations.

How We Learn Social Skills Interpreting social information can often result in difficulties if social cues are misinterpreted, resulting in a social mismatch. At a basic level, social information comes to us in much the same way as we learn other information.

DIDYOUKNOW

Interpreting social information follows the same process as interpreting other information from our environment:

Recognition of social cues → Interpretation of social cues → Response to social cues

---

Difficulties with the recognition of social cues may result from poor ability to attend to information that is presented verbally, visually, or motorically (for example, through touch). A great deal of information can be misinterpreted if we do not pay attention to subtle auditory cues like tone and emphasis. Misinterpretation at this level often results in missing the main message. If we don't pay attention to a person's facial expression or body posture, we may miss important signals about how receptive a person is to our approaching them at this time.

For example, is the person sending signals that say "Approach me" or "Leave me alone"? Finally, not recognizing the difference between a soft pat and a more intrusive touch may result in conveying a completely different meaning than was intended in a given interchange.

Children who have difficulties with academics due to weak attention to visual details may readily miss visual details in social situations as well. Errors in visual attention may result in a lack of attention to visual indicators such as subtle changes in facial expression that provide clues to a person's current emotional status or changes in body posture that can signal fatigue or a high energy level. Similarly, a child who demonstrates poor listening skills in the classroom may also misinterpret social communication by not tuning in at the correct time or by missing important parts of a message.

Interpretation of Social Information   Provided that we have recognized the cues appropriately, how can we be sure that we have interpreted the cues in the best way, given the context of the situation?

We learn appropriate social responses through the four competency skills discussed that are acquired over time through our exposure to social input in the home, at school, and in previous social interactions. Interpreting a particular social situation requires that we are able to draw on previous experience to help us sort out what we are dealing with. In order to learn, we need to find predictability in our environment, which allows us to organize social responses into categories of successful and unsuccessful attempts. We also need to be able to make comparisons between similar situations or to generalize the information from situation to situation so that we don't keep repeating our errors over and over again.

Children with specific learning disabilities often have difficulties in the following areas:

- Organizing information

- Attention span

- Memory and expression

- Sequencing information

- Isolating key elements of information

- Transferring information from one situation to another

Can you see how all these areas could affect our success or lack of success in social relationships? All these elements play a crucial role in the interpretation of social events. The skills necessary for the correct interpretation of social exchanges are the same skills required for problem solving in many academic situations. These abilities allow us to learn from our past experiences by storing information about how we acted and what we did in similar social situations. Drawing on information from past experiences also allows us to use our reasoning skills to compare a current situation to other situations in terms of how similar or different it might be and what did or didn't work in the past. Being able to correctly sequence which events came first and how they unfolded is crucial to the ability to understand and anticipate the consequences of our actions. Children who are impulsive often have considerable difficulty in this area.

Social Responding Responses to social situations can cause trouble if the response does not match the situation in terms of timing and/or intensity. Children who are hyperactive or impulsive often overreact to social stimulation; their reactions are inflated compared with what triggered the reaction. Extremely impulsive children, such as those with ADHD, seem to bypass the interpretation component completely, as if they go directly from *INPUT* $\longrightarrow$ *RESPONSE* without taking the time to interpret or problem solve.

Children who are passive or hypoactive (slow to respond) may take too long to respond and also miss the appropriate opportunity for reaction. Some children who have expressive language problems take a long time to process information and seldom get their verbal responses together quickly enough to participate. These are the children who take so long to answer that people often end up finishing their sentences for them. Children who are overly passive may be the opposite of the impulsive responder in their passive or nonresponsive manner (for example, providing minimal facial expressions or verbal feedback). These children, in their passivity, give off few social cues to which others can respond. These children are often called "hard to read" and may be avoided by others socially because people are unsure how to respond to them since they provide so little feedback.

Social Responding and the Social Self-Concept A final word of emphasis on the chain of information that takes place in the building of social self-concept. Other people evaluate us by our social responses and they, in turn, direct their responses to us based on their interpretations. It is often from this feedback that our positive or negative social self-concept is formed.

Interventions to Help Social Skills and Social Competence Because social competence is an acquired skill, children who do not pick up social skills naturally can often be helped through direct instruction and role playing. Discussing stories or movies can help children better understand subtleties and nuances in social communication that they may not pay attention to. In addition, discussing social rules—such as turn taking, giving compliments to others, and how to respond to criticism—can all help a child's understanding of social situations and facilitate success in social circumstances. In order to find out more about what areas of social skills a child might be having difficulty with, review the *Social Problems* checklists in Appendix B.

CHAPTER

14

INTERVENTIONS TO IMPROVE BEHAVIOR AND DISCIPLINE

Discipline is essential both at home and in school. It can help children to understand which behaviors are acceptable and which are not. As they mature, they will begin to see that their behavior at home is also related to the quality of the social interactions they have with other children. Discipline is a significant contributor to children's development at home, at school, and in their social relationships.

In this chapter, we will discuss how to provide structure at home and in school; show you how to teach children to display appropriate behaviors; discuss what to do when behavior problems arise; and address the different types of effective discipline.

SHAPING BEHAVIOR AT HOME AND IN SCHOOL

All children need structure. Creating a predictable environment for a child is an important part of fostering his physical growth and mental development. Structure provides a safe environment in which to develop healthy self-esteem. Clearly defined rules and expectations that are consistently reinforced can limit the need for discipline.

> ## DIDYOUKNOW
>
> In order to create structure, parents and teachers need to establish boundaries; follow routines but bend the rules when necessary; and set limits. Structure provides an excellent framework for appropriate behavior.

Step 1: Establish Boundaries

Children do not have natural behavioral boundaries. Parents need to help their children establish boundaries of what is and is not acceptable behavior for a given situation. This can be done by creating rules, establishing consequences, and providing reinforcement.

Creating Rules   Rules are needed both in the classroom and in the home. Teachers, parents, and children should work together to think of rules that should be followed at school and at home. Allowing a child to help create the rules gives her some ownership of them and increases the likelihood that they will be followed. No more than five or ten rules should be created; the more rules there are, the more likely a child is to forget them. In order to help a child remember the rules, post them in a few places around your classroom or home, such as in the play area, near the classroom door or the board, in the kitchen, or in her bedroom. Periodically reviewing the rules also is helpful, just to be sure she remembers them. If a child's behavior is getting worse in one area, it may be helpful to create a new rule to address this behavior.

For older children, it is acceptable to state actual rules—for example, "Toys are to be put away after I play with them"; "I will put all of my clothes in the hamper before I go to bed"; or "There is no running in the hallway." The "House Rules" and "Classroom Rules" charts in Appendix D can be used to post the rules and the consequences for breaking them, which we'll talk about in the next section. Verbally reminding the child ("Mark, remember the rule that says 'no running in the house'") helps him to remember the rules; you may need to use this strategy after a new rule is implemented. You can use a check mark or a tick mark to indicate whether the child followed the rule. Again, before he goes to bed, review with him how well he did that day. Encouragement and praise will go a long way in helping a child to change his behavior.

Young children may not fully understand how to follow rules, so it's often better to set positive behavior goals instead of rules. For example, "I will wash my hands before I eat"; "I will put away my toys"; and "I will brush my teeth in the morning and before I go to bed" are common goals. You can use the "Positive Behavior Chart" in Appendix D to record the goals and the child's daily progress. When he completes a goal, draw a smiley face in that column. If he forgets the goal, draw a frowning face in that column. The faces provide a visual reminder of his daily performance. It is a good idea to review that day's progress with him so that he can see how well he did. Verbally praise him when he does well, and encourage him to do better when he does not.

DIDYOUKNOW

Many children are visual learners and benefit from having a chart about rules or behavior posted near their desk at home or at school. Use our charts (see Appendix D) or create your own. You may want to laminate your chart and use a dry erase marker to monitor daily behaviors. Avoid using a red marker, however; it may seem too punitive.

Establishing Consequences   Establishing consequences helps a child understand the relationship between misbehavior and its consequences. In order to learn right from wrong, she must learn that if she breaks the rules, there will be consequences. We like the idea of using a Consequences Jar—a jar that contains a number of consequences written on small pieces of paper or index cards that have been created collaboratively by you and the child. This technique can be used at home or in the classroom. Brainstorming about consequences can be a productive and meaningful activity that promotes creativity and personal responsibility. If a child misbehaves and you feel she deserves a consequence, ask her to choose one of the consequences out of the jar. This procedure also helps to minimize verbal backtalk such as "That's not fair!" because she chose the consequences herself. Examples of consequences include "No dessert," "No TV after dinner," or "Going to bed thirty minutes early."

Providing Reinforcement   It is important to praise a child when his behavior has been good on a particular day. If he has earned many smiley faces on the Positive Behavior Chart or few negative check marks on the "House Rules" or "Classroom Rules" chart, you should tell him that he did a good job, that he should keep up the good work, and that you are proud of him. There are many ways to provide a child with positive reinforcement, both verbally ("Good job!" or "I like your good behavior!") and nonverbally (a smile or hug). It is important that you make a conscious effort to provide this type of reinforcement on a regular basis. Positive reinforcement will help a child build self-confidence. Children want to please their parents and teachers, and this type of reinforcement increases the chances that he will continue to exhibit good behavior. Children have both good days and bad days, just as adults do, but the goal is to maximize the number of good days. These good days will serve as a model for positive behavior in the future.

Step 2: Follow Routines

Establishing routines brings consistency to a child's life. Parents can work with their children to create morning, after school and homework, and bedtime routines. These routines should be followed each school day.

Morning Morning routines should be the same every day so that a child knows what to expect and can learn to get ready with little supervision. A typical pattern might look like this:

Get out of bed → Brush teeth → Wash face →
Get dressed → Make bed →
Eat breakfast → Go to school

Once you decide on the pattern that works best for you and your child, you may want to list the tasks and post them in her room or the bathroom so that she can follow them more easily. For younger children and those with reading problems, you can use pictures to represent each of the tasks.

School A child's school routine will depend largely on the classroom schedule and the services the child is receiving. He may follow the classroom schedule for part of the day but leave at a certain point in order to receive speech services or other special education services in another classroom. He should have a set schedule soon after a school year begins, and once a schedule is set, it can be written down for him to follow.

After School and Homework Whether a child goes straight home or to after-school care, a routine can be established. If she goes home, decide whether you want her to do all, some, or none of her homework before she gets time to play. Some parents prefer that their child complete work as soon as she gets home so that the day's lesson is still fresh in her mind; others say "Let kids be kids" and give their child some free time first, believing that playtime right after school is important in order to give the child a break from academics. You must choose the routine that works best for you and your child. In making a decision about your child's routine, it is important to realize that your child should follow the same routine each day. The routine for homework will depend on whether the child has homework, how much, and the amount of help and supervision she will require. For younger children and children who have no homework, create a routine that includes a snack, playtime outside for exercise, dinner, TV time, book time, and individual time with you. In establishing homework routines, it is very important to set aside a consistent place where homework is to be completed. If at all possible, it is best to restrict homework to locations that are away from high-traffic areas. (For example, doing homework on the kitchen table can be a good thing unless this area is where the family often congregates to talk and share daily information.)

The amount of time a child is expected to spend on homework will depend on your school district's curriculum, the difficulty level of a class, the child's ability, and the child's own expectations. For example, the amount of time a child spends on homework may be correlated with the grade that he or she receives. If a child wants high grades, he will likely invest the time to complete all of his homework. If a child's doesn't care about school and has low expectations for his grade, he will likely not spend much time on homework. We recommend the following guidelines for the number of homework minutes, which are based on a child's developmental level. The time spent on homework may also vary according to the severity of a child's disability.

Grade	Maximum Homework Time
Kindergarten and Grade 1	15 minutes
Grade 2	20 minutes
Grade 3	30 minutes
Grade 4	45 minutes
Grade 5	60 minutes
Grade 6	75 minutes
Grades 7 and 8	2 hours
Grades 9–12	2–3 hours

The time spent on homework at each sitting may vary according to a child's age and disability. A child with ADHD, for example, may be too inattentive to sit through a forty-five-minute homework session; it may be necessary to break homework time into several sessions. A child with a physical disability may also find it difficult to sit up for an extended period of time and may need multiple homework sessions.

Bedtime   A nighttime routine helps a child prepare for a good night's sleep. Like a morning routine, a bedtime routine should follow a typical pattern such as this one:

Brush teeth → Wash face → Take a bath (on days when the child needs one) →
Put on pajamas → Read book with parent →
Talk about the day's events and what he learned → Go to sleep

Giving a child a thirty-minute period to wind down will help him to relax and fall asleep more easily. A sleep routine is important, and children benefit from positive sleep habits even at an early age. A good sleep routine includes waking up and going to bed at roughly the same time each night, including weekends. In general, children need between nine and eleven hours of sleep; some children may require more or less, depending on their day's activity level.

When to Change a Routine   Sometimes a change in routine may be necessary. Here are three instances when you might want or need to change a routine:

A special occasion necessitates an exception. It may be necessary to change a routine because of a special event such as a party, a vacation, or a sporting event. When such a change occurs, it is important to point out to your child that you are making the change because it is a special time, but that she will go back to her regular routine when it is over. In certain situations, an exception to a routine may be a reward for good behavior.

A routine is no longer appropriate. Much of what you do with a child depends on his developmental level. As the child matures, you may find it necessary to change his routine to provide additional homework time, for example. And as he gets older, his bedtime may be pushed to a later hour or he may need to get up earlier for school. You may also ask him about his routine and give him the opportunity to give you feedback.

A child is not adapting to the routine. Some children may have difficulty making a transition from one routine to another. If a child has never had a good routine, she may initially struggle when a routine is implemented. Give her some time to adjust. After a reasonable period—say, a month—if you find that she is not adapting well, you will need to adjust the routine accordingly. Maybe she is not getting enough sleep or she needs more free time to play. Again, if you think she is mature enough, be sure to ask her about it. Older children are able to verbalize what they see as not working in their routine.

Step 3: Set Limits

It is important for parents to set limits. Children need to understand that there are rules that must be maintained on a consistent basis. Parents can set time, material, and behavioral limits.

Time Limits   A child must learn to minimize time spent on certain activities and maximize time spent on others. At home, parents may need to teach him that time for watching TV, talking on the phone, playing video games, and playing on the computer is a privilege and as such must be earned by displaying good behavior. Even when the privileges have been earned, we recommend that you limit these activities to a reasonable number of hours per week and instead maximize your child's time with reading, puzzles, games, the arts, and creative play. In the classroom, children must learn to increase their on-task behavior and minimize time spent in socializing, playing with objects in their desk, and other nonproductive activities that can interfere with classroom performance.

Material Limits   It is in a child's best interest to place limits on material items. Children tend to think that the sky's the limit when it comes to owning things. If they have too many toys, they tend to play only with the new ones and a few select favorites, forgetting about the rest. A child does not need all of the latest toys, games, and electronic equipment; purchasing a few new toys for your child at major holidays is fine. Limiting the number of toys, games, and other play materials will help her to learn self-control and promote creativity. Parents and teachers should have a common understanding about whether it is a good idea for a child to bring play materials from home to school and which toys a child is allowed to bring from home.

For some children, having a TV in their bedroom may interfere with good study or sleep habits. In such a case, emphasize books and the importance of reading prior to bedtime and perhaps read with the child, if she is still young enough to enjoy that. It is often advisable to take a child to the local library in order to develop her interest in books or story reading. Mature children should have their own library card and be responsible for returning and renewing their borrowed materials.

Behavioral Limits   Children must learn that the appropriateness of some behaviors depends on the setting and situation. It is often acceptable, for example, to yell outside but not inside a house, school, or store, which leads to a difference between "inside voice" and "outside voice." Learning to control impulses is a complex process that is affected by a child's developmental level, personality, environment, and disability.

Children must also recognize the difference between requesting something once and asking for it repeatedly. Requesting a cookie once or twice is fine, but not ten times. The limits imposed on this behavior have implications for their social interactions, too, because many peers may find such insistent behavior annoying.

DIDYOUKNOW

Children see and often repeat almost everything adults do, even if the adults don't witness the children noticing it. Children are often a reflection of important adults in their environment, which is why adults must remember to be a good role model for children.

ADULTS AS ROLE MODELS

Distinguishing between appropriate and inappropriate behaviors is only the beginning. It is important that adults model good behavior so that children can see appropriate behavior in action. You can be a good role model by demonstrating appropriate behaviors, thinking before you act, and explaining your behavior when you do something inappropriate.

Demonstrate Appropriate Behavior

Each time a child misbehaves, the adult should use it as an opportunity to show him how he should have acted differently. He'll not only understand that his behavior was incorrect, but if an adult demonstrates the appropriate behavior, he will learn an alternative way to act. For example, if your child grabs a toy from another child's hand, explain to him how to ask for the toy ("Jimmy, when you are done with the toy, may I please play with it?") and then discuss why it's important to wait his turn (Jimmy may find him unfriendly, and he probably would not like it if Jimmy did the same thing and grabbed his toy). Teaching your child social skills and manners will help foster positive social interactions. Role-playing different scenarios with him while discussing and demonstrating the appropriate behaviors can also be helpful.

Think Before You Act

Children model their behavior after adults. They observe you, your behavior, and your reactions to different situations. If you want a child to act appropriately in different situations, the best way to teach him is to set a good example. The apple truly does not fall far from the tree.

Explain Your Behavior

Although you may be an excellent role model, there will be times when you say or do something you shouldn't. When this occurs, use it as a learning opportunity. Tell your child that what you did was wrong and what you should have done instead. If you don't, she will think your behavior was acceptable, and it will confuse her if she gets into trouble later for exhibiting the same behavior.

DIDYOUKNOW

You should consider a child's behavior in the context of several factors. Behavior problems can be complex, and it is important to use our five-question assessment in order to gather information about why a child may be misbehaving.

WHEN BEHAVIOR PROBLEMS ARISE AT HOME OR IN SCHOOL

To better understand a child's behavior, it is important to look at it in the context of several factors, a number of which may be occurring at the same time. We advocate a five-question assessment to gather information about his behavior. This will not only help you to understand the child a little better, but it can help you to choose appropriate discipline, which we'll talk about in the next section.

Question 1: Is the Behavior Developmentally Appropriate?

You must first consider whether the behavior is typical for the child's age group. Your response to the child's behavior will depend on his developmental level. If the behavior is typical for a child his age, you probably should not discipline him unless he is putting himself or others at risk. Children with cognitive delays often exhibit behaviors that are typical of children at a younger developmental level, so this must be considered as well.

Question 2: What Is the Situation?

Situational factors can have an effect on behavior. Factors ranging from use of medication to physical, emotional, or sexual abuse to other difficulties (for example, social problems or the death of a friend, family member, or pet) can cause a child to display atypical behavior. When a child displays a distinct change in behavior, you should consider whether something has changed in the child's life. When in doubt, ask him. You might say, "It seems that you may be feeling really bad about something. What do you think may be bothering you?" Things that bother children often seem trivial to us. A child may exhibit behavior problems because he was not chosen for his friend's team in gym class or because his friend did not sit next to him at lunch. While you may want to downplay the situation because you think it's unimportant, it is very real to the child. You should never tell a child not to feel a certain way, even if you think that what he thinks about the situation is wrong or stupid. The child cannot help how he feels; he needs help with sorting out why he is feeling that way and help with moving away from negative feelings toward positive ones.

Question 3: When Does the Behavior Occur?

Parents and teachers can observe whether children behave differently at different times of the day, and the timing of the behavior may provide important clues. For example, if a parent notes that a child misbehaves in the morning before leaving for school, it could mean that the problem is related to school and that the parent needs to investigate what may be occurring. Maybe the child has a test and does not feel prepared, or maybe he is being bullied and is scared. If a child misbehaves at the end of a school day and is fearful of going home, perhaps there are problems going on at home. A school counselor may want to talk with him to make sure that he is not being abused or neglected. Behavior problems that occur immediately after school may be an indication that something happened at school that is bothering him. If this is the case, ask. Behavior problems right before going to bed could indicate that a child has nightmares and does not want to go to bed, although they are often related to the fact that what the child is doing before bedtime is more exciting than going to bed. If a teacher notes that a child comes to school in a bad mood and is upset before the day gets started, then problems may be occurring at home that need to be investigated or, possibly, on the school bus on his way to school. Behavior problems at recess may mean that a child is trying to vent academic frustrations or is being teased or bullied on the school grounds. If a child is on medication, does the behavior problem peak when the medication has started to wear off? Does the child misbehave during some subjects and not others? Are problems related to transitions between classes or free-time periods when there is less structure? All of these questions can help teachers and parents better understand the context in which problems are occurring.

Question 4: What Is the Child's Emotional State?

Like adults, children behave differently because of changes in their emotional state. When a child misbehaves, you may want to consider things such as whether he is tired, hungry, frustrated, ill, bored, anxious, or depressed. These feelings can often lead to misbehaviors, so take a moment to ask him how he is feeling. Young children are often unable to express how they are feeling; in the absence of verbal feedback from a child, you may be able to obtain important information from his demeanor and posture.

Question 5: What Is the Child's Temperament?

A child's temperament should also be a consideration. Is he typically shy? Active? Outgoing? Temperament can affect how he reacts to others and to specific situations. What is believed to be a behavior problem may instead be the typical behaviors of an extroverted child. Once you better understand who a child is, you can understand why he behaves a certain way. A school psychologist can assess a child's temperament. The Student Styles Questionnaire and the Murphy-Meisgeier Type Indicator for Children are used to detect individual differences in students' preferences, temperaments, and personal styles.

DISCIPLINING A CHILD

Methods of child discipline depend on many factors. Parents and teachers must consider the age of the child, the nature and severity of his disability, and the behavior he displays, in addition to their own feelings about discipline. Most experts agree, however, that some form of discipline is necessary in order for a child to understand the consequences of her behaviors. Let's talk a bit about different forms of discipline, including positive reinforcement, negative reinforcement, time-out procedures, and punishment.

Positive Reinforcement

Positive reinforcement is one of the easiest, most effective forms of discipline. It involves catching the child being good—engaging in good behavior—and rewarding it quickly and often. When you see a behavior you like, point it out to her. Feedback may include comments such as "I like how you are playing with your brother"; "I liked the way you put away your crayons when you were finished coloring"; or "I like how you are using good table manners." Rewards you give a child may be a smile, a hug, a kiss, a smiley face on a chart, a choice of what movie to watch that night, or special time with you. We don't recommend using material rewards like money because then the child may have an expectation that she will get a monetary reward each time you catch her being good.

Negative Reinforcement

You can increase behavior in two important ways: positive reinforcement (reward for good behavior) and negative reinforcement (removing a negative consequence or penalty as a result of the desired behavior). For example, if Mary's teacher says to her, "If you do all your work in class, you won't have to do any homework tonight," the predicted response is that Mary would increase her behavior of working at school in order to avoid having to work at home (negative consequence). In doing so, she does not have to complete her work as homework, which would take up some of her playtime. Mary has learned that she can avoid homework (aversive) by completing her assignments at school (reinforced behavior).

Time-Out Procedures

Time out can be an effective behavioral intervention. Time out involves removing a child from the environment in which she is displaying unacceptable behavior and moving her to an isolated area—for example, a quiet section of the classroom or a chair in her room—for a short period of time. In doing so, you are removing her from the situation and removing her audience (which could be a parent, a teacher, or other children). Children will often stop their inappropriate behavior when there is no one around to see it or give attention to it. In addition, many children benefit from having a cooling-off period. If a child has a temper tantrum, calmly say, "Your behavior is unacceptable. Please go to time out." This should be said only once, and you can either walk her to her chair or, in cases of extreme behavior, carry her.

What if a child misbehaves in a store or during a field trip? It can be more difficult to implement time out, but you can still use it effectively. When a child starts misbehaving, walk her to a quiet area and ask her to stand there quietly. She will want to engage you in conversation, but there should be no verbal communication while she is in time out. Each of the child's attempts to speak should be followed by repeating, "There is no talking while in time out." She will soon learn that she is not going to get and maintain your attention while in time out. In cases of severe misbehavior, you may wish to leave the store and use a time out outside or, if you are on a field trip, bring the child to a private area away from the other children.

> ## DIDYOUKNOW
>
> A digital timer or egg timer has many uses. Not only can a timer be helpful during time out, but it can also be used to time academic drills when a child is completing math problems, to set a limit on TV watching, or to indicate the number of minutes until bedtime.

Time out can help to reduce behavior problems such as hitting, temper tantrums, biting, spitting, and not following directions. Time out can be used with children as young as two and as old as ten or eleven. Once she is in her room, set a timer (keep it on a shelf or somewhere high so that she can't reach it) and tell her that time out will be over when the timer goes off. When the timer goes off, ask her whether she has calmed down and can display acceptable behavior. The only acceptable answer should be "yes" (or a variation thereof), and the answer should not be given in an angry or nasty tone. If the child's behavior has not improved or if she says she is not ready, she shouldn't remain in time out but instead should play in a quiet area until she is ready.

> ## DIDYOUKNOW
>
> A rule of thumb is to place a child in time out for two minutes for each year of their age but never for more than ten minutes. Time out loses its effectiveness when the period of isolation is too lengthy for a child's developmental level.

Punishment

While both positive and negative reinforcements work to increase behaviors, punishments work to decrease behaviors. There are different types of punishments. The type of punishment you use will depend on the situation, including factors such as the child's response to different punishments and your personal preference. Removing privileges is one form of punishment (also called a *penalty*) that is effective. If a child misbehaves, you may choose to not allow her to go to a special center in the class or to her friend's house to play, or you may cancel plans to go to the park or to the movies. You should make it clear that she has lost the privilege because she did not have good behavior and that she may lose other privileges if you do not see an immediate improvement in her behavior.

Removing material items is another type of punishment. Taking away a favorite toy or video game when a child misbehaves can be effective. The item that you choose to take away must mean something to the child, or she won't care that she no longer has access to it. Let the child earn the item back with good behavior. If her behavior changes, you may want to give it back to her in an hour; if there is no improvement in behavior, you may not want to return it until the next day.

Spanking, a form of corporal punishment, remains questionable as an effective type of discipline at home. When done correctly, spanking provides an intense short-term consequence that is negative to the child and sends a strong message that her behavior was unacceptable. On the other hand, spanking models aggressive behavior and teaches a child that aggression is an acceptable way to deal with issues; it may result in her engaging in hands-on physical behavior with other children. If you decide to use spanking, it should be used with caution because it can have negative effects on behavior when not done correctly. For example, if there is too much time between the child's misbehavior and the spanking, she may not see the relationship between the two. Spanking that is too rough can injure a child, and you must also question whether you are doing it to change the child's behavior or as an outlet for your frustration. In the end, for parents, the use of spanking remains a matter of personal choice.

DIDYOUKNOW

Paddling, a form of spanking, is still in use in American schools. While more than half the states ban it, a few hundred thousand paddlings are administered to children and adolescents each year. The National Association of School Psychologists is opposed to the use of corporal punishment in schools because of its harmful physical, educational, psychological, and social effects on students. The American Academy of Pediatrics also recommends that corporal punishment in schools be abolished in all states by law and that alternative forms of student behavior management be used.

SUMMARY

We want to emphasize that, whatever discipline method you choose, you must be consistent in applying your methods. We have already discussed several guidelines for disciplining children. In closing, however, we want to emphasize that in order for discipline to be effective, it must be consistent and predictable, have a definite time limit, and be well suited to a child's developmental level. A school psychologist or behavior specialist can provide tips on behavior modification to parents and teachers.

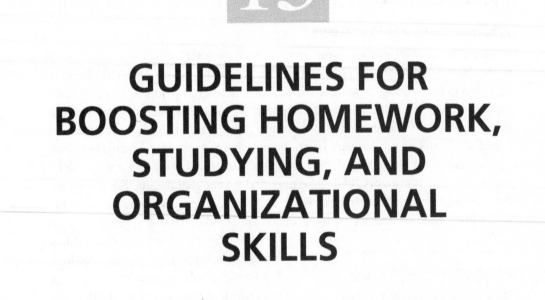

GUIDELINES FOR BOOSTING HOMEWORK, STUDYING, AND ORGANIZATIONAL SKILLS

School is designed to benefit children who can sit still and concentrate. Those who succeed are likely the ones who can sit in their seat, listen attentively, read well, and complete tasks independently. Children with special needs may be good at only some or, possibly, none of these. Consequently, many of them have difficulty completing homework, studying for tests, and organizing their work environment and may require a lot of parental and teacher help in order to be successful. While it isn't always the school's fault, parents may become frustrated with the process of trying to find ways to help their child be successful in this type of environment.

In this chapter, we will provide information for parents and teachers about ways to improve children's performance and increase their chances for academic success.

HOMEWORK

Homework is an important task. It gives children the opportunity to practice what they have learned in school. This practice helps them to demonstrate that they have mastered the material and are ready to move on to more difficult work. The amount of time a child is expected to spend on homework relative to the grade level was discussed in the previous chapter (page 181). Some additional considerations for parents to keep in mind are when and where their child will complete his homework.

When to Complete Homework

By the time a child comes home from school, he may have used up a lot of energy getting through a typical school day. Over the course of a day, he may have had to focus on what the teacher said, take notes, remember to raise his hand instead of blurting out an answer, finish his work in the allotted time without being distracted by everything around him, take a test or quiz, participate in group work, and so on. He may be completely burned out once he arrives home.

Getting children to complete their homework can be quite a chore. Many don't like to do homework, and some may find it very challenging. Some suggest that children complete their homework as soon as they get home because the information will be fresher in their mind, while others say it's better to give them a chance to unwind before they begin their homework. Some children, for example, may do a better job on their homework if they complete it after dinner or after a bath, when they are more relaxed.

> REMEMBER that the best thing is to be flexible when trying to figure out the best solution; it may be a trial-and-error process. Give yourself and your child time to decide what works best.

Which way is better? It depends. Our best advice is to figure out what works best for your child. We can't advocate one choice over another because children are so different; what works for one child may not work for another. It is important to ask your child for his input and then see what results you get from the different methods.

Where to Complete Homework

For some children, where they complete their homework is not an issue. They may not have any trouble completing it at a noisy kitchen table or in the living room with the TV blasting. Others may require the solitude of a quiet room, especially if they have attention problems.

A child's bedroom may be a good place to complete homework. It's likely to be quiet and away from the hustle and bustle of home life. However, it may offer too many distractions. A TV, a computer, video games, an iPod, books, or a telephone may be within arm's reach, and if a child is bored with the homework, other activities may be very tempting. A parent may also be too far away should the child have a question. Nonetheless, most of the children with whom we have worked find the solitude of a bedroom to be a good work setting.

Children may respond well to adjustments to their environment that help them to concentrate. Classical music playing quietly in the background may help to drown out other noises in the house. A white noise machine may also be very helpful in blocking out unwanted noises. It can be used during the day when outside noises or other noises within the home are loud or at night to help children who have difficulty falling asleep.

DIDYOUKNOW

Once you find a homework routine that works, it is important to be consistent and stick to the routine. Many children thrive on a routine, and they will likely benefit from the day-to-day consistency and parental expectations.

Keeping Track of Homework

Getting children to complete their homework is one thing; getting them to turn it in is another. How many times has your child spent an hour on homework only to forget to turn it in to the teacher? This type of lapse can be a very common occurrence, especially among young children. Many teachers check backpacks and binders for completed homework sheets, but not all do, and as children get older, teachers are likely to do this much less frequently, if at all.

Parents want their children to bring home their homework assignments, including the correct worksheets; complete their homework without any drama; and remember to turn it in the next morning. While this scenario may seem like a tall order, it's not only possible, but it's important for your child's success. Parents and teachers can work collaboratively to help students succeed in completing their homework.

Many schools require children to use a planner. Children often find a planner helpful because they can write down their homework for each subject and keep track of what they need to do each night. It is most effective when teachers check it for accuracy at the end of the day and parents review and sign it each day, too. Children will quickly realize that they will be held accountable—by both their teacher and their parents—for their own homework. If a child's teachers do not require the use of a planner, the child's parent can ask for the child's IEP to require that a planner be used and that teachers check it every day. Parents should also check the planner daily to see what assignments are due and to read any teacher comments.

Parents can also put all of their child's homework in one folder to minimize the number of things a child needs to look through each morning. While each subject may have its own notebook and folder, one folder for all homework makes it easier for children to keep track of their work. Plus, if teachers need to look for the homework because the child forgot to turn it in, finding it is easier.

Parents may need to pack their child's book bag each night to ensure that homework not only is completed but actually makes it to school. As a child gets older and she packs her book bag herself, parents may only need to double-check to ensure that she has packed everything successfully. This check needs to be performed every day. If a child forgets an assignment, additional oversight may be needed until she does this task successfully 100 percent of the time.

Things to Consider

What Motivates or Frustrates a Child   As a parent, you need to watch your child for clues. Note when he gets frustrated or feels overwhelmed, and also observe what makes him feel good about himself. If he says things like "I did all my homework!" that is a good start. He feels success in completing this task, and simply completing it can be the challenge at first. You can then continue to build on what you know works to motivate your child do his home-work and do it well. Let your child take responsibility—and enjoy the resulting pride—for being successful. If his level of frustration continues, however, he may require additional assistance with his homework. You may need to check his work frequently and give him feedback. If your child is continually overwhelmed with the amount of homework, it may be a good idea to meet with his teacher(s) to see if it is possible to decrease the amount he is required to complete each night.

Family Schedule   When planning homework time, take into consideration the family schedule and the amount of homework to be completed. If a child has to balance homework with extracurricular activities, he may be very tired. We definitely encourage participation in extracurricular activities, but not at the expense of time to complete homework or a child's energy level. Children who are tired all the time may find it difficult to be academically successful. Therefore, we recommend just one extracurricular activity at a time. Also, if there are multiple children or a crying baby in a household, distractions may keep a child from staying on task and may limit the amount of time that parents have to help each child. These factors are why everyone's work, study, and sleep schedules must be taken into consideration.

STUDYING

Everyone agrees that children need to study for tests and quizzes in order to do well. While some don't study and are still very successful, we find this to be unusual. Many children—especially those with learning problems—have difficulty with long-term retrieval of information. That is, they have trouble recalling previously learned information that is stored in their brain. The goal is to help them to recall this information more easily, so they can improve their performance on classroom assessments.

Let's talk about some ways in which we can help children recall information.

What Helps Children Remember Information?

Children may not recall information because they did not do a good job of storing the information initially. Several techniques can be used to increase the likelihood of remembering the information when it is needed later. You may be familiar with some of these, while others may be new to you. We suggest that you have your child or student try different ones. Give them some time to work; generally, you will not see results overnight.

Proper Note Taking   Taking good notes is an important first step. For some children, the notes are all they have to study at home. Some school districts no longer allow children to take their textbooks home, which underscores the importance of taking good notes. If the notes are poor or are incorrect, the child will not be successful in reviewing and studying for a test. Some IEPs include a requirement that children be provided with notes, which is a good way to ensure that they have access to all of the information that their teacher shared with the class.

Writing or Rewriting Notes   While teacher-provided notes are helpful, the act of writing notes helps the brain to process and store the information. Whenever possible, we encourage children to take notes themselves, even if teachers will provide them later on. Rewriting notes can also help children remember information. While they may find rewriting their notes to be a boring task, it's something they can do to help themselves organize and relearn information when they are at home.

Note taking is not necessarily a skill we teach. The goal is for children to learn to listen to the teacher and write down the important information. But which information is considered important? Some children have difficulty understanding the difference between relevant and irrelevant information. A child can compare her notes with teacher-provided notes to see how well she was able to pull out the important points. Additional practice can improve this skill. Note taking is even more important at the secondary level because lectures are likely to move along at a quicker pace. It is helpful for children to use a separate notebook for each class and keep them organized in a large three-ring binder. We'll discuss organization in more detail later in this chapter.

DIDYOUKNOW

A child may use an audio recorder to record a teacher's lesson. He can listen to it later and perhaps take notes from this recording. Recording may only be necessary for a subject that is particularly difficult or when the lesson content is difficult to understand. Some students are auditory learners or may have attention problems and may benefit from the ability to replay the recording for information that they may have missed the first time. The student should always ask for permission before recording the teacher.

Mnemonics   Mnemonics can be a good learning aid. Many of us have used mnemonics to remember information, although children today don't seem to rely on this skill. Perhaps it's not being taught by parents or teachers or it's because rote facts are easy to access online.

An acronym is one type of mnemonic device that can be used to remember information on any subject. For example,

- In U.S. geography, *HOMES* is used to remember the five Great Lakes: Huron, Ontario, Michigan, Erie, and Superior.

- In math, the phrase "**P**lease **e**xcuse **m**y **d**ear Aunt **S**ally" represents the order of operations: **p**arentheses, **e**xponents, **m**ultiplication and **d**ivision, and **a**ddition and **s**ubtraction.

- And in science, *Roy G. Biv* is used to remember the sequence of hues in a rainbow: red, orange, yellow, green, blue, indigo, and violet.

While some of these mnemonics can be taught to children, they can and should create their own mnemonic devices, for they are more likely to remember mnemonic devices that they created themselves.

Songs   Children learn by repetition. Setting information to a song can make it easier for them to repeat, retain, and, later, recall the information. Many young children, for example, learn the alphabet by singing the ABC song. Children can create their own mnemonic songs by using any song familiar to them, keeping the melody and changing the lyrics to reflect the information they are trying to remember. As they sing the song over and over, it increases the likelihood that the information will be remembered later. This practice can help them to hold on to the information.

Flash Cards   Flash cards remain a good way for children to quiz themselves. A word can be placed on the front of an index card, for example, and on the back a definition of the word or a fact relating to it can be listed. Flash cards can be used for almost any subject, and children can review them quickly right before a test. Flash cards are commercially available, but self-made cards are better because children learn through the act of creating them. Flash cards are inexpensive, portable, and easy to create.

How Long Should a Child Study?

The length of time that a child needs to study varies. Factors such as intelligence level, strength of memory, age, and complexity of information must be considered. Some children may need to study for a test for an hour, while others may require only thirty minutes. Through trial and error, you will come to know what works best for your child. The trick is to find a balance between studying enough and studying too much. Children who do not study enough may miss important concepts that are likely to show up on a test. Conversely, those who study too much may become burned out or very disinterested in the material. The ideal balance may change, depending on a child's age and the subject, so watch for clues to indicate that he has reached his tolerance level.

ORGANIZATION

Organization does not come naturally to many children. In elementary school, activities are very structured. Parents and teacher help ensure that children have everything they need to complete a particular task. But as children get older, they are expected to increase their level of independence. With this independence comes the need to organize their own materials, their own workspace, and their own time.

Organization of Materials

It is important that children organize their materials. Better organization can help ensure that they have the necessary materials available when needed. Materials must be organized both at school and at home.

School A locker can be stocked with the materials that a child needs—things like notebooks and pens or pencils. A child can go to her locker between classes to get what she needs for the next class or the next several classes. A couple of drawbacks to keeping materials in a locker are that it is sometimes not very convenient and not all children have a locker.

A book bag or duffel bag can be used instead of or in conjunction with a locker. The advantage is that a child will have his materials with him at all times. If the bag is too heavy because of the number of textbooks, a child may keep his books in his locker and all of his other materials in the bag.

Home As we mentioned earlier, some schools no longer allow children to take their books home at night. But in an IEP, a parent can request that a set of books be provided for home use. These books can help children who have trouble remembering information. Rather than relying on their memory, they can look up information in the textbook. Having this reference available increases the accuracy of the information that they learn. For children who are allowed to bring their books home, a set of books that always remain at home alleviates the problems associated with forgetting books at school.

REMEMBER that parents need to check with their child to find out what materials she needs. A child may run out of paper or pens and forget to mention it. For children to be successful, they need to have the materials necessary to complete their work.

Children need materials to help them stay organized. Notebooks, pens and pencils, erasers, dictionary, a thesaurus, and self-adhesive notes are some of the items they will need to complete their work. Self-adhesive notes are particularly helpful. Children can use them to remind themselves to complete tasks or to ask the teacher certain questions. Parents can also use them as reminders for children. A sticky note on the refrigerator, for example, can remind a child to study for a spelling test.

Organization of Workspace

Children need to keep their workspace clean and organized. At home, many children work at their desk, while others may work elsewhere—for example, at a kitchen table. Their space should not be messy, and it should not include any distractions (like a TV).

A child's desk at school should also be neat. Desks need to be cleaned out regularly. We've seen desks stuffed with old food, used juice boxes, and dozens of old worksheets. We suggest that children be encouraged to clean out their desk at least once per week to get rid of anything unnecessary and to ensure that it is stocked with needed materials such as those mentioned in the preceding section. Lockers, book bags, and duffel bags should also be cleaned out regularly.

Organization of Time

Children may have a lot of work to do in a short period of time. The goal is to maximize their efficiency so that they can complete their work and be successful. Teachers need to be mindful of the total amount of homework a child may have each night, while parents must be mindful of the time it takes a child to complete work. Finding the right balance between homework and other activities is especially important when extracurricular activities are taking up some of a child's free time.

Children need to learn to budget their time. If they have a test on Friday, they need to start studying, say, on Monday or Tuesday, not on Thursday. If they study each night, they break up the amount of information that needs to be learned each day. Studying information on multiple nights also provides repetition, which may help children retain information. If they wait until the last day and they have other work to complete or they don't feel well, they're not likely to be well prepared for the test.

Planning ahead also allows children to break a project into smaller, manageable parts. Some children have a lot of difficulty completing large projects. Parents can help children set deadlines for individual parts of a project to help ensure that the final project is completed on time. This method alleviates the stress of having to stay up late the night before a project is due. Some IEPs may state that teachers will set deadlines for reviewing different parts of a project and providing feedback. Such reviews help a child to understand whether he is on the right track or needs to correct his work.

> *REMEMBER to ask your child daily, "Is there anything I need to see or sign?" This simple question will remind your child that a parental signature is required on a test, for example, or to tell you that a new project has been assigned.*

Four

Planning for Success and Monitoring Change

CHAPTER

16

THE IEP AND BEYOND

Tips for Successful Parent-Teacher Collaboration

The *Individualized Education Program* (IEP) is perhaps the most important document in a child's special education file. An IEP guides the delivery of special education services for a child who has been identified as qualified to receive them. As its name indicates, IEPs are individualized for each child according to his needs. IEPs are based on input from a variety of people. Parents often provide important information and feedback, and school personnel such as special education and regular education teachers, teacher assistants, administrators, school psychologists, school counselors, speech-language pathologists, occupational therapists, or physical therapists may each have important contributions to make in regard to meeting a child's needs.

The IEP, as well as the special education process, require parent-teacher collaboration. Parental input is beneficial to teachers because parents may provide important insight on their child's problems and his or her progress at mastering goals at home. Later in this chapter we will discuss ways in which to initiate and maintain communication between parents and teachers. In addition, we will discuss how to prepare for a collaborative parent-teacher meeting. Preparation is key, and we will share some important steps to follow before and during a meeting.

THE INDIVIDUALIZED EDUCATION PROGRAM

The IEP is the most important legal document in a child's file. It outlines the goals and objectives for the next year—or multiple years—in states that allow multi-year IEPs. The IEP requires input from many individuals, such as teachers, parents, school psychologist, speech-language pathologist, and related services personnel such as occupational therapists or physical therapists. A multidisciplinary approach is important because it allows different perspectives about which goals and objectives are appropriate for the child.

DIDYOUKNOW

IDEA 2004 recognizes the need for increased efficiency and effectiveness in streamlining education for students with disabilities by increasing convenience for parents who wish to participate in their child's education and by reducing the need for teachers to complete excessive paperwork.

Development of the IEP

Although IEP forms vary from district to district, each contains the same basic information. This section provides you with important information about each of the essential parts of an IEP.

Present Level of Performance   An IEP describes a child's current progress in the classroom. Teacher input, homework and class assignments, tests, and observations all help to answer the question "How is the child doing?" Any ways in which a child is not meeting the goals of the general curriculum will be noted, especially if the lack of progress is caused by the disability.

Annual Goals   Annual goals set targets for a child's progress during the next twelve months. Goals may address academics, behavior, physical needs, or socialization. IEP goals should be very clear, and they must be measurable, which means that the desired results can be counted or observed. While all goals should be achievable, a parent or the IEP team can call a meeting at any time to adjust the annual goals. Such an adjustment is likely to occur if a child falls far behind and it is inconceivable that she will meet a particular goal or if she is progressing at a faster rate than was expected and has already met a goal.

Under the Individuals with Disabilities Education Improvement Act of 2004 (IDEA 2004), short-term objectives are no longer mandatory unless a child is considered severely disabled. This mandate includes students with severe cognitive disabilities. Many of them take alternative assessments, which are created by the IEP team and used in place of national standardized achievement tests such as the Iowa Test of Basic Skills or the Stanford Achievement Test. The alternative achievement standards created for severely disabled children benefit from short-term objectives because they may need to be reviewed and revised rather frequently. These students may make incremental progress toward their goals and may need short-term objectives that can be updated regularly as they meet their goals.

DIDYOUKNOW

Under IDEA 2004, a parent and a school district can agree not to convene an IEP meeting to make needed changes to an IEP. Instead, a written document can be created to amend or modify the current IEP and this new paperwork can be sent to the parent. Parents still have a right to request an IEP meeting in order to be sure that their requests are incorporated in the revisions.

Another change under IDEA 2004 was to allow fifteen states to participate in a pilot paperwork reduction program. This change allowed states to give parents and school districts (local educational agencies) the opportunity for long-term planning by offering them the option of developing a comprehensive multi-year IEP (for a term not to exceed three years) rather than a yearly IEP. Parents retain the right to request a yearly IEP if they prefer that option. Changes to IEPs can be made via videoconferences or conference calls if all IEP team members agree on the proposed changes.

DIDYOUKNOW

All special education and related services must be provided at no cost to parents. Parents must provide transportation for students who are home-schooled.

Special Education, Related Services, and Supplementary Aids and Services
An IEP describes the special education services a child will receive. Decisions will also be made about issues such as whether a child needs an extended school year and what types of physical education or vocational education are needed. Physical therapy and occupational therapy are considered *related services*. The frequency and duration of physical therapy or occupational therapy visits will be specified in the IEP. Other related services might include speech therapy or counseling. Some children may need help from a teacher assistant, a person to take notes, or access to a time-out room; these types of items are referred to as *supplementary aids and services*. In addition, any program modifications or supports for school personnel, such as computer software and hardware or a training workshop on autism for the regular education teacher, are included as supplementary aids and services.

Participation with Nondisabled Students   As part of the IEP, a determination will be made about the amount of time a child may spend in the regular education classroom. The goal is always to keep a child in the least restrictive environment to the maximum extent possible. For most students, the least restrictive environment is a regular education classroom. If a child's behavior is so severe that making transitions back and forth between special education and regular education settings would be too upsetting, his participation in regular education may be minimized for his benefit. An IEP also addresses whether a student will participate with his regular education peers in physical education, computer lab, art or music classes, recess, meals in the lunchroom, or extracurricular activities.

DIDYOUKNOW

Parents and regular classroom teachers must be invited to IEP and placement meetings, which are held at a mutually convenient time. Although parental presence is not required, we recommend that parents try to attend all IEP meetings, particularly the first one and any meetings in which a change of placement is being considered.

Participation in State and District Testing   An IEP addresses whether a child will take state and district tests. Such tests are not given to children in every grade; however, if an IEP is being written in May when a child is in second grade and state tests are completed by third graders each spring, the IEP must address this future testing, which falls within the term of the IEP. Any modifications—such as allowing a child to work with a small group while taking the test, extended time, or reading the test to a child (that is, all sections other than reading comprehension)—must be included in the IEP. These modifications can be changed as needed, based on teacher and parent feedback on what works best for the child, given that it is sometimes difficult to know a year in advance what modifications will be needed. If a child will not participate in state or district tests, perhaps because of a severe cognitive disability, her IEP will state why these tests are not appropriate and will specify a different way of assessing her.

Dates and Places   An IEP specifies when services start, how long they will last, how often they will be provided, and where they will take place. Most services will last for one year, but services such as physical therapy or occupational therapy may be provided for a specified period of time at one frequency (for example, thirty minutes weekly for the first three months) and then at a decreased frequency (for example, thirty minutes monthly for the remaining nine months) for the duration of the IEP. The actual frequency will depend on the child's needs.

DIDYOUKNOW

Schools value parental input into the IEP. No one knows a child better than his parents. Some teachers prefer to write some of the goals prior to the meeting in order to save time, and these goals are based on current evaluation results, the student's progress toward meeting previous goals, or the student's current level of performance. Any of these goals can be changed or deleted and new ones created on the basis of input from parents or other members of the IEP team.

Transition Services   Transition services are designed to help a child move from school to activities such as postsecondary education (college), vocational training, employment, and independent living. When a child turns fourteen, the IEP committee must begin to discuss her future plans. The committee will be interested in knowing her desires and abilities in regard to education, employment, and independent living. The idea is to identify her interests and goals and provide her with the skills needed to meet these goals after she is finished with high school. For example, if a student has lower ability functioning and is not going to attend college, but wants to live on his own, the committee may help him locate supported employment and other community resources that offer independent living. The student may participate in community-based instruction (CBI) while in high school in an effort to gain supervised work experience.

Needed Transition Services   When a student is sixteen, her IEP committee will confirm her interests and goals and will assess the services, programs, or supports that are needed to help her achieve those goals. Those transition services will ensure that she is prepared for education, employment, or independent living after she leaves high school. The IEP must list any needed transition services and may include future possibilities in regard to community agencies that can provide the student with training or assistance in finding employment.

Age of Majority   At least a year before the age of majority (eighteen, in most states), the student's IEP must include a statement that says she's been informed that her rights will transfer to her once she reaches the age of majority. Once rights have been transferred, the student—not the parent—must agree to any testing, changes in eligibility, or changes in placement.

Measuring Progress   Measuring a child's progress is an important part of his education, and an IEP will specify the ways in which his progress will be measured. Parental updates on progress might be notes in a daily journal, a weekly summary, or a monthly report card. We advocate for more frequent progress reports, perhaps weekly or, in most instances, biweekly, although we do see the benefit of weekly reports, especially right after special education services are first initiated.

DIDYOUKNOW

A child can be a member of his own IEP committee. Having a student on his own IEP committee is especially important when discussing his postsecondary plans. The IEP team will want to hear about his plans for his immediate and distant future so that plans can be put in place to work toward his goals.

The IEP Meeting

Who will attend the IEP meeting? Most likely the parents, regular education teachers, special education teachers, a school administrator, school psychologist, and others who may have been involved in the assessment of a child (such as a speech-language pathologist, physical therapist, or occupational therapist). We always recommend that both parents attend the meeting, if at all possible; an IEP is extremely important and requires input from both parents.

During the creation of the IEP, input from parents and school personnel will be requested. This is the opportunity for parents to suggest goals they would like to see added to the IEP. Some schools may create a draft of the IEP and present it at the meeting in an effort to save time, but anything can be changed during the IEP meeting. Parents can request changes, though they may not be incorporated into the document if the committee does not feel these changes are appropriate. If parents want to make any changes at a later date, they have the right to call an IEP meeting and ask that the IEP be reviewed and amended, if necessary.

Once the IEP meeting is over, parents will receive a copy of the IEP. Typically, they are given a copy right away; occasionally, it is sent to the home the next day or a few days later. We advocate for obtaining a copy of the IEP immediately after the meeting in order to give parents the opportunity to review it or to share it with the parent who could not attend. When the meeting is scheduled, we encourage parents to tell the school that they would like a copy of the IEP before leaving the meeting. Parents, it is important that you understand the contents of an IEP so that you can advocate for your child. If you don't understand something, just ask. You have a right to a clear explanation of everything discussed during the meeting. You may wish to bring this book with you in case you wish to look up any of the acronyms in Appendix A.

Implementation of the IEP

Writing an IEP is only part of the story. The other part involves its implementation. All persons who will provide services to a child must receive a copy of her IEP. The IEP spells out the types of services, their frequency and duration, and the setting in which they will be provided, all of which are very important information for the service providers.

DIDYOUKNOW

If parents do not think an IEP is adequately addressing their child's needs, they can request a meeting to review and, perhaps, update the IEP. Some goals in the IEP may prove too difficult for the child to master, and some goals may be mastered quite easily. In these instances, another IEP should be written, including revised goals.

Parents' feedback to the IEP committee is helpful, important, and appreciated at any time. The committee will want to know whether the child's behavior is improving, if he finds it easier to complete his homework, or if he socializes better with his neighborhood peers. This kind of information gives the committee members an idea of what's going on in the child's home and, in conjunction with teacher feedback, provides a good sense of a child's progress and how he is meeting his goals. It is to a child's advantage for parents and teachers to work together. Next, we will discuss ways for parents and teachers to initiate and maintain communication with one another.

PARENT-TEACHER COLLABORATION

After an IEP is created, parents will likely have ongoing contact with teachers, who will share with parents on a regular basis a student's grades and progress. Consequently, it is important for parents to collaborate with teachers on issues related to their child's mastery of goals. Parent-teacher communication is an important part of a child's education. Her success depends, in large part, on the combined efforts of her teachers and parents to maintain ongoing contact. Not only do teachers communicate with one another and with school administrators, but they also communicate with parents—sometimes on a regular basis. Parents are a very important partner in a child's education, and good communication between school and home is essential.

Initiating Communication Between Parents and Teachers

The first step in parent-teacher communication is for parents and teachers to create a positive relationship with one another. Let's talk about some of the more popular methods of cultivating a good relationship.

Attend an Open House   We recommend that parents attend each open house that their child's school holds. This is an excellent opportunity for parents to meet their child's teachers face to face and get to know who they are. An open house is an informal setting that allows parents to ask general questions about what their child is doing in each class and to meet other parents, too. Teachers also have an opportunity to get to know parents and to learn more about the child. During an open house, teachers often display children's work as a way of displaying some of their accomplishments. If a child's work is displayed, it can be very rewarding for the child if his parent mentions the work and praises him for having his achievement recognized.

Volunteer in the Classroom   Another way for parents to be involved in their child's class is to be a classroom volunteer. While some principals will not assign parents to their child's room, being a room mother (or room father) is a possibility in many districts. Volunteering in another class can still provide many insights into what goes on in the school or in the classroom—for example, what happens daily or how a teacher manages her classroom. Volunteering provides the teacher with an extra set of hands and some welcome help. Teaching is a big responsibility that requires a great deal of planning and hard work, and typically, parents' offers to help are greatly appreciated.

DIDYOUKNOW

It is not always a good idea to volunteer in your child's classroom, especially if she is very young. Younger children tend to cling to their parents, and they may come to expect to see their parent in the classroom every day, leading to problems when the parent is not present. On the other hand, having a parent in the classroom may embarrass a child or make her feel uncomfortable. Be sure to ask your child if she wants you to be a classroom volunteer. If she says no, it's best that you not volunteer in her classroom.

Meet Early in the School Year   It's a good idea for parents to meet with their child's teacher (or teachers) before or immediately after a new school year starts. This meeting gives them an opportunity to discuss possible concerns, including the child's disability, his needs, and which classroom interventions have and have not worked. Parents should ensure that the new teacher has a copy of the child's special education file, including the IEP. While schools usually do a good job of making sure each teacher is aware of every student with a disability, a change in school leadership or teaching staff or a change in schools on the student's part may cause some things to be accidentally overlooked at the beginning of the school year, when things are likely to be very hectic.

DIDYOUKNOW

The Parent Teacher Association (PTA) was started in 1897. According to the PTA, there are approximately 26,000 local units, including units in every state, the District of Columbia, the U.S. Virgin Islands, and the Department of Defense schools in Europe and the Pacific. You can learn more about the National PTA at http://www.pta.org/.

Maintaining Communication Between Parents and Teachers

Parents and teachers use many methods to stay in contact with one another. Some require technology; others are old-fashioned ways of communicating. Regardless of which method is chosen, it is important that parents and teacher maintain a regular, open, and positive channel of communication with one another. In this section, we list some of the most successful ways of maintaining parent-teacher communication.

Student Planner   A student planner, sometimes called a *homework agenda,* is a notebook that is used to help children keep track of their daily homework assignments. While many teachers will write the assignments that are due in the planner, older children may be required to do this task themselves in order to increase their independence and responsibility. Teachers may write out the assignments for children with motor impairments or for those with written expression problems. When children are responsible for writing their assignments in the planner, the teacher will sometimes check their notebook to see whether they completed the task accurately. Parents and teachers can communicate daily through a child's planner.

Message Notebook   A message notebook may be used so that a teacher can communicate what is going on at school and a parent can communicate what is happening at home. Notebook comments from a teacher may discuss a child's progress, her behavior, her attitude, the rate at which she completes class work, or other relevant information. A message notebook also provides an opportunity for a parent to ask questions she may have for the teacher or provide information about her child to the teacher. For example, a parent might want to know which pages her child should be reading over a weekend or holiday break to give the child an opportunity to get ahead, or a parent might wonder whether the interventions she is trying at home have helped her child at school. Thus, using a message notebook or a planner can be an excellent method of two-way communication.

Phone Calls   Whether parents call their child's teacher or vice versa, phone conversations can be a good way to communicate because each party can ask more detailed questions. Telephone conversations often do not provide the ongoing dialogue that corresponding through a message notebook does. However, for complex issues, a phone call may be the better choice. Although we suggest that a face-to-face meeting is usually the best way to communicate, a phone conversation is a good alternative.

Scheduling phone calls can be difficult. Perhaps a parent's employment situation is not suitable for personal conversations; for example, the parent may work in an open area where everyone can hear the call or in a busy environment that does not allow personal calls. Teachers are often very difficult to reach during school hours because of classroom obligations. Parents also may not realize that in the late afternoon or evening after school, teachers are often engaged in meetings, after-school programs, college courses, or training. It sometimes is best to leave a message for the teacher and ask that she return your call at a time that is convenient for her. This allows teachers to call you when they have free time during the day. E-mail can be used to schedule time for a phone call. If you have a quick question and know that the call will take only ten minutes, or if you have many questions and will require a thirty-minute phone call, say so ahead of time so that the teacher can plan her time accordingly.

E-Mail   E-mail has become a very common and convenient method of communication. If parents and teachers both have an e-mail address, e-mail may be a convenient way for them to communicate. E-mail can also be used to support the other forms of communication mentioned earlier in this section. Many individuals who have access to e-mail, especially teachers, are much more likely to respond to an e-mail than to return a phone call during the day. E-mail has the advantage that each party can respond at a time that is convenient rather than having to schedule a time that works for both.

Homework Hot Line   Some districts use a homework hot line that allows teachers to communicate homework information to parents and students. Parents can call a certain number in order to hear the day's homework assignments for their child. Of course, a hot line may be used in conjunction with other forms of communication.

Web-Based Homework List   Similar to a homework hot line, a Web-based homework list provides a list of reading and homework assignments for the night. The site may also include links to relevant Internet resources. A homework list is often offered as part of a program that allows parents to log in and access their child's grades. This feature allows parents to continually monitor their child's progress, which is particularly important if parents are concerned that their child's grades may be slipping because of extracurricular activities or after-school employment.

Preparing for a Collaborative Parent-Teacher Meeting

Sometimes it is necessary for a parent and a teacher to meet. A parent may have medical documentation, for example, or a child's work samples to show the teacher. A parent may also have a question about a child's grade, amount of homework, or the teacher's classroom management skills and feels more comfortable discussing this in a face-to-face meeting. In this section, we suggest a six-step process for engaging in an informal meeting with a teacher or parent. These tips will help ensure a successful, productive meeting.

Step 1: List Your Concerns   It is appropriate to bring a list of questions to the meeting. The concerns do not need to be detailed in paragraph or even sentence form; a numbered or bulleted list may suffice.

Step 2: Listen to the Other Party   It's probably best to take turns talking. If a parent goes first, the teacher should answer all of the parent's questions before asking her own. A collaborative discussion may commence after both parties have asked their questions. Allowing each person time to address his or her points is important. Of course, how each responds and what is said is important, too.

Step 3: Ask Questions   Now is the time to ask your questions. It's best to raise one question or concern at a time; a rapid-fire approach can be very confusing. Once the other person answers your question to your satisfaction, move on to the next point. If the answer is unclear, be sure to ask for clarification. If necessary, take notes.

Step 4: Be Prepared to Brainstorm   Parents and teachers may meet because a child has problems with his behavior, academics, social skills, or some other issue—or perhaps more than one of these areas. Brainstorming allows parents and teachers to generate creative and imaginative solutions to his challenges. There may be many obvious solutions to these problems, but if they don't work, some creativity may be required. If they can work together, parents and teachers have a better chance of finding solutions that will help a child in the classroom and at home.

Step 5: Be Open to the Other Person's Suggestions   Brainstorming requires both creativity and patience. You need to allow the other person to share suggestions with you, even though they might not necessarily make sense to you at first. The best solutions are not always the most obvious ones. Try to be flexible in your thinking and open to the other person's suggestions and listen to the reasons behind the suggestions. A teacher may suggest a particular approach, for example, because that intervention has been effective with other students in the past.

Step 6: Remain Positive   We understand that meetings can be stressful. A good deal of time may be spent on discussing a child's problems, how he misbehaves, how he does not understand class work or homework, and so on. At times like these, it is not uncommon for both parents and teachers to feel somewhat defensive or to feel that they should have been able to solve the problem on their own. *But sometimes it takes two*. It is extremely important to try to remain positive and work together. In order to come up with the best solutions to a child's problems, parents and teachers need to discuss the problems in detail. Although such discussions may be difficult, they are necessary in order to develop interventions that can be implemented consistently in the classroom and at home. With the right interventions, most children will improve, although it may take a while. Stay positive, work collaboratively, and think about how all of this time and effort will ultimately benefit the child.

CHAPTER

17

TRANSITIONS

Moving, Changing Schools, or Transitioning from Elementary to Secondary School

As adults, we recognize that major life changes (positive or negative) can be stressful. Facing the unknown can place individuals at a disadvantage, not knowing what to expect or anticipate. For some, hoping for the best but anticipating the worst can be a lifelong challenge. For children, school transitions can be stressful and can have as much or even more impact than a job change has for adults. In fact, it has been found that for children and youth, visits to health care professionals for complaints of stomach aches, headaches, and body pains peak during two key periods: transition to elementary school (six years of age) and entry into middle school or junior high school (Schor, 1986). Even four-year-olds have been found to show elevations in their stress levels in anticipation of beginning school within the next six months (Turner-Cobb, Rixon, & Jessop, 2008). Preschoolers who had the most difficulty with attention and impulse control were the most stressed upon school entry and in the first six months of enrolling in the school program. Children who exhibit uncontrolled behaviors (difficult temperament with hyperactivity and poor ability to control impulses) are at the greatest risk for negative outcomes, including school adjustment problems.

However, children who are overly shy or wary are also at risk for difficult adjustment to school entry or school changes (Kagan, 1997). Children who are very shy are apt to respond to the unknown with increased activation of physical responses (for example, increased heart rate, rapid breathing), becoming more fearful with increasing attempts to withdraw in order to avoid the anxiety-producing situation. Shy and reticent children are more likely to be exposed to peer rejection, exclusion, loneliness, and victimization in their early school years (Coplan, Closson, & Arbeau, 2007). At least one study reported that some teachers believe shyness to have as much of a negative impact on social and school adjustment as aggression (Arbeau & Coplan, 2007).

Problems that can cause school adjustment difficulties include disabilities that interfere with a child's ability to learn, such as learning disabilities, problems with attention and concentration, emotional and social difficulties, physical disabilities, aggressive peers, and child perceptions of parent and teacher support. Children who have pre-existing learning, emotional, or social problems are at increased risk for school adjustment problems. Adding additional risks can have a *multiplier effect* on a child's opportunities for success decreasing the chance for positive outcomes significantly as the number of risk factors increases. Parent and teacher support have been found to protect children from this effect. Researchers have found that positive teacher support can be a protective factor when children have issues caused by multiple school moves. As anticipated, researchers found that school changes predicted declines in academic performance and classroom participation. However, negative effects could be offset by peer acceptance and teacher support, and teacher support was significantly related to positive attitudes toward school among children who had experienced the most school changes (Gruman, Harachi, Abbott, Catalano, & Fleming, 2008).

Studies have shown that among students who do not have disabilities, there is a significant decline in interest, motivation, academic performance, and motivation across adolescence, especially during the transition from elementary to secondary school (Barber & Olsen, 2004). It has been suggested that these declines may be related to changes in the school setting and expectations that accompany the transition from elementary school to secondary school—for example, settings with close teacher contact and direct supervision are replaced with larger classes, multiple teachers, higher expectations, and less guidance and supervision. Furthermore, as the number of life changes increase (for example, school transition, pubertal development, onset of dating, residential moves, family conflict), academic performance decreases accordingly. Therefore, it is not surprising that children who have disabilities may be at greater risk for problems associated with transitions to secondary school education.

As outlined in the preceding paragraphs, many children who do not have disabilities experience school transitions as a stressful experience. Therefore, it would seem logical that children who have disabilities would also be vulnerable to the same stressors—or, even more vulnerable. Therefore, it is important for parents and teachers to consider what a child or adolescent is going through as a result of the school change. We will talk about the ramifications of school transitions in two ways. First, we will address the psychological aspects of change and how to reduce the stress associated with school adjustment. Then we will discuss how IDEA 2004 has addressed transitions during three important time periods: transition from preschool to elementary school, transition to secondary school, and postsecondary school transitions.

THE PSYCHOLOGICAL IMPACT OF SCHOOL TRANSITIONS

As we discussed in the introductory comments to this chapter, school moves can represent a stressful experience for the majority of children. However, for children with disabilities, a change of schools can be particularly unsettling for many reasons. We can find situations stressful or distressing when there is a change in our environment that increases our lack of predictability or lack of control. For children with disabilities, structure is an integral part of their ability to adapt to their surroundings. Structure provides a consistent framework, set of limits, expectations, and procedures that are familiar and predictable. When the structure is clear, consistent, and well-defined, the child is able to handle age-appropriate tasks more successfully.

Reactions to stress and unpredictability can occur physically, emotionally, behaviorally, and mentally. At a physical level, when placed under stress our body mobilizes to respond to the stressful threat by *fight or flight*. Our body responds by increasing its heart rate and adrenaline production. While in this state of alert, we are mobilized to combat the stressor. However, this physical response is very taxing on our system and if we remain in this state of alert for too long, we become exhausted. One of the consequences of being in a state of heightened alert is that ultimately it drains our reserves, resulting in increased susceptibility to illness. Other physical symptoms can include sleep problems and eating problems (overeating or undereating). Our thinking can also be impaired. We can make errors in judgment and make impulsive and rash decisions. Emotionally, we can become irritable, angry, and act out our frustrations toward others.

Children who are stressed may respond with a wide variety of symptoms. Some children may become weepy and break into tears at a moment's notice. Other children withdraw, attempting to avoid the stressful situation. Fantasy play may help some children avoid a too-stressful reality, while others respond to stress on a physical level, complaining of headaches or stomach aches or exhibiting sleep problems (for example, needing too much sleep or having problems falling asleep or staying asleep). Some children demonstrate regressive behavior; for example, a five-year-old may want a bottle because her new baby sister is getting too much attention. Acting out in an aggressive way is also a common childhood reaction to stress. Many children will use denial to avoid acknowledging a stressful situation; for example, a child may continually forget to bring his schoolbooks home because he is at a loss as to how to do the work.

Easing School Adjustment Problems

If a change of schools is imminent either due to relocation or moving from one school level to another, children should be made aware of the move in advance so that they can prepare for it. If at all possible, especially if moving any distance, it would be helpful to find the school's Web site and introduce the child to pictures of the new school to ease the fear of the unknown. If possible, a visit to the new school can also be a positive way to ease the stress of adjusting to a new location.

As for special education services, make sure that you talk to educators in the new location to become familiar with how they process their cases for special education placement. Even though a child may currently be placed in special education, the same criteria may not be used by a different state or school district. Your child may have to undergo further assessment in order to see whether he or she meets the criteria for placement in the new location. To assist educators at the new school in their efforts to help your child succeed, make sure that copies of all reports, IEPs and assessment results are sent to the new school district.

Helping a Child to Cope with Stress

Children can also be helped to manage stress in many ways. Knowing how to identify stressful symptoms in a child is the first step toward helping the child develop ways to successfully cope with stressful situations. The following steps can be helpful in teaching children to manage stress more effectively:

- Teach children how to recognize the symptoms of stress they may be experiencing.

- Help the child learn how to relax through deep breathing, stretching, muscle relaxation, or using visual imagery to calm the mind and body.

- Help the child to develop a framework for problem solving that will help to reduce stress and increase opportunities for success.

1. **Stop:** What is the problem?

2. **Think:** What can I do about it?

3. **Try:** A response

- Encourage the child to use positive methods to solve the problem or to back away and release tensions prior to attempting a solution.

- Normalize stress for the child by talking about how stress can influence anyone, at any age.

- Don't involve a young child in discussions about adult matters. Children who are given too much information may feel more powerless to help and may feel that they are to blame for difficult times.

- Praise the child's efforts and help the child understand that sometimes not getting what we want can be a powerful lesson that helps us learn how to try different approaches in the future.

- Help the child to understand that stress often comes from having to make difficult choices. If the child did not make the best choice, help him or her to understand how to problem solve in order to make better choices in the future.

- A daily planner can be a great stress buster. Teach the child that a daily planner (student agenda) is a best friend. Knowing what to expect can help the child to be prepared, and being prepared is one of the best ways to fight stress.

- If the child is stressed about a social situation or event, help the child role-play what might happen and what possible responses might be appropriate.

Finally, it is important to remember that there are both positive and negative ways of coping with stress. Inappropriate ways of attempting to deal with stress involve withdrawal, avoidance, denial, acting out, and blaming others. Positive ways of coping with stressful experiences result from viewing stressful experiences as learning experiences. Knowing what to expect and preparing for the unexpected are healthy ways of using stressful experiences to motivate change in a positive way. And don't forget, having a good sense of humor can be a positive way to relieve stress.

IDEA 2004 AND SCHOOL TRANSITIONS

With the implementation of IDEA 2004, transition planning for students who have disabilities has been increasingly emphasized and widened to include other key points in a student's school history. While we will focus on preparing for school entry (when a child is three years old) and school exit (when a child is sixteen years old), transition planning also can involve students transitioning from elementary school to middle school and from middle school to high school. The intent of transition planning is to make the transition as seamless as possible. Transition planning is also being provided for students who will be making a transition from high school to college or other postsecondary learning environments.

Transition Services When a Child Turns Three

Although the majority of information in this book relates to special education services that are available for children between the ages of three and twenty-one, under IDEA 2004, infants and toddlers with disabilities and developmental delays who are eligible for services can receive intervention programs to assist with delays in physical, cognitive, speech and language, social, emotional and behavioral, or adaptive functioning. Services for children under the age of three are coordinated through an *individualized family service plan* (IFSP), the nature of which can vary in details from state to state. Most family service plans are monitored by a coordinator and include information about a child's current levels of functioning and the types and locations of services that will be put in place. IDEA 2004 emphasizes the need to develop an effective **transition plan** in order to provide a smooth and effective transition from interventions provided under Part C of IDEA 2004 (which covers infants and toddlers with disabilities and delays) to Part B (which pertains to children between three and twenty-one years of age who have disabilities and delays). To ensure a smooth transition, an IEP or an IFSP must be implemented prior to a child's third birthday and discussed at a conference in which representatives from the child's school district are invited to participate.

Transition Services When a Child Turns Sixteen

Under IDEA 2004, significant emphasis has been placed on transition planning for life after high school. Although we will highlight only the main points here, individuals who want to obtain additional information on transitions and transition planning can visit the Web site where the IDEA 2004 transition guidelines are summarized (http://www.ncset.org/publications/related/ideatransition.asp). It is the mandate of IDEA 2004 to "ensure that all children with disabilities have available to them a free appropriate public education that emphasizes special education and related services designed to meet their unique needs *and prepare them for further education, employment, and independent living*" [italics added]. To meet this goal, Section 602 of IDEA 2004 discusses the need for *transition services,* which it defines as

> a coordinated set of activities for a child with a disability that—
>
> (A)   is designed to be within a results-oriented process, that is focused on improving the academic and functional achievement of the child with a disability to facilitate the child's movement from school to post-school activities, including post-secondary education, vocational education, integrated employment (including supported employment), continuing and adult education, adult services, independent living, or community participation;
>
> (B)   is based on the individual child's needs, taking into account the child's strengths, preferences, and interests; and
>
> (C)   includes instruction, related services, community experiences, the development of employment and other post-school adult living objectives, and when appropriate, acquisition of daily living skills and functional vocational evaluation.

These transition plans must be in place by the time a child turns sixteen and are considered to be part of the student's Individualized Education Program (IEP).

Because increasing numbers of students continue their education after they leave high school, the assistant secretary for civil rights in the U.S. Department of Education, Stephanie Monroe, working from the Office for Civil Rights (OCR), has prepared a series of online letters to inform parents, educators, and youth about their rights. The letters were developed to "raise awareness of issues and to share information about legal rights and responsibilities that will affect students with disabilities as they transition from high school to institutions of postsecondary education." The letters can be accessed online at http://dpi.wi.gov/sped/transition.html. The letters are highly informative and outline some of the challenges facing students with disabilities as they leave the school system under the protection of IDEA 2004 and embark on a journey that will be far different from the one that they have previously known; on the new journey, they will shift from having services provided for them to having to advocate for services on their own behalf. The letters are insightful in addressing the many changes that students—especially those who have been receiving services under IDEA 2004—will face and discussing how to obtain academic adjustments at a postsecondary institution under Section 504 of the Rehabilitation Act of 1973.

The Department of Education administers IDEA 2004 through the Office of Special Education and Rehabilitative Services (OSERS). OSERS also administers the State Vocational Rehabilitation (VR) Services Program, a formula grant program that provides funds to state vocational rehabilitation (VR) agencies in order to assist eligible individuals with disabilities to obtain employment, including funding for the provision of services designed to facilitate the transition of eligible students with disabilities from school to post-school. Although institutions of postsecondary education have no legal obligations under IDEA 2004, individuals attending such institutions can qualify for services under Section 504 of the Rehabilitation Act of 1973 or Title II of the Americans with Disabilities Act (ADA). However, IDEA 2004 states that prior to graduation from high school, students must be invited to attend the IEP meetings surrounding the transition process. Because students will soon have to take responsibility for advocating on their own behalf after graduation, it is important that they take an active role in the IEP meetings when transition planning is discussed.

Five

Laws and Regulations Related to Special Education

CHAPTER

18

AN OVERVIEW OF THE INDIVIDUALS WITH DISABILITIES EDUCATION IMPROVEMENT ACT OF 2004

In this chapter, we will discuss a brief history of how the Individuals with Disabilities Education Act (IDEA) came to be and how this law mandates special education and related services for children with disabilities. We will also provide an overview of the latest version—IDEA 2004—which became law on July 1, 2005.

A BRIEF HISTORY OF IDEA

Special education for children with disabilities was first initiated in 1975 with the passage of Public Law 94-142, the Education for All Handicapped Children Act, which legislated grants to states specifically for the education of children with disabilities. The law has been amended several times since then, and in 1990, the law was renamed the Individuals with Disabilities Education Act (IDEA). This law sets guidelines for how schools should deliver special education and related services to students with disabilities. The law has been changed many times, and more regulations and procedures have been added with each change. Congress last reauthorized IDEA in November 2004, passing the Individuals with Disabilities Education Improvement Act of 2004, which President George W. Bush signed into law on December 3, 2004. The last revision of the act before that was in 1997. The entire contents of the congressional report can be accessed at http://thomas.loc.gov/ under H.R. 1350. In our discussion, we will include the section numbers (for example, Sec. 614) to indicate which portion of the law to check for additional information.

IDEA 2004 is a federal law that was developed to protect the rights of students with disabilities. It defines a disability as "a natural part of the human experience" (Sec. 601) and seeks to equalize educational opportunities for individuals with disabilities. IDEA 2004 lists specific categories of disabilities that children may experience, mandating services for any child (i) with mental retardation, hearing impairments (including deafness), speech or language impairments, visual impairments (including blindness), deaf-blindness, serious emotional disturbance, orthopedic impairments, autism, traumatic brain injury, other health impairments, or specific learning disabilities; and who needs special education and related services as a result of their disability. We discuss disabilities and special education disability categories in Chapters Two and Three.

In addition to specifying these thirteen categories of disabilities, IDEA 2004 also states that at the discretion of the state and the school district, children aged three through nine (or any subset of that age range, including ages three through five) may also receive special education and related services if they are experiencing developmental delays. It is important to understand, however, that under IDEA 2004, states are not required to provide services for children with developmental delays, and if they do, they may choose to serve a limited age span. We will discuss this topic at greater length when we focus on how the act applies to school-age children in the section called "IDEA 2004, Part B."

The major goals of IDEA 2004 are to improve educational results for children with disabilities and to ensure that they have the same opportunities for participation, independent living, and economic self-sufficiency as their nondisabled peers. Specifically, the legislation strives to

- Ensure that children with disabilities have access to a free appropriate public education (FAPE) that includes special education and related services when such services are required to address a child's individual learning needs

- Ensure that undiagnosed disabilities do not prevent children from having a successful educational experience

- Ensure that public schools provide the necessary services for children with disabilities to have an FAPE

- Protect the rights of children with disabilities and their parents

- Ensure that funds are available to support states and local school districts and agencies in providing special education and related services

- Monitor the effectiveness of educational programs in meeting the needs of children with disabilities

The law has four main parts:

- *Parts A and B*. These sections cover eligibility procedures, regulations, and required services for children between three years and twenty-one years of age.

- *Part C*. This section pertains to services for infants and toddlers with disabilities who are under three years of age.

- *Part D*. This section discusses activities that are promoted by the federal government in order to enhance educational services for children with disabilities.

DIDYOUKNOW

Under IDEA 2004, infants and toddlers (under age three) with disabilities and developmental delays can receive *intervention services* as part of their *individualized family service plan* (IFSP). Also, children with disabilities between the ages of three and twenty-one can receive *special education* and *related services* that are part of their *individualized education program* (IEP).

According to IDEA 2004, improving educational success for children with disabilities can only be achieved in an environment that supports

- High expectations for success and meeting developmental goals with maximum access to the general curriculum

- Increased parent participation in their child's educational program

- Coordination of the efforts of IDEA 2004 with other educational laws, such as the Elementary and Secondary Education Act of 1965 (ESEA), as amended by the No Child Left Behind Act of 2001 (NCLB), to increase the emphasis on providing children with disabilities with the same opportunities for education as their nondisabled peers. IDEA 2004 includes over sixty references to ESEA or NCLB, importing terms directly from these laws; for example, IDEA 2004 refers to achievement in the "core academic subjects"; discusses qualifications for special education teachers in terms of standards for "highly qualified teachers" noted in NCLB; and refers to "homeless children," who were not mentioned in previous versions of IDEA.

- Supplementing the regular curriculum with special education and related services when required

- Development and use of technology to maximize access to education

- Increased effort to reduce mislabeling and high dropout rates of minority children. IDEA 2004 requires states to develop policies and procedures to minimize over-identification of students from racially and ethnically diverse cultures as requiring special education

IDEA 2004, PART C: THE INFANTS AND TODDLERS WITH DISABILITIES PROGRAM (AGES BIRTH TO TWO YEARS)

Although most of this chapter will discuss special education and related services for children between the ages of three and twenty-one, we provide a brief explanation of how IDEA 2004 addresses intervention services for children from birth to the end of a child's second year.

Under Part C of IDEA 2004 (Sec. 631), financial assistance is provided to each state

- To develop multidisciplinary inter-agency systems to provide early intervention services for infants and toddlers with disabilities and their families

- To encourage expansion of services for children under three years of age who would be at risk of having substantial developmental delay if they did not receive early intervention services

- To evaluate, identify, and meet the needs of all children, particularly minority, low-income, inner-city, and rural children, as well as infants and toddlers in foster care. According to IDEA 2004, early intervention services include services that may be required to assist in identification and remediation of problems of infants and toddlers with identified developmental delays or may include services for children at risk for developmental delays that could have a negative influence on their ability to learn. IDEA 2004 uses the term *at-risk infant or toddler* to refer to a child under three years of age who would be at risk of being substantially delayed if early intervention services were not provided. IDEA uses the term *developmental delay* (Sec. 635) to refer to a delay of

- 35 percent or more in one of the developmental areas listed in the next sentence; or

- 25 percent or more in two or more of the developmental areas

Delays (Sec. 632) may be evident in one of five developmental areas:

- How the child learns (cognitive development)

- Physical development (motor skills)

- Communication skills (speech and language development)

- Social or emotional development

- Adaptive functioning

Adaptive functioning includes daily living and self-help skills—for example, dressing or feeding oneself. Parents who believe that their infant or toddler may be eligible for intervention services should contact the agency in their state that is responsible for early intervention programs.

IDEA 2004 also mandates services for infants and toddlers who have a diagnosed physical or mental condition that has a high likelihood of resulting in a developmental delay.

Congress has allocated funds to help states develop early intervention services. If the state chooses, it can also use these funds to develop programs for children who are at risk of developing disabilities. For children under three years of age, services are provided by a number of different agencies. In some states, the department of education may be responsible for programs for children of all ages; however, in other states, other agencies, such as the health department, may be responsible for programs designed for infants and toddlers. When multiple agencies are involved, a lead agency will be established and a service coordinator to oversee the intervention services will be selected from that agency.

How Will I Know Whether a Child Needs Intervention Services?

According to IDEA 2004, an evaluation will be provided at no cost to parents in order to determine whether a child meets eligibility criteria for services.

Information will be collected by a multidisciplinary intervention team that may include a social worker, school psychologist, school counselor, behavior therapist, speech-language pathologist, physical therapist, occupational therapist, or other professionals.

What Types of Information Will Be Required?

The intervention team will evaluate eligibility for intervention services on the basis of information collected from a number of professionals who are familiar with the child. Information may be obtained from

- Family social history, including information about developmental milestones (at what age the child sat up, walked, talked, and so on)

- Medical history and physicians' reports

- Results of developmental tests that evaluate cognitive ability, language, motor functioning, and so on

- Observations of the child by members of the intervention team

What Types of Intervention Services Are Provided?

Under IDEA 2004, infants and toddlers with disabilities and delays who are eligible for services can participate in intervention programs designed to target specific types of delay:

- Physical

- Cognitive

- Speech and language (communication)

- Social, emotional, or behavioral

- Adaptive functioning

Once it is determined that a child is eligible for intervention services, a service coordinator will be assigned to the family and will assist the family in locating appropriate resources in the community. The service coordinator will provide assistance to the family until the child no longer requires services or until the child reaches three years of age. At this time, the coordinator will assist the family in the transition to appropriate services for children three years and older.

Who Pays for the Intervention Services?

Although the evaluation is free for families, some parts of the services may be charged to parents, depending on state policies and regulations. Most services, if they are not free of charge, are priced on a sliding scale that is based on the family's income. Some services may be covered by Medicaid or other health insurance plans.

Individualized Family Service Plan

In IDEA 2004, the family is seen as the child's foundation for support; therefore, the services are integrated into a plan that has family at the core: the individualized family service plan (IFSP).

Under Part C of IDEA 2004 (Sec. 636), each infant or toddler with a disability, as well as the infant's or toddler's family, are entitled to

- A multidisciplinary assessment of the child's strengths and individual needs, as well as identification of services appropriate to meet such needs

- A family-based assessment to determine the family's needs (for example, their concerns and available resources) and available community resources and services to assist the family in meeting the child's developmental needs

- An individualized family service plan (IFSP) written by the multidisciplinary team and the child's parents, outlining the child's needs and appropriate resources and transition services that are available for the child

Although IDEA 2004 outlines the goals for the family service plan, specific guidelines concerning how the plans are to be developed are determined by each state. While these plans differ from state to state, most family service plans include some or all of the following:

- The child's current levels of functioning

- Services required and who will provide the services

- Expected outcomes

- Where the services will be provided, with emphasis on services within the natural environment—that is, the environment where your child will be, such as the home or a daycare setting

- When services will be initiated, the length of each session, the frequency of the services, and how many weeks or months of services will be provided

- Designation of the service coordinator

- Plans for transition to other programs

IDEA 2004 mandates that parent permission be obtained prior to the provision of early intervention services described in the IFSP. Only services for which parents have given consent can be provided. Although IDEA 2004 determines that the IFSP is to be evaluated annually, the family will receive a review of the plan at six-month intervals (or more often, if needed).

IDEA 2004 stresses the importance of developing an effective plan to facilitate a smooth transition from interventions covered under Part C (Infants and Toddlers with Disabilities Program) to preschool programs covered under Part B (Assistance for Education of All Children with Disabilities). IDEA 2004 mandates that by a child's third birthday, an IEP or an IFSP must be developed and implemented. The service coordinator will be responsible for arranging a conference and inviting the school district to participate in the transition planning process.

IDEA 2004, PART B

Part B of IDEA 2004 covers students age three to twenty-one. It addresses programs for preschool and school-age children with disabilities. It is important to be aware of all aspects of Part B because we find that some parents do not realize that special education services are available for students with a disability who are not yet enrolled in school.

Special Education Programs and Services for Preschoolers (Ages Three to Five)

Under Part B of IDEA 2004, all public schools must provide free special education services for eligible children with disabilities once they reach three years of age. IDEA also mandates special education preschool programs for eligible children with disabilities who are between three and five years of age.

How Will I Know Whether a Child Is Eligible for a Special Education Preschool Program?   According to IDEA 2004, children can become eligible for special education services if they meet the following three criteria:

1. They have received an individual evaluation (as set out in the regulations).

2. The evaluation has confirmed the existence of a disability in one of thirteen specified areas.

3. The disability interferes with the child's ability to learn.

A comprehensive discussion of the types of individual evaluations that may be conducted and how to interpret and understand the results of an assessment is presented in Part Two.

Children with Developmental Delays Prior to the 1997 reauthorization of IDEA, the law stipulated that preschoolers aged three to five years who demonstrated developmental delays could be eligible for special education services if a comprehensive initial evaluation determined that they had significant developmental delays. However, the "developmental delay" classification was to be removed prior to the child's sixth birthday. At that time, further evaluation would be conducted to determine whether the child would continue to receive services under one or more of the thirteen categories of disabilities or was no longer eligible to receive services under IDEA.

With the 1997 reauthorization of IDEA, the age range for consideration of developmental delay was expanded from "3 to 5 years" to "3 through 9 years." Under IDEA 2004, this expanded age range of three through nine has been retained and the phrase "including the subset of ages 3 through 5" has been added to the age description. Children with identified delays in one of the five developmental areas (physical, cognitive, communication, social or emotional, or adaptive) may be granted access to special education and related services at the discretion of the state, if these services are needed because of a child's developmental delays. However, as noted previously, IDEA 2004 did not change the discretionary nature of this service, and states are not mandated to provide special education and related services for children with developmental delays.

Controversy about whether the expanded age range should be adopted has resulted in wide variations in age criteria for the developmental delay category among the states. Proponents of extending the age of eligibility for the developmental delay classification believe that standardized tests are not as reliable in early childhood and that their use could lead to misdiagnosis. Furthermore, the need to have children meet criteria for one of the thirteen disability categories might also lead to inappropriate diagnoses or ineligibility for services at a time when increased services might have the most impact. Those who are not in favor of increasing the age span are concerned about over-identification of children as eligible for special education services.

Special Education Services for School-Age Children (Ages Three to Twenty-One)

According to IDEA 2004, if a child aged three to twenty-one years has a disability that interferes with his ability to learn, then he is legally entitled to a free appropriate public education (FAPE) in the least restrictive environment. Special education and related services (such as special transportation, speech and language therapy, or assistive technology) must be available from the child's third birthday until receipt of a high school diploma or the end of the school year that contains the student's twenty-first birthday, whichever is earlier. However, under IDEA 2004, it has been more clearly noted that schools are not required to conduct an exit evaluation in order to terminate special education services when a child graduates with a standard diploma or is no longer eligible for services due to his age (that is, if he is twenty-two years old).

Who Determines Eligibility for Special Education Services?   A child who is suspected of having a disability that is interfering with her ability to learn can be identified by either the child's teacher or the child's parent. Under IDEA 2004 (Sec. 614), the school district must conduct a full and individual initial evaluation to determine whether a child meets eligibility criteria for special education and related services. IDEA 2004 notes that an initial evaluation can be requested by a parent, a state department of education or other state agency, or a school district.

If a parent suspects a disability, he or she should contact the school in person or in writing to request a meeting to discuss the child's problem. The parents will be invited to a meeting to discuss ways to address the problem. If at some point an evaluation is requested by either a parent or the school, it will be conducted at no cost to the parents.

If school personnel suspect a disability and feel that an evaluation is necessary, the child's parents will be advised that the school is recommending an evaluation to help determine whether the child is eligible for special education and related services. Parents must be informed about the nature of the evaluation proposed and must provide written consent for the initial evaluation.

Consent for Evaluation and Services   If a parent refuses to provide consent for initial evaluation, the school district may choose to engage in due process or mediation. Under IDEA 2004, if a parent refuses special education services for a child with a disability, the school district will not be considered to be in violation of the law by not providing an FAPE, nor will the district be responsible for developing an IEP for the child.

The evaluation process under IDEA 2004 requires that a comprehensive assessment be conducted. This evaluation, often referred to as an *initial referral for evaluation,* may include the administration of specialized assessment measures (such as those discussed in Part Two); review of school history; parent, teacher and student interviews; completion of behavioral rating scales and other forms; and classroom observations.

IDEA 2004 recognizes the increasing number of schoolchildren who have limited English proficiency and emphasizes the need to provide assessments for these children in a language and form that is likely to yield the most accurate picture of their knowledge and understanding. IDEA 2004 also cautions against placing too many minority children in special education programs relative to their non-minority peers.

Once sufficient information is obtained to make an informed decision about whether a child has a disability and the extent to which that disability impairs the child's academic performance, the child's parents will be invited to attend an educational meeting at which the results of the evaluation will be discussed and eligibility for special education services will be determined.

DIDYOUKNOW

Under IDEA 2004, once a child has been referred for initial evaluation, the school district has sixty days from the time of parental consent for evaluation (or as set out in state regulations) in which to complete the evaluation and convene an educational meeting to discuss the results of that evaluation.

Under IDEA 2004, eligibility determination must rule out that learning was negatively influenced by

- Lack of appropriate instruction in reading (as set out in NCLB)

- Lack of appropriate instruction in mathematics

- Limited English proficiency

Determination of Learning Disability Under IDEA 2004 Under IDEA 2004, a school district is no longer required to demonstrate a significant discrepancy between achievement and intelligence in order to determine that a child has a specific learning disability. Instead, a district may choose to determine eligibility under the category of specific learning disability if an evaluation reveals that a child has failed to respond adequately to a research-based intervention program aimed at increasing skills in the area in which she is exhibiting a deficit. We discuss this response-to-intervention approach in Chapter Four.

Procedural Safeguards   IDEA 2004 contains procedural safeguards for students with disabilities. The text of these procedural safeguards is provided to parents

- When their child is referred for an initial evaluation

- Upon notification of subsequent educational meetings of their child's IEP team (yearly)

- When they file a complaint

- When they request it

These safeguards are designed to help parents understand how federal and state laws protect their rights in such areas as prior written notice of meetings; consent; independent educational evaluation; records; mediation; disciplinary hearings; due process hearings; and appeals. The procedural safeguards are discussed at length in Appendix E.

Delivery of Special Education Services   *Special education* refers to educational instruction that is specifically designed to meet the needs of a child with a disability. This instruction may differ from regular education in content, delivery, or the location in which the instruction takes place. Instruction may occur in the regular education classroom or one of two special education classroom settings: a resource room, where children can receive specialized help (generally, in one or two academic areas) for brief periods during the day, or a self-contained room, where children remain for the majority of their day. Special education instruction can also be provided in the student's home, in a hospital, or in other alternative settings. School districts are responsible for providing a continuum of special education placements that adhere to the policy of offering the least restrictive environment, ranging from minimal services (for example, twenty minutes weekly) to full-time placement in an alternative setting.

Specialized instruction is developed and documented in an individualized education program (IEP). We discuss IEPs in Chapter Sixteen.

DIDYOUKNOW

Under IDEA 2004, children must be educated in their home school (local school), unless alternative placement is recommended in the child's IEP because services cannot be provided adequately in the home school.

HOW CAN I LEARN MORE ABOUT IDEA 2004?

The Office of Special Education Programs (OSEP) in the U.S. Department of Education maintains a Web site that includes a great deal of information about the current IDEA legislation (http://idea.ed.gov/explore/home). This site is an excellent resource for learning about IDEA 2004 alignment with the No Child Left Behind Act, discipline requirements that schools must follow, disproportionality of certain student groups in special education, early intervening services, evaluation and re-evaluation, funding of special education services, highly qualified teachers, identification of specific learning disabilities, individualized education programs, procedural safeguards, transition from high school to postsecondary activities, statewide and districtwide assessments, and other topics.

Obtaining a Copy of a State's Special Education Regulations

To find out more about your state's special education laws and regulations, contact your state's department of special education. Contact information is included in Appendix G.

Summary of Selected Changes in IDEA 2004

Following is an outline of some of the major changes in IDEA 2004 that we think will be of interest to parents and teachers. Some of these were addressed earlier, but we are summarizing the changes in one location for your convenience.

State and School District Accountability

- Allows federal funds for special educational programs to be withheld if states do not meet federal standards dictated by IDEA 2004

- Makes states accountable for meeting standards of educational achievement

- Emphasizes empirically based interventions

- Requires state policies and procedures to prevent over-identification or disproportionate representation by race or ethnicity of children with disabilities, including children with a particular impairment

Educational Accountability

- Includes provisions on how the concept of adequate yearly progress relates to children with disabilities

- Eliminates requirements for short-term objectives in IEPs

- Requires that IEPs include a child's current levels of academic achievement and functional performance
- Requires progress updates that provide parents with specific, meaningful, and understandable information on the progress their child is making

Evaluation Requirements

- Requires that tests and evaluations that are used to determine eligibility be in the language and form most likely to yield accurate information about a child's academic, developmental, and functional status
- Allows some children with disabilities to obtain certain necessary accommodations related to assessments or even to use an alternative assessment
- Revises requirements for exit evaluations under certain circumstances

Efficiency

- Encourages school districts to combine IEP meetings and re-evaluation meetings
- Allows a member of an IEP team to be excused from an IEP meeting under certain circumstances
- Provides an option for a resolution session, to give parents and school districts an opportunity to resolve their differences before going to a due process hearing
- Sets a two-year statute of limitations for parents who wish to request a hearing on claims for reimbursed or ongoing compensatory education services (such as private school), unless there is a state timeline

Student Conduct

- Requires IEP teams to provide positive behavioral interventions and supports for children with disabilities whose behavior impedes their learning or the learning of others
- Allows schools to consider unique circumstances on a case-by-case basis when determining whether to order a change in placement for a child with a disability who violates a code of student conduct
- Gives schools the right to make decisions about educational placement changes when behavior is not a result of the child's disability, although parents can appeal the decision

- Allows students to be placed in an alternative educational setting for forty-five school days rather than forty-five calendar days.

Early Intervention

- *For preschool children:* Previously, funds were allocated for early intervention programs at two separate levels: infants and toddlers (under three years of age) could receive funds for early intervention services, which would be implemented through an IFSP, and children three to twenty-one years of age could receive special education or related services, which would be developed and implemented according to an IEP. Under IDEA 2004, it is possible for states to develop a seamless system of service to serve children from birth through five years of age.

- *For school-age children:* IDEA 2004 allows districts to use up to 15 percent of their IDEA funding for students in regular education who are at risk of needing special education services in the future for academic and behavioral problems. The funds can be used for direct service or teacher training.

CHAPTER

504 PLANS

An Alternative to Special Education Placement

In Chapter Eighteen, we talked about IDEA 2004 as it relates to special education services. However, all children identified with a disability do not necessarily require these services. Some have a disability but are not eligible for special education under IDEA 2004. In this chapter, we will provide information about Section 504 of the Rehabilitation Act of 1973 and the new Americans with Disabilities Act Amendments Act of 2008 (ADAAA) and then discuss how modifications can be implemented in the regular education setting through a 504 plan.

SECTION 504 OF THE REHABILITATION ACT OF 1973

Section 504 of the Rehabilitation Act of 1973, which will be referred to as *504* from this point on, is a civil rights law. It protects individuals with disabilities from discrimination, and it ensures that children with disabilities have equal access to education. Special accommodations to a child's program are required if she has a substantial mental or physical impairment that limits, to a considerable or large degree, one or more of her major life activities: caring for herself, performing manual tasks, walking, seeing, hearing, speaking, breathing, learning, or working. A physical or mental impairment may be a facial disfigurement, blindness or visual impairment, cancer, diabetes, mental illness, specific learning disability, intellectual disability, heart disease, AIDS, and deafness or hearing impairment.

A child may also qualify for accommodations if he has a physical or mental impairment that substantially limits major life activities due to the attitudes of others toward such impairment (peers' reaction to burn scars, for example); has a physical or mental impairment that does not substantially limit major life activities but is treated by others as having a limitation; or has none of the mental or physical impairments mentioned earlier but is treated as having such an impairment. Therefore, even if a person's disability does not directly impair functioning, the act covers impaired functioning resulting from discrimination based on others' attitudes or responses to the disability. The last two options offer some flexibility. If your child is treated as having substantial limitations or impairments, he may qualify under 504.

DIDYOUKNOW

The nondiscrimination requirements of Section 504 apply to organizations that receive financial assistance from any federal department or agency and thus include school districts.

THE AMERICANS WITH DISABILITIES ACT AMENDMENTS ACT OF 2008

President George Bush signed the Americans with Disabilities Act Amendments Act of 2008 (ADAAA) on September 25, 2008. ADAAA, which updates the Americans with Disabilities Act of 1990, became effective on January 1, 2009. It broadens the definition of *disability* by making changes to important parts of the definition. In addition to expanding the definition of *major life activities,* it redefines who is regarded as having a disability, modifies the definition of *substantially limits,* specifies that a disability includes any impairment—even one that is episodic or in remission—if it would substantially limit a major life activity when active, and prohibits consideration of the effects of mitigating measures when assessing whether an impairment substantially limits major life activities. Examples of mitigating measures include medications, prosthetics, hearing aids or cochlear implants, and assistive technology. Ordinary eyeglasses or contact lenses are excluded. ADAAA requirements for schools are the same as those in Section 504 of the Rehabilitation Act of 1973.

DETERMINING ELIGIBILITY

Determining eligibility under 504 is a team decision. Team members may include regular education teachers, a school administrator, school psychologist, school counselor, speech-language pathologist, school social worker, school nurse, occupational therapist, physical therapist, the parent, and the child. The members of the 504 team will review all of the information presented to them and determine whether the child qualifies for assistance. Having a physical or mental impairment does not guarantee that the child will qualify. A medical report from the child's doctor or a psychological evaluation by the school psychologist or a psychologist in private practice may be required. The nature and severity of the disability as well as its expected duration will be considered.

Under 504, unlike IDEA 2004, a child does not need to have a specific disease or medical condition. Section 504 only requires that the physical or mental impairment affect one of the body systems (neurological; musculoskeletal; special sense organs; respiratory, including speech organs; cardiovascular; reproductive; digestive; genitourinary; hemic and lymphatic; skin; or endocrine) or that the disability be considered a mental or psychological disorder.

Let's take a look at Figure 19.1 to illustrate the differences between IDEA 2004 and Section 504. The largest circle represents all children in a school district. Out of all children, some qualify for coverage under 504 (the middle circle). And of those, some meet the more rigid eligibility standards under IDEA 2004 (the smallest circle).

A 504 PLAN

A 504 plan is a legal document designed to create a program of instructional services for a child with special needs in order to assist her in a regular education setting. The 504 team writes the plan after receiving input from everyone on the team. A 504 plan includes reasonable instructional accommodations and modifications to meet a child's individual needs. We'll discuss some typical accommodations in this section. After the 504 plan has been developed and everyone on the 504 team agrees on its contents, the general education team is responsible for implementation of the plan. A sample 504 plan is included in Appendix C.

FIGURE 19.1 *Children Qualifying Under IDEA 2004 and Section 504*

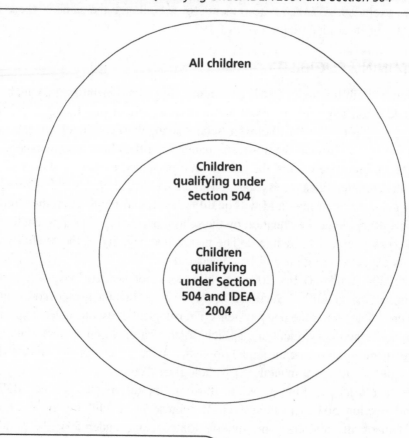

DIDYOUKNOW

Unlike IDEA 2004, Section 504 does not grant federal financial support to school districts for providing additional services to students. Therefore, districts may appear unwilling to provide these services and may instead push for finding your child eligible under IDEA 2004. If you do not want your child to receive special education services and would prefer that accommodations be made in the regular education classroom, discuss a 504 plan with the school.

Plan Accommodations and Helpful Strategies

Accommodations provided to a child in the classroom are decided on by his 504 team, depending on his needs. Two children with the same disability may require very different accommodations. In our experience, the following classroom accommodations are helpful to many children, although many others are equally effective. We outline some accommodations for the classroom and also include suggestions that can improve a child's performance at home.

Behavioral Strategies

At school, teachers can

- Post rules and consequences for classroom behavior

- Use a daily journal to report a child's behavior to her parents

- Encourage children to self-monitor their behavior by using a journal or a sheet to tally behaviors

- Use a behavioral contract to provide the child with structure and self-management skills

- Use positive verbal or nonverbal cues and reinforcements

At home, parents can

- Post house rules and responsibilities in a conspicuous place (for example, on the refrigerator)

- Check their child's daily planner to monitor his assignments and read his teacher's comments

- Encourage their child to monitor and record his own behaviors

- Praise their child for bringing his planner home and for following through on assignments

- Develop a behavioral contract with clear expectations and rewards or consequences for specific behaviors or completion of tasks or goals

Organizational Strategies

At school, teachers can

- Use an organizational system such as folders for different assignments or classes. Each folder should be labeled with the name of a subject; a different colored folder for each subject works best.

- Provide a homework journal in which students can record their assignments. Teachers should check the journal before students leave the classroom.

- Set a time limit on assignments. For example, a child with obsessive-compulsive disorder may benefit from the use of an egg timer so that she knows when to stop working on one assignment and move on to another.

At home, parents can

- Make sure their child's workspace is clear

- Provide a child with the supplies necessary to complete her work

- Use a timer if their child has difficulty completing her work in a timely manner, setting it for a certain amount of time (thirty minutes, for example), after which she can take a short break

- Review a child's work once he is finished, to make sure that he has completed all of his work.

Environmental Strategies

At school, teachers can

- Provide a structured learning environment. It is helpful to post a daily schedule that indicates when each subject will be discussed. The schedule should also include break times and art, music, computer lab, or physical education classes. Some children require the guidance provided by a daily schedule in order to be successful.

- Provide preferential seating. For example, a child with ADHD may need to sit next to the teacher's desk so that his behavior can be monitored more closely, while a child with a visual impairment, even one that has been corrected, may need to sit close to the board. A child with ADHD also should not sit in a high-traffic area—for example, near the pencil sharpener or the classroom door—because this location increases distractions and opportunities to talk to others.

- Provide a study carrel to minimize distractions. This strategy can be especially helpful when a child needs to complete class work or a test.

- Change the location of classroom supplies for easier access or to minimize distraction. A child using crutches should not have to navigate a maze of desks to get to a pencil sharpener.

At home, parents can

- Provide their child with a quiet place in which to work, without distractions from TV, radio, games, toys, or conversations

- Keep their child visible, in order to monitor her progress and provide assistance, if needed

Presentation Strategies

At school, teachers can

- Provide a lesson outline for each day's lesson so that students know what to expect that day

- Post the lesson outline in the same location each day—for example, in the upper-right corner of the blackboard—and direct students to review the outline prior to beginning the lesson

- Provide a study guide for tests

- Use alternative textbooks and workbooks, such as ones with enlarged text font size or books on tape

- Highlight the main ideas of a passage in the textbook or workbook

- Make audio recordings of lessons so that a child can review them later

At home, parents can

- Sit down with their child and provide an overview of the work that must be completed that night

- Have their child circle the signs on math worksheets so he does not do the wrong operation

Evaluation Methods

At school, teachers can

- Provide a practice test

- Provide oral testing for children who have difficulty with written expression or manual dexterity

- Limit the amount of material that is presented on a single page

- Allow students with special needs to take extra time in completing their work

- Require the completion of fewer test items

At home, parents can

- Use math drills

- Encourage their child to practice writing spelling words repeatedly

- Have their child read aloud, keeping track of the words that are difficult for him, and then keep a bank of those words or put them on flash cards for later practice

DIDYOUKNOW

If a child is not responding well to the accommodations in a 504 plan, parents or teachers can request a meeting in order to create a new one. A new 504 plan will be written and will include the accommodations that are working as well as new ones to be implemented and monitored. The plan should be revised as often as needed in order to find interventions that work for the child.

Accommodations for Specific Disabilities

The accommodations provided for a child vary according to his needs as well as his strengths and weaknesses. In general, children who have a particular disability receive a common set of accommodations. In this section, we discuss accommodations that may be helpful for children with specific disabilities.

Asthma

Major life activity affected: Learning

- Provide rest periods.

- Share information on the child's medical needs with school personnel.

- Train appropriate school personnel to properly dispense medication and monitor the child for side effects (as needed).

- Develop health care and emergency plans (for example, what to do if a child does not respond to medical intervention).

- Assist with inhalant therapy.

- Adjust the child's schedule to allow for administration of medications.

- Allow time to make up work when the child is absent for medical reasons.

- Have the child's peers help her carry books and other supplies as needed.

- Adapt the child's activity level at recess, during physical education, and at other times as needed.

- Minimize allergens (such as perfume, cologne, lotions, or paint) in the child's vicinity.

DIDYOUKNOW

The National Institute of Allergy and Infectious Diseases reports that nearly 7 million children in the United States have asthma (National Institute of Allergy and Infectious Diseases, 2010).

Attention Deficit Hyperactivity Disorder (ADHD)

Major life activity affected: Learning and, possibly, social interactions

- Provide appropriate staff training about ADHD.

- Seat the child in close proximity to the teacher; seat him away from distractions.

- Provide the child with a peer helper for class work and projects.

- Inform school personnel of the child's potential need for excessive movement; allow him to stand or move while working.

- Ensure that school personnel understand the child's tendency to be inattentive; establish nonverbal cues that allow the teacher to get the child's attention and help him increase on-task behavior.

- Post classroom rules, and review them on a regular basis.

- Provide reinforcement when the child displays appropriate behavior.

- Give a five-minute warning of a change in activity so that the child can begin to disengage from his current task.

- Provide supervision during transition times (for example, when switching from one activity to another or moving from one class to another).

- Ask the child to restate directions.

- Assist the child with organizational strategies.

- Allow the child to complete tests in several short sessions.
- Provide extended time for the child to complete assignments and tests.
- Train appropriate school personnel to properly dispense medication and monitor the child for side effects (as needed). Use a "study buddy" so that the child can work with another student.
- Allow small-group work with two or three other students.
- Allow the child to tutor younger students.
- Develop a friendship plan for the home setting to help the child learn to initiate and maintain friendships.
- Help the child learn how to resolve conflict in friendships.

DIDYOUKNOW

As of 2006, approximately 4.5 million children between the ages of five and seventeen have been diagnosed with ADHD at some point in their lives, according to the Centers for Disease Control and Prevention (2010). Between 3 percent and 7 percent of school-aged children have ADHD.

Bipolar Disorder

Major life activity affected: Learning

- Provide staff members with appropriate training on bipolar disorder.
- Implement a crisis intervention plan in case the child becomes uncontrollable, impulsive, or dangerous.
- Immediately report any suicidal comments to the school psychologist, the school counselor, and the child's parents.
- Give the child advance notice of transitions.
- Create strategies for handling unpredictable mood swings.
- Allow the child to complete difficult class work at times when she is more alert.
- Provide extended time for the child to complete assignments and tests.

- Monitor the child's understanding of directions.
- Break assignments into manageable parts.
- Train appropriate school personnel to properly dispense medication and monitor the child for side effects (as needed).

DIDYOUKNOW

Some researchers suspect that a significant number of children in the United States who have been diagnosed with ADHD have early-onset bipolar disorder instead of or along with ADHD. Bipolar disorder is one of the many ADHD look-alikes.

Emotional Disturbance

Major life activity affected: Learning

- Provide staff members with appropriate training on emotional disturbance.
- Post classroom rules, and review them on a regular basis.
- Create effective behavior modification plans.
- Ensure that behavioral interventions are used both at home and at school and are monitored closely. The child's parents and teachers should work collaboratively to maintain consistency.
- Be consistent in setting behavioral expectations and following through with reinforcements or consequences.
- Create a behavior contract for the child.
- Ask the child to keep a daily journal in order to record and monitor his own behaviors.
- Allow the child to participate in group counseling sessions with the school counselor or the school psychologist.
- Train appropriate school personnel to properly dispense medication and monitor the child for side effects (as needed).

DIDYOUKNOW

Results from the National Health and Nutrition Examination Survey indicate that 13 percent of children and adolescents ages eight to fifteen met criteria for having generalized anxiety disorder, panic disorder, eating disorders (anorexia and bulimia), depression, ADHD, and/or conduct disorder within the previous year (National Institute of Mental Health, 2009).

Epilepsy

Major life activity affected: Learning

- Provide staff members with appropriate training on epilepsy.
- Train both staff and children on what to do if the child has a seizure.
- Look for consistent triggers of seizures.
- Document the characteristics of each seizure that occurs.
- Seat the child in an area where she will not be injured if she has a seizure.
- Prepare an emergency plan to follow if a seizure occurs; for example, (1) protect the child from injury by clearing space around her; (2) ask other children to keep the area clear; (3) loosen tight clothing and protect her head from injury; (4) do not insert objects into her mouth; (5) if she is unconscious, place her on her side in order to keep her from choking on vomit; and (6) stay with her until she fully recovers.
- Do not allow the child to be unsupervised, especially during physical education or field trips.
- Give the child time to make up any work she misses because of absence due to seizures.
- Train appropriate school personnel to properly dispense medication and monitor the child for side effects (as needed).

DIDYOUKNOW

The brain of a child is more prone to seizures than the brain of an adult. Causes of childhood epilepsy may include genetics, brain tumors, head injury, and infections of the brain, among others. According to the Epilepsy Foundation (2010), there is no known cause in 70 percent of cases.

CHAPTER

20

A COMPARISON OF IDEA 2004 AND SECTION 504, AND A BRIEF LOOK AT NO CHILD LEFT BEHIND

When considering placement options, IDEA 2004 and Section 504 of the Rehabilitation Act of 1973 require school districts to adhere to the following guidelines in the interpretation of data and in making placement decisions.

- Draw on information from a variety of sources.

- Ensure that all information is current, documented, and considered.

- Ensure that eligibility decisions are made by a group of individuals who are knowledgeable about the student and can interpret the available data appropriately in order to make informed decisions about placement options.

- Ensure that the student will be educated with nondisabled students to the maximum extent possible (that is, in the least restrictive environment).

IDEA 2004 AND SECTION 504: A COMPARISON

The fundamental difference between IDEA 2004 and Section 504 is as follows:

- IDEA 2004 is a federally funded statute that was developed to provide states with financial assistance in order to ensure that students with disabilities receive free, appropriate services.

- Section 504 is a civil rights law. The law was designed to protect the rights of individuals with disabilities who are served in programs that receive federal financial assistance from the U.S. Department of Education.

The following question and answer (Q&A) dialogue is based on frequently asked questions about similarities and differences between regulations and procedures under IDEA 2004 and Section 504. We hope that the answers will assist parents and educators in making more informed decisions about how to advocate for children with disabilities and to assist in determining which laws will best meet the needs of a child's unique disability.

Q: Who is protected under IDEA 2004 and Section 504?

A: If a child is of school age (three to twenty-one years old) and meets eligibility criteria for one of the thirteen disability categories listed under IDEA 2004, and if that disability is significantly interfering with the child's ability to learn, then that child is covered under IDEA 2004.

If the child, adolescent, or adult has a disability (physical or mental impairment) that significantly interferes with one or more major life activities,* or is regarded as disabled by others, and the individual is in a program that receives federal financial assistance from the U.S. Department of Education, then that individual is covered under Section 504.

This is an important distinction because individuals in postsecondary institutions are not protected under IDEA 2004, but may be protected under Section 504. For further information, see Chapter Seventeen on transition planning for postsecondary school students.

*Major life activities include walking, seeing, hearing, speaking, breathing, learning, working, caring for oneself, and performance on manual tasks.

Q: **What are the regulations regarding a free and appropriate public education (FAPE)?**

A: Individuals who qualify under IDEA 2004 receive FAPE, which may include individual instruction but must include a written IEP and an IEP meeting held at least annually.

Under Section 504, there is provision for FAPE for eligible students and the possibility of individual instruction; however, an IEP is not part of the process. Instead there is a written plan that is discussed during an educational meeting.

Q: **How would modifications to programming or curriculum differ for a student under IDEA 2004 versus Section 504?**

A: Under IDEA 2004, students receive an individualized education program (IEP) that is designed to meet their individual educational needs and any related services (for example, speech and language therapy, physical therapy) that may be necessary to enhance learning.

Under Section 504, students with disabilities will be provided with accommodations that will help them to benefit from the educational programming that is received by their nondisabled peers.

Q: **Can a child with a 504 Plan receive the benefit of individual special education programming?**

A: While all children who are deemed eligible for services under IDEA 2004 will also qualify for services under Section 504, the reverse is not necessarily true. Under IDEA 2004, students are deemed eligible for special education services because they have one of the thirteen disabilities listed under IDEA 2004 and *the disability adversely affects the student's ability to learn*. These children are provided with an IEP developed as part of special education and related services.

Under Section 504, a child will be considered as "disabled," but there is no burden of proof that the disability is negatively affecting learning. Accommodations will be provided in the regular educational program to assist the individual to access educational opportunities to the same extent as his or her nondisabled peers.

Q: **To what extent can a child's educational program be modified under IDEA 2004 and Section 504?**

A: Under IDEA 2004, any eligible student can have their program modified to the extent necessary to achieve FAPE.

Under Section 504, appropriate accommodations might include equal access to buildings (physical accommodations); enhanced communication systems (for example, an FM system to help students who have hearing impairments); use of a note taker; or extra time to complete tasks and tests.

Q: **Who enforces IDEA 2004 and Section 504?**

A: IDEA 2004 is a federal law that falls under the U.S. Office of Special Education Programs and is compliant to the law monitored by the State Departments of Education and the Office of Special Education Programs (OSEP).

Section 504 is an anti-discrimination law and is the responsibility of the U.S. Office for Civil Rights, and is not part of the State Department of Education.

Q: **Who funds the laws?**

A: IDEA 2004 is federally funded; school districts receive funding for students who are eligible for special education under IDEA 2004. Section 504 provides protection against discrimination but does not fund students who receive services under Section 504.

NO CHILD LEFT BEHIND

The No Child Left Behind Act of 2001 (NCLB) was designed to improve student achievement and change America's schools. We will provide an overview of NCLB and address the many ways in which it can benefit children. With the passage of NCLB, Congress reauthorized the Elementary and Secondary Education Act (ESEA), the federal law affecting education from kindergarten through twelfth grade. In amending ESEA, the new law represents a dramatic overhaul of the federal government's efforts to address these areas:

- Accountability for results, an emphasis on doing

- What works is based on scientific research

- Expanded parental options

- Expanded school district control and flexibility

There has been much controversy surrounding the goals of NCLB. The legislation has strong supporters and harsh critics, and many have called for changes in the law that some view as unrealistic. However, IDEA 2004 has aligned itself more closely with NCLB, and for these reasons, rather than discussing the pros and cons of NCLB, this book outlines its potential benefits as envisioned by sponsors of the legislation and discusses how IDEA 2004 has attempted to align itself with sections of NCLB.

No Child Left Behind supports learning in the early years, which can prevent many learning problems when children are older.

Students who begin school with language skills and pre-reading skills (for example, understanding that print reads from left to right and top to bottom) are more likely to learn to read well in the early grades and succeed in later years. Researchers have found that most reading problems in adolescence and adulthood are the result of problems that could have been prevented through good instruction in early childhood.

IDEA 2004 recognizes the need for early intervention in two important ways: attempting to create a seamless delivery of service from preschool (infants and toddlers) to school-age programs (three to twenty-one years of age) and in allocating a percentage of funds (up to 15 percent of a school district's IDEA 2004 funds) that may be used to develop early intervention educational services for students not receiving special education, but who would likely require educational or behavioral support from special education programs in the future.

No Child Left Behind provides more information about a child's progress.

Under NCLB, each state must assess every public school student's progress in reading and math in each of grades 3 through 8, and at least once between grades 10 and 12. Starting in 2007–08 assessments in science were also added. These assessments, which must be aligned with state academic content and achievement standards, measure each child's level of academic achievement.

IDEA 2004 now requires IEPs to include a statement of measurable annual goals that relate to academic and functional goals. In order that children with disabilities may participate in statewide assessments, IDEA 2004 has revised the requirements for accommodations and alternative assessments.

No Child Left Behind provides important information about the performance of a child's school.

NCLB requires that states and school districts provide the public with information in understandable, detailed report cards on schools and districts. These report cards indicate student achievement data by race, ethnicity, gender, English language proficiency, migrant status, disability status, and low-income status. Information about the professional qualifications of teachers is also included.

No Child Left Behind provides children with educational support and options.

Under NCLB, low-performing schools must use their federal funds to make needed improvements. If a school continues to perform poorly, parents have the option to transfer their child to a higher-performing school nearby or allow their child to receive tutoring, after-school programs, or remedial classes.

No Child Left Behind improves teaching and learning by providing better information to teachers and principals.

Annual testing to measure students' progress provides teachers with data on each student's strengths and weaknesses. Teachers can use this information in the development of their lessons to create opportunities to help students meet or exceed the standards. IDEA 2004 revises standards of academic achievement and functional performance of children with disabilities to conform to accountability systems established by NCLB and ensures that the adequate yearly progress (AYP) of children with disabilities is evaluated as an appropriate subgroup.

No Child Left Behind ensures that teacher quality is a high priority.

NCLB defines the qualifications needed by teachers and paraprofessionals (such as teacher assistants) who instruct students. It requires states to develop plans to achieve the goal that all teachers of the core academic subjects (English, reading or language arts, math, science, foreign languages, civics and government, economics, arts, history, and geography) be highly qualified. This can help teachers by ensuring that districts provide them with the necessary training and professional development support to meet this goal.

IDEA 2004 requires states to ensure that teachers of special education programs are highly qualified according to standards set by NCLB, and it removes the waiver in the cases of emergency or provisional basis for personnel who have not met certification or licensure requirements.

No Child Left Behind gives more resources to schools.

NCLB initially provided $23.7 billion worth of federal funding, most of which was used during the 2003–04 school year. A large portion of the money went toward grants for states and school districts. These grants were awarded to help them improve the education of disadvantaged students, turn around low-performing schools, improve teacher quality, and increase choices for parents.

IDEA 2004 allocates 15 percent of the federal funds reserved for special education and related services to direct service for high-risk students or to teacher training and professional development programs to train teachers to work with children who are likely to require special education services in the future.

No Child Left Behind allows more flexibility.

NCLB gives states and school districts more flexibility in how they can use their education funding. This gives school district administrators the freedom to implement innovative programs based on the needs of their district and feedback from parents.

IDEA 2004 authorizes more flexible use of up to 15 percent of IDEA 2004 funds, which may be used for direct student intervention for at-risk students or for teacher training or as previously outlined, to ensure professional development for teachers providing educational and behavioral evaluations and supports or scientifically based literacy instruction.

No Child Left Behind (NCLB) focuses on what works.

Focus is placed on well-designed research studies that demonstrate which educational programs and practices are considered effective. These programs will receive federal funding. IDEA 2004 has allocated funds for professional development for teachers to deliver scientifically based academic and behavioral interventions. IDEA 2004 has also altered the criteria for determining eligibility for special education services for students with learning disabilities to include an inability to benefit from a scientific, research-based intervention, and excluded eligibility for students who have not had the benefit of adequate instruction.

SUMMARY

On paper, NCLB has lofty goals for improving our schools and our children's education. In time, we will see whether all of these goals will be achieved. We understand that changes will be made in future years in response to feedback from states, parents, and the performance of students and school districts. However, many believe that the four areas of focus—accountability for results, an emphasis on doing what works based on scientific research, expanded parental options, and expanded school district control and flexibility—will most likely remain the same as they serve to support the legislation's core values.

ACKNOWLEDGMENT

The information in this section was drawn in part from *No Child Left Behind: A Parents Guide*, published in 2003 by the U.S. Department of Education, Office of the Secretary, Office of Public Affairs in Washington, D.C. To order your copy of this free thirty-seven-page document, write to ED Pubs, Education Publications Center, U.S. Department of Education, P.O. Box 1398, Jessup, MD 20794-1398. You can also request it by phone (877-433-7827), fax (301-470-1244), or visit the Web site (retrieved April 24, 2010, from http://ed.gov/nclb/landing.jhtml).

REFERENCES

CHAPTER ONE

Association of State Units on Aging. (2005). Retrieved November 15, 2009, from http://www.nasua.org/.

Council for Exceptional Children. Retrieved December 1, 2009, from http://www.cec.sped.org//AM/Template.cfm?Section=Home.

Farkas, S., Johnson, J., Duffett, A., Foleno, T., & Foley, P. (2001). *Trying to stay ahead of the game; Superintendents and principals talk about school leadership.* New York: Public Agenda. Retrieved November 20, 2009, from http://www.publicagenda.org/files/pdf/ahead_of_the_game.pdf.

Horn, W., & Tynan, D. (2001). Revamping special education. *Public Interest*, Issue 144.

Johnson, J., & Duffett, A., Farkas, S., & Wilson, L. (2002). *When it's your own child: A report on special education from the families who use it.* New York: Public Agenda. Retrieved November 25, 2009, from http://www.publicagenda.org/files/pdf/when_its_your_own_child.pdf.

National Center for Educational Statistics. U.S. Department of Education Institute of Educational Statistics. (2009). Retrieved April 1, 2010, from http://nces.ed.gov/programs/coe/2009/section1/indicator09.asp.

Texas Center for Educational Research. (2006). Results from the Texas Study of Personnel Needs in Special Education. Retrieved November 13, 2009, from http://www.tcer.org/research/special_ed/documents/sped_tasbtasa_presen.pdf.

U.S. Department of Education. Digest of Education Statistics. (2003). Retrieved November 19, 2009, from http://nces.ed.gov/pubsearch/pubsinfo.asp?pubid=2005025.

U.S. Department of Education, Office of Special Education Programs. (2006). Retrieved March 10, 2010, from http://nces.ed.gov/programs/coe/2009/section1/indicator09.asp.

CHAPTER TWO

American Association on Intellectual and Developmental Disabilities (AAIDD). (2007). Retrieved March 15, 2010, from http://www.aamr.org.

American Psychiatric Association (APA). (2000). *Diagnostic and statistical manual of mental disorders* (4th ed., Text Revision). Washington, DC: American Psychiatric Press.

Rosenthal, R., & Jacobson, L. (2003). *Pygmalion in the classroom: Teacher expectation and pupils' intellectual development.* New York: Crown House.

CHAPTER THREE

American Psychiatric Association (APA). (2000). *Diagnostic and statistical manual of mental disorders* (4th ed., Text Revision). Washington, DC: American Psychiatric Press.

Centers for Disease Control. (2009, Dec. 19). Prevalence of autism spectrum disorders—Autism and Developmental Disabilities Monitoring Network, United States, 2006. Surveillance summaries. *MMWR, 58*(SS 10), 1–20.

Individuals with Disabilities Education Act. (2004). *Code of federal regulations.* Retrieved May 29, 2009, from www.ed.gov/offices/ OSERS/ IDEA/index.html.

MTA Cooperative Group. (2004). National Institute of Mental Health Treatment Study of ADHD (NIMH:MTA) follow up: 24-month outcomes of treatment strategies for attention deficit hyperactivity disorder. *Archives of General Psychiatry, 56*, 1073–1086.

Scheeringa, M. S. (2001). The differential diagnosis of impaired reciprocal social interaction in children: A review of disorders. *Child Psychiatry and Human Development, 32*(1), 71–89.

U.S. Department of Education. Office of Special Education and Rehabilitative Services, Office of Special Education Programs. (2004). *24th annual report to Congress on the implementation of the Individuals with Disabilities Education Act* (Vol.1). Washington, DC. Retrieved January 15, 2009, from http://www.ed.gov/about/reports/annual/osep/2004/26th-vol-1.pdf.

U.S. Department of Health and Human Services (USDHHS). (1999). *Mental health: A report of the Surgeon General.* Rockville, MD: Author.

Wilens, T. E. (2003). *Straight talk about psychiatric medications for kids.* New York: Guilford Press.

CHAPTER SIX

Wechsler, D. (2003). *Manual for the Wechsler Intelligence Scale for Children* (4th ed.). *(WISC-IV).* San Antonio, TX: Harcourt Assessment..

CHAPTER TEN

Barkley, R. A. (1997). *Attention deficit hyperactivity disorder: A handbook for diagnosis and treatment* (2nd ed.). New York: Guilford.

Gioia, G. A. (2005, November). *Executive functions in the schools: Concepts, assessments and intervention.* Paper presented at the annual meeting of the Florida Association of School Psychologists, Hollywood, FL.

Gioia, G. A., Isquith, P. K., Guy, S. C., & Kenworthy, L. (2000). *BRIEF: Behavior rating inventory of executive function, professional manual.* Odessa, FL: PAR.

Gioia, G. A., Isquith, P. K., Kenworthy, L., & Barton, R. M. (2002). Profiles of everyday executive function in acquired and developmental disorders. *Child Neuropsychology, 8*, 121–137.

National Center for Learning Disabilities. (2009). *Executive function fact sheet.* Retrieved April 24, 2010, from http://www.ncld.org/ld-basics/ld-aamp-executive-functioning/basic-ef-facts/executive-function-fact-sheet.

CHAPTER TWELVE

Gioia, G. A. (2005, November). *Executive functions in the schools: Concepts, assessments and intervention.* Paper presented at the annual meeting of the Florida Association of School Psychologists, Hollywood, FL.

Ylvisaker, M., Szekeres, S., & Feeney, T. (1998). Cognitive rehabilitation: Executive functions. In M. Ylvisaker (Ed.), *Traumatic brain injury rehabilitation: Children and adolescents* (2nd ed., pp. 221–269). Boston: Butterworth-Heinemann.

CHAPTER SEVENTEEN

Arbeau, A., & Coplan, R. J. (2007). Kindergarten teachers' beliefs and responses to hypothetical prosocial, asocial and antisocial children. *Merrill-Palmer Quarterly, 53*, 291–318.

Barber, B. K., & Olsen, J. A. (2004). Assessing the transitions to middle and high school. *Journal of Adolescent Research, 19*, 3–30.

Coplan, R. J., Closson, L., & Arbeau, A. (2007). Gender differences in the behavioral associates of loneliness and social dissatisfaction in kindergarten. *Journal of Child Psychology and Psychiatry, 48* [Special issue on preschool mental health], 988–995.

Gruman, D., Harachi, T., Abbott, R. D., Catalano, R. F., & Fleming, C. B. (2008). Longitudinal effects of student mobility on three dimensions of elementary school engagement. *Child Development, 79*(6), 1833–1852.

Kagan, J. (1997). Temperament and the reactions to unfamiliarity. *Child Development, 68*, 139–143.

Schor, E. (1986). Use of health care services by children and diagnoses received during presumably stressful life transitions. *Pediatrics, 77*, 834–841.

Turner-Cobb, J., Rixon, L., & Jessop, D. (2008). A prospective study of diurnal cortisol responses to the social experience of school transition in four-year-old children: Anticipation, exposure, and adaptation. *Developmental Psychobiology, 50*(4), 377–389.

CHAPTER NINETEEN

Centers for Disease Control and Prevention. (2010). *Attention-deficit/hyperactivity disorder.* Retrieved April 29, 2010, from http://www.cdc.gov/ncbddd/adhd/data.html.

Epilepsy Foundation. (2010). *Causes of childhood epilepsy.* Retrieved April 29, 2010, from http://www.epilepsyfoundation.org/about/types/causes/childcauses.cfm.

National Institute of Allergy and Infectious Diseases. (2010). *Asthma.* Retrieved April 29, 2010, from http://www.niaid.nih.gov/topics/asthma/Pages/facts.aspx.

National Institute of Mental Health. (2009). *National survey tracks rates of common mental disorders among American youth.* Retrieved April 29, 2010, from http://www.nimh.nih.gov/science-news/2009/national-survey-tracks-rates-of-common-mental-disorders-among-american-youth.shtml.

APPENDIX

EDUCATIONAL ACRONYMS AND WHAT THEY MEAN

Like most professions, the field of education has its own set of acronyms that are used to communicate information. While they can be a time-saver for school professionals, acronyms can be intimidating to parents, teachers, or others who are unfamiliar with the lingo. You are at a disadvantage if you do not know what is being said. Here is a list of acronyms we have either heard or used ourselves in schools.

AAD   **adaptive assistive devices:** assistive technology devices that are designed or altered for use by children with developmental delays.

ABA   **applied behavior analysis:** an intervention technique that can be used to teach children with autism. The teacher breaks skills into very small components and teaches them systematically, so that each skill forms the foundation for the next one.

ADA   **Americans with Disabilities Act:** legislation enacted in 1990 that provides civil rights protections for individuals with disabilities similar to protections provided for individuals on the basis of race, ethnicity, gender, age, and religion. It guarantees equal opportunity for individuals with disabilities in public accommodations, employment, transportation, state and local government services, and telecommunications.

ADHD   **attention deficit hyperactivity disorder:** developmentally inappropriate behavior, including poor attention skills, impulsivity, and hyperactivity. A person can be predominantly inattentive (often referred to as *ADD*), predominantly hyperactive-impulsive, or a combination of the two.

ADL   **activities of daily living:** personal care activities necessary in everyday life, including eating, dressing, bathing, grooming, and toileting.

AEP   **alternative education placement:** an alternative classroom setting that is used to improve classroom behavior and address needs that cannot be met in a regular classroom setting.

AG   **annual goal:** a goal that a student will strive to achieve in a 12-month period, documented in an individualized education program (IEP); for example, "David will read at a second-grade level by the end of the next school year."

AI   **auditorily impaired:** an inability to hear within normal limits because of physical impairment or dysfunction of auditory mechanisms.

AP   **assistant principal** or **associate principal:** an administrator who assists the principal of a school. May also be called a *vice principal.*

APD   **antisocial personality disorder:** a psychiatric condition characterized by chronic behavior (often criminal) that manipulates, exploits, or violates the rights of others. This diagnosis cannot be made until an individual is over eighteen years old; prior to that, a teenager may be categorized as conduct-disordered.

auditory processing disorder: an inability to accurately process and interpret sound information. Students with APD often do not recognize subtle differences between sounds in words (for example, "hit" versus "hat").

APE   **adapted physical education:** alternative physical education for students who cannot participate in the regular program.

ASD   **autism spectrum disorders:** several disorders characterized by varying degrees of impairment in communication skills and social interactions and by restricted repetitive and stereotyped patterns of behavior. Examples include preoccupation with parts of objects or repetitive motor movements like hand or finger flapping.

ASL   **American Sign Language:** a language used among deaf persons that uses signs formed by specific movements and shapes of the hand and arms, eyes, face, head, and body posture.

AT   **assistive technology:** technological devices used by children with disabilities. (See also AAD.)

AUT   **autism:** the category of special education services for students with autism. (See also ASD.)

AYP   **adequate yearly progress:** All public school campuses, school districts, and states are required by the No Child Left Behind Act to be evaluated for AYP. AYP is determined by how well students perform on standardized tests. Each is required to meet AYP criteria on three measures: reading/language arts, mathematics, and either graduation rate (for high schools and districts) or attendance rate (for elementary schools, middle schools, and junior high schools).

BD   **behaviorally disordered:** the category of special education services for students with a behavior disorder.
brain damage: damage to the brain that has occurred as a result of head trauma, infections, bleeding into the brain, lack of oxygen, failure of the brain to develop properly, or neurological damage.

BIL   **bilingual:** the ability to use two languages with equal or nearly equal fluency.

BIP	**behavior intervention plan:** a plan that includes positive strategies, program modifications, and supplementary aids and supports that address a student's disruptive behaviors and allow the child to be educated in the least restrictive environment.
BMP	**behavior management plan:** See BIP.
CA	**chronological age:** a student's actual age in years and months, calculated when intelligence and achievement measures are administered to a child, because these tests are scored on the basis of chronological age.
CAI	**computer-assisted instruction:** drill-and-practice, tutorial, or simulation activities presented through computer programs and used by students alone or in conjunction with classroom instruction.
CAP	**central auditory processing:** brain functions that allow a person interpret and store information that is received orally. Examples include auditory discrimination (being able to distinguish between similar sounds such as short *a,* short *e,* and short *i*) or being able to attend to some sounds while purposefully ignoring other sounds.
CAPD	**central auditory processing disorders:** difficulty in understanding speech or oral instructions despite normal hearing sensitivity. Although a child with CAPD has normal hearing, he cannot understand oral communication at the same level as other children his age.
CBA	**curriculum-based assessment:** ongoing assessment of a student's ability to meet expected performance standards based on the state's education curriculum for behaviors in the developmental areas of cognitive, communication, social, motor, and adaptive behaviors.
CBM	**curriculum-based measurement:** a method that teachers use to measure how students are progressing in basic academic areas such as math, reading, writing, and spelling. The measures are based on how well a student masters the curriculum goals. The teacher gives the student brief, timed samples (called *probes*), which are created from material from the school curriculum. To keep the measurements standardized, the teacher reads the same

directions every time that he gives a specific probe. The probes are timed and may last from one to five minutes, depending on the child's age and the skill being measured. The child's performance on a probe is scored for speed and accuracy. The probes may be used repeatedly as practice drills, in which case the student's results are charted to monitor her rate of academic progress.

CD — **conduct disorder:** a group of behavioral and emotional problems in children and adolescents that result in great difficulty in following rules and behaving in a socially acceptable way. Behaviors may include aggression toward people and animals; destruction of property; deceitfulness, lying, or stealing; or serious violations of rules.

CHI — **closed head injury:** an injury (for example, a concussion) that occurs when the head is struck by a blunt object.

CLD — **culturally and linguistically diverse:** refers to students who come from a different culture from mainstream American culture and whose background includes a language other than English.

COTA — **certified occupational therapist assistant:** a trained professional who works under the direction and supervision of an occupational therapist. In schools, a COTA provides rehabilitative services to students with developmental, physical, mental, or emotional impairments.

CP — **cerebral palsy:** a term that encompasses many different disorders of movement and posture.

DAP — **developmentally appropriate practices:** practices that are age-appropriate, individually appropriate, and culturally appropriate for each student.

DB or DBL — **deaf-blind:** students who are both deaf and blind.

DD — **developmental disabilities:** a diverse group of severe chronic conditions due to mental or physical impairments.

developmentally delayed: lagging in cognitive development, communication development, social or emotional development, physical or motor development, or adaptive or self-help development. Some districts place an age limit on children with this categorical label; for example, in some districts, children can be categorized as DD only prior to their sixth birthday. After that time, further assessment is required in order to provide a more appropriate designation.

DSM   *Diagnostic and Statistical Manual of Mental Disorders:* a handbook that provides descriptions and diagnostic criteria for the most common mental disorders, as well as information on treatments and research findings.

EBD   **emotional and behavioral disorders:** the category of special education services for students with both emotional and behavioral problems.

EC   **early childhood:** the stage of a child's growth or development from birth through eight years of age.

exceptional children: children who have special needs. This term is often used to refer to those receiving special education services.

ECE   **early childhood education:** the education of a child through third grade (birth through eight years of age).

ECI   **early childhood intervention:** programs designed to provide assistance to preschool children with physical or developmental problems.

ED   **emotionally disturbed:** the category of special education services for students who demonstrate emotional problems.

emotional disturbance: an inability to learn that cannot be explained by intellectual, sensory, or health factors; an inability to build or maintain satisfactory interpersonal relationships with peers and teachers; inappropriate types of behavior or feelings under normal circumstances; a general pervasive mood of unhappiness or depression; a tendency to develop physical symptoms or fears associated with personal or school problems. At various times, students with severe emotional disturbance can feel extremely sad, angry, worthless, anxious or worried, fearful, or afraid that they are not in control of their mind or behavior. These behaviors occur with such intensity, frequency, and duration that they are considered disabling to a child.

ELL   **English language learner:** someone who is learning to speak and understand the English language.

ESE	**exceptional students education:** special education services for students who qualify for such services.
ESL	**English as a second language:** English learned in an environment in which it is the predominant language of communication.
ESOL	**English for speakers of other languages:** English instruction for persons who speak a language other than English.
ESY	**extended school year:** Students who are receiving special education services may qualify for ESY services, which extend beyond the regular school year (summer school). A student's IEP team determines her eligibility for ESY services.
FAPE	**free appropriate public education:** special education and related services that are designed for the individual educational needs of disabled children, provided at no cost to the child or parents.
FBA	**functional behavioral assessment:** a problem-solving process for addressing a student's behavior problems that uses strategies to identify what precipitates or triggers a given behavior and to select interventions that directly address the problem behaviors.
FERPA	**Family Educational Rights and Privacy Act:** a federal law that protects the privacy of students' education records.
FY	**fiscal year:** a twelve-month period used in calculating yearly financial reports. Most schools use a July 1–June 30 fiscal year.
HI	**hearing impairment:** a category of special education services for students with impaired hearing, whether it is permanent or fluctuating.
HS	**Head Start:** a child development program for children ages three to five and their families that focuses on increasing the school readiness of young children from low-income families by increasing opportunities for learning.
	high school: a secondary school offering the final years of high school, usually grades 9–12.
ID	**intellectual disability:** the category of special education services for students with an intellectual disability (previously called *mental retardation*)—significantly below-average intellectual

functioning and significant deficits in adaptive behavior. Intellectual disabilities are classified in three different ways by three different sources: the DSM-IV (which uses the diagnosis of mental retardation); the American Association on Intellectual and Developmental Disabilities; and the educational system. Each has its own definition of intellectual disability and the diagnostic criteria that must be met for this category. The causes of intellectual disabilities are not always known, but they can be caused by trauma before or after birth (lack of oxygen to the brain or a severe head injury); infectious diseases (meningitis, encephalitis); chromosomal abnormalities (Down syndrome, fragile X syndrome, Angelman syndrome, Prader-Willi syndrome); genetic abnormalities or inherited metabolic disorders (Tay-Sachs disease, phenylketonuria, Rett syndrome); metabolic disorders (Reye's syndrome, hypoglycemia); toxins (lead poisoning or intrauterine exposure to alcohol, cocaine, amphetamines, or other drugs); nutritional problems (malnutrition); or environmental factors (poverty, low socioeconomic status).

IDEA 2004 — **Individuals with Disabilities Education Improvement Act of 2004:** a federal law mandating that all children with disabilities have access to a free, appropriate public education that emphasizes special education and related services that are designed to meet their unique needs and prepare them for employment and independent living. (See Chapter Eighteen for more information on IDEA 2004.)

IED — **intermittent explosive disorder:** a disorder that is characterized by frequent and often unpredictable episodes of extreme anger or physical outbursts. Typically, there is no evidence of violence or physical threats between these episodes.

IEE — **independent educational evaluation:** an evaluation conducted by a qualified examiner who is not employed by the school district, at the public's expense.

IEP — **individualized education program:** a document written for each child who is found eligible for special education services. It addresses each child's unique needs and includes, among many other things, goals and measurable objectives that a child will strive to achieve. (See Chapter Sixteen for more information on IEPs.)

IFA **individualized functional assessment:** an assessment that examines whether a child can effectively engage in age-appropriate activities.

IQ **intelligence quotient:** a measure of someone's intelligence as indicated by an intelligence test with an average score of 100. An IQ score is the ratio of a person's mental age to his chronological age multiplied by 100. For example, if the mental age of a child is 130 months, and he is exactly 10 years old (120 months), the child's IQ is 108 ($130/120 \times 100 = 108$).

ISS **in-school suspension:** an alternative placement program that allows students to come to school but not to attend regular class. They are placed in an isolated, supervised small-group setting in which they can still complete their schoolwork.

ITP **individualized transition plan:** Transition services start when a student begins to prepare for the transition from high school to postsecondary education, vocational training, independent employment, supported employment, continuing education, adult education, adult disability services, or independent living. When transition services begin for students with an IEP, the IEP team holds a transition planning interview in order to identify their needs. The IEP team uses this information to develop an ITP, which is designed to accomplish the student's goals.

LD **learning disability:** a neurological disorder that affects the brain's ability to receive, process, store, or respond to information. A person may have difficulty in reading, writing, mathematics, listening, or speaking.

LEA **local education agency:** a school district, for example. It may include a private school or a regional educational service agency.

LEP **limited English proficient:** describes a student who is not fully proficient in English, speaks a language other than English at home, and does not demonstrate English language skills of comprehension, speaking, reading, and writing at a level that would allow him to be placed in a mainstream class setting in which only English is spoken.

LRE
least restrictive environment: The least restrictive environment means that a student with a disability should have an opportunity to be educated with his nondisabled peers to the greatest extent possible. For most students, the least restrictive environment is the regular classroom, but a student's IEP team must determine the LRE for that student on the basis of her individual needs.

MA
mental age: an individual's level of intellectual development as measured by an intelligence test. For example, if an eight-year-old is able to successfully answer only questions that the average six-year-old could handle, then his mental age is six years.

MDT
multidisciplinary team: a group of school professionals that conducts an in-depth evaluation of the psychological, academic, behavioral, and communication skills, as well as the physical health, hearing, and vision of a student because it is suspected that she has a disability that is hampering her learning.

manifest determination team: a group of school personnel who meet to review the case of a student who is receiving special education services when his behavior has resulted in expulsion or a change in placement. The team determines whether the student's behavior is related to his disability.

MI
multiple intelligences: Howard Gardner's theory, which states that our conception of intelligence, which is based on IQ testing, is too limited. Gardner proposes there are eight different intelligences: linguistic intelligence ("word smart"), logical-mathematical intelligence ("number/reasoning smart"), spatial intelligence ("picture smart"), bodily-kinesthetic intelligence ("body smart"), musical intelligence ("music smart"), interpersonal intelligence ("people smart"), intrapersonal intelligence ("self smart"), and naturalist intelligence ("nature smart").

MR
mental retardation: See ID.

NCLB
No Child Left Behind Act of 2001: legislation whose purpose is to ensure that all children have a fair, equal, and significant opportunity to obtain a high-quality education and reach, at a

minimum, proficiency on challenging state academic achievement standards and state academic assessments.

O&M **orientation and mobility:** instruction that teaches individuals who are visually impaired, blind, or deaf-blind to move about safely and independently in a familiar or unfamiliar environment.

OCD **obsessive-compulsive disorder:** a disorder characterized by recurrent obsessions (thoughts or images) or compulsions (actions). *Obsessions* are recurrent and persistent thoughts, impulses, or images that are unwanted and cause a great deal of anxiety. *Compulsions* are repetitive behaviors or rituals (for example, hand washing, keeping things in order, or checking to make sure a light it turned off) or mental acts (for example, counting or repeating words silently). Often, the actions are attempts to reduce the anxious thoughts or images.

OCR **Office for Civil Rights:** the federal agency that serves student populations that face discrimination as well as the advocates and institutions that promote solutions to civil rights problems. An important responsibility of OCR is resolving complaints of discrimination in addition to developing creative approaches to preventing and addressing discrimination.

ODD **oppositional defiant disorder:** a disorder characterized by an ongoing pattern of uncooperative, defiant, and hostile behavior toward authority figures that seriously interferes with a student's daily functioning. A high percentage of children with ODD are also diagnosed with ADHD.

OH **orthopedically handicapped:** the category of special education services for students with severe orthopedic impairments.

OHI **other health impairment:** the category of special education services for students with limited strength, vitality, or alertness due to chronic or acute health problems (such as asthma, ADHD, diabetes, or a heart condition).

OSEP **Office of Special Education Programs:** a section of the U.S. Department of Education whose goal is to improve results for infants, toddlers, children, and adolescents with disabilities (ages birth through twenty-one) by providing leadership and financial support to assist states and local districts.

OSS   **out-of-school suspension:** a form of discipline that is used when a student has significant behavior problems and is not allowed to remain in school.

OT   **occupational therapy:** a rehabilitative service for persons with mental, physical, emotional, or developmental impairments. In a school setting, OT can reduce barriers that limit a student's participation in the school environment—for example, facilitating the use of assistive technology to support student success. Other examples of OT include helping a student with his pencil grip, providing physical exercises to increase a student's strength and dexterity, or teaching a student some exercises to improve hand-eye coordination.

occupational therapist: a trained professional who provides occupational therapy.

OT/PT   **occupational therapy/physical therapy:** a designation used for a student who is receiving both occupational therapy and physical therapy services.

PDD   **pervasive developmental disorder:** the category of special education services for students with delays or deviance in social, language, motor, or cognitive development.

PLOP   **present level of performance:** a statement that describes how a child is currently performing.

Pre-K   **pre-kindergarten:** the year of education that occurs before kindergarten. The goal of pre-K is to promote school readiness so that children have a better chance of success in their later school years.

PT   **physical therapy:** instructional support and treatment of physical disabilities provided by a trained physical therapist, under a doctor's prescription, that helps a person improve the use of bones, muscles, joints, and nerves.

physical therapist: a trained professional who provides physical therapy.

PTA   **physical therapist assistant:** a professional who works under the supervision of a physical therapist and provides rehabilitative services to students with physical or developmental impairments.

Parent-Teacher Association: a school district–based group that is part of the National PTA. Its purpose is to help increase parental participation in public or private schools.

PTO **Parent-Teacher Organization:** a school-based group that helps to create activities that support and enhance students' educational experience.

PTSD **post-traumatic stress disorder:** a DSM-IV psychiatric disorder that can result from experiencing or witnessing life-threatening events such as a natural disaster or serious accident. Persons suffering from PTSD often relive a traumatic experience through nightmares and flashbacks, have difficulty sleeping, and feel detached or estranged from others. Children with PTSD often re-experience trauma through play.

RAD **reactive attachment disorder:** the failure of a child to bond with a caretaker in infancy or early childhood. It is often precipitated by severe attachment trauma (for example, abuse or neglect). As children with RAD develop, they may either treat all people as if they were their best friend or show mistrust of nearly everyone.

RTI **response to intervention:** the response-to-invention (RTI) model is also often called the *three-tier model.* Under IDEA 2004, school districts can use this model as an alternative to the discrepancy model (which compares standard scores for achievement and intelligence) as a method for determining whether a student has a learning disability. (See Chapter Four for more information on RTI.)

SAT **student assistance team:** See SST.

SDD **significant developmental delay:** a category of special education services for young children who have delayed development in adaptive behavior (daily living skills), cognition (learning), communication, motor development (walking, running), or social development.

SEA **state education agency:** a state department of education

SEBD **serious emotional and behavioral disorder:** a category of special education services for students who are experiencing significant emotional disturbance. (See ED.)

SED	**seriously emotionally disturbed:** a category of special education services for students who are experiencing significant emotional disturbance. (See ED.)
SI	**speech impaired:** the category of special education services for students with a speech impairment.
SIB	**self-injurious behavior:** behavior that involves self-inflicted tissue damage such as bruises, redness, or open wounds. Examples of self-injurious behaviors include cutting, hand biting, head banging, and excessive scratching or rubbing.
SLD	**specific learning disability:** a category of special education services for students with a disability in one or more of the basic psychological processes involved in understanding or in using language, spoken or written, that may manifest itself in an imperfect ability to listen, think, speak, read, write, spell, or to do mathematical calculations.
SLP	**speech-language pathologist:** a professional who assesses, diagnoses, treats, and helps to prevent disorders of speech, language, cognition, communication, voice, swallowing, and fluency. Speech-language pathologists are sometimes referred to as *speech therapists* or *speech teachers*.
SPED	**special education:** services offered to children who have one or more of the following disabilities: specific learning disability, speech or language impairment, intellectual disability, emotional disturbance, multiple disabilities, hearing impairment, orthopedic impairment, visual impairment, autism, deafness, combined deafness and blindness, traumatic brain injury, or other health impairment.
SST	**student support team** or **student study team:** a team of school professionals (including, for example, classroom teachers, a curriculum specialist, school psychologist, speech-language therapist, and principal or assistant principal) and parents who meet to discuss the problems a child is having in regular education classes. The goal of an SST is to discuss ways to assist a child in order to minimize the effect that learning or behavior problems have on her education. An SST can also be called a *student assistance team* (SAT).

TBI	**traumatic brain injury:** the category of special education services for students with a traumatic brain injury, which occurs when sudden physical trauma to the head causes damage to the brain.
TDD	**telecommunication devices for the deaf:** special telephones with typewriter keyboards and visual displays that provide people who are deaf with access to telephones.
TPP	**transition planning process:** how an IEP team helps a student make the transition from school to adult life through effective planning, school experiences, services, and supports in order to help him achieve his desired outcomes.
VI	**visually impaired:** a category of special education services for students with an impairment in vision (including blindness).

APPENDIX

CHECKLISTS FOR CHILD PROBLEMS

ATTENTION DEFICIT HYPERACTIVITY DISORDER (ADHD)

There are three major types of ADHD, and the following checklist can help you to understand the types of behaviors and symptoms that children with ADHD share. In addition to having the appropriate number of symptoms, it is also important that the child display the symptoms across situations, such as at home and at school. Although the symptoms may be more obvious in the classroom setting, where it is more important that the child remain seated and concentrate on schoolwork, the behaviors should also be observable at home as well. It is also important to understand that other problems can have similar symptoms. For example, you will find similar symptoms in the checklists for anxiety disorders and depression, especially the bipolar version of depression. So if the child is demonstrating a number of these symptoms, it might be helpful to look at the checklists for depression and anxiety as well.

Attention Deficit Hyperactivity Disorder (ADHD) Checklist

Three Types		
1. Predominantly Inattentive (six symptoms)		
2. Predominantly Hyperactive-Impulsive (six symptoms)		
3. Combined Type (twelve symptoms; meet criteria for both 1 and 2)		
Six Symptoms	**Six Symptoms**	
Inattention	**Hyperactivity**	**Impulsivity**
☐ Poor attention to details (misses key parts of information)	☐ Fidgets, squirmy	☐ Problems waiting for his or her turn
☐ Problems sustaining attention in boring or repetitious tasks	☐ Problems remaining seated when required to sit	☐ Blurts out answers
☐ High level of distractibility; distractions interfere with task completion	☐ Runs, climbs, excessively (or is restless if a teenager)	☐ Intrusive, interrupts others
☐ Insufficient attention to details and organizational framework	☐ Loud play and problems playing quietly	
☐ Doesn't "seem" to listen	☐ Always on the go, driven like a motor	
☐ Problems organizing information	☐ Excessive talking	
☐ Avoids and dislikes tasks requiring sustained mental effort		
☐ Forgetfulness		
☐ Loss of tools required to accomplish tasks (misplaces notes, pens, pencils, books, etc.)		

Additional Criteria for ADHD		
• Some symptoms present before age seven		
• Symptoms evident in more than one setting		
Other Possible Symptoms ☐ Problems with sleep ☐ Anxious ☐ Irritable	☐ Depression ☐ Physical complaints ☐ Oppositional Defiant	☐ Aggression ☐ Social skills ☐ Learning problems

ANXIETY PROBLEMS AND ANXIETY DISORDERS

Anxiety is one of the most common problems in childhood and adolescence, with as high as 13 percent reporting some degree of anxiety. Children who experience problems with anxiety often feel a sense of uncontrollable worry in the face of unpredictable events. Often situations or events can trigger uncomfortable levels of emotional and physical arousal such as increased heart rate, rapid breathing, feeling threatened, and a strong desire to withdraw, avoid, or escape. Young children are especially likely to feel a mixture of both anxious and depressed feelings.

Anxiety Symptom Checklist

Type of Anxiety	Symptom Examples		
Anxious/ Depressed	☐ Cries a lot ☐ Worries ☐ Many fears ☐ Nervous	☐ Overly self-conscious ☐ Feels unloved ☐ Feels need to be perfect	☐ Blames self ☐ Feels worthless ☐ Fears at school ☐ Avoids situations
Specific Phobias: *Persistent, irrational fear*	☐ Fear of animals ☐ Fear of thunder ☐ Fear of lightning	☐ Fear of injections ☐ Fear of situations (flying, school)	☐ Fear of heights ☐ Fear of choking ☐ Fear of clowns
Separation Anxiety Disorder *Intense avoidance and fear of separation from caregiver*	☐ Separation causes intense distress ☐ Fear that harm will come to caregiver	☐ Worry over future separations ☐ School refusal ☐ Fear of being alone	☐ Fear of sleeping alone ☐ Nightmares about separation ☐ Complains of head aches, stomachaches
General Anxiety Disorder *Overly worried about family, friends, school, performance, health, and so on*	☐ Overly restless ☐ Tires easily ☐ Irritable	☐ Problems sleeping ☐ Tension in muscles ☐ Frequent physical complaints	☐ Problems with concentration ☐ Perfectionistic ☐ Vague worries
Obsessive Compulsive Disorder (OCD) *Persistent thoughts (obsessions) → behaviors (compulsions)*	*Preoccupation with* ☐ Fear of contamination ☐ Excessive cleanliness ☐ Excess hand washing, showers, teeth brushing	☐ Order, symmetry ☐ Obsessive neatness ☐ Safety (check doors, locks) ☐ Repetitive rituals	☐ Hoarding, collecting useless objects ☐ Compulsive list making

Type of Anxiety	Symptom Examples		
Social Phobia *Intense fear of public embarrassment*	☐ Avoids social situations ☐ Avoids eating in public ☐ Panic attacks	☐ Avoids public speaking ☐ Avoids writing in public	☐ Fear may result in tremors, blushing ☐ Discomfort in social situations
Panic Attacks *Intense feeling of panic*	☐ Palpitations ☐ Sweating ☐ Trembling	☐ Dizziness ☐ Urge to escape ☐ Loss of control	☐ Breathing problems ☐ Chest pain
Post-Traumatic Stress Disorder (PTSD) *Response to experiencing or witnessing traumatic event; may appear disorganized and agitated*	*Re-experiencing* ☐ Repetitive trauma play ☐ Dreams of monsters or rescue ☐ Distress to triggers of event	*Avoidance and Numbing* ☐ Detachment ☐ Diminished interest ☐ Flat affect ☐ Believe they can foresee the future ☐ Can't recall event ☐ Avoid activities associated with event	*Increased Arousal* ☐ Sleep problems ☐ Irritable/angry outbursts ☐ Hypervigilance ☐ Concentration problems

AUTISM

The majority of children with autism (approximately 75 percent) will also have some degree of intellectual disability. Autism is one of the Pervasive Developmental Disorders (PDD), all of which share a number of the same characteristics. The disorder is observable prior to three years of age, although early development may appear normal. There are three major areas of atypical functioning and qualitative impairment.

Autism Symptom Checklist (Pervasive Developmental Disorders: PDD)

Impairment in Communication	Impairment in Social Interaction	Restrictive, Repetitive, or Stereotyped Behaviors
Delay or lack of speech ☐ Lack of speech-related gestures	**Lack of nonverbal behavior** ☐ Lack of social gestures ☐ Lack of eye contact ☐ Flat facial expression	**Preoccupation with interests with intense focus** ☐ Interest in dates, numbers ☐ Intense interest in one area (maps, dinosaurs, bottle caps)
Lack of initiating/sustaining speech ☐ Failure to maintain conversation ☐ Responds to questions inappropriately	**Lack of appropriate peer relationships** ☐ Remains aloof, standoffish ☐ Lacks understanding of social rules	**Preoccupation with nonfunctional routines or rituals** ☐ Lining up objects ☐ Using the same route every day
Repetitive or stereotyped speech ☐ Repeats or echoes words or phrases ☐ Odd monotone (robotlike) ☐ Uses "I" inappropriately ☐ Refers to self in third person	**Does not engage in social referencing** ☐ Does not spontaneously share ☐ Does not point or share interest in objects, activities ☐ Does not include others in activities	**Repetitive and stereotyped mannerisms** ☐ Hand flapping ☐ Twirling ☐ Clapping ☐ Rocking ☐ Swaying

Impairment in Communication	Impairment in Social Interaction	Restrictive, Repetitive, or Stereotyped Behaviors
Lack of typical play ☐ Lack of imitative play ☐ Lack of imaginative play ☐ Lack of make-believe play ☐ Lack of spontaneous play	**Lack of social or emotional reciprocity** ☐ Does not share feelings ☐ Does not share a smile ☐ Does not return a social gesture ☐ Prefers solitary activities ☐ Includes others only as mechanical aid ☐ Unaware of others' feelings or distress	**Preoccupation with parts of objects** ☐ Spinning a wheel on a car, or propeller on an airplane ☐ Buttons ☐ Opening and closing doors ☐ Attached to an inanimate object (button, rubber band)

Additional Criteria

- Onset prior to three years of age

- Abnormal functioning in at least one of three areas: (1) social interaction; (2) social communication; or (3) symbolic or imaginative play

| *Other Possible Symptoms*
☐ Stares blankly
☐ Walks on tiptoes
☐ Resists physical contact | ☐ Laughs or giggles inappropriately
☐ Highly resistant to any change in routine
☐ Tantrums when upset | ☐ Does not understand jokes
☐ Unreasonably fearful
☐ Easily frustrated
☐ Makes odd sounds |

DISORDERS AND PROBLEMS OF MOOD: DEPRESSION AND BIPOLAR DISORDER

Unlike adults, children who are upset show depression through irritability. Depressed mood can be a temporary reaction, which self-corrects when the distress subsides. Difficult adjustments (moving to a new house or changing schools) may result in a temporary (less than six months) depressive response. Sometimes, children will exhibit a number of symptoms of depression that cluster together, referred to as a syndrome. Children and youth can also experience more severe forms of depression, such as dysthymic disorder (DD), lasting for a year, or major depressive disorder (MDD), a severe disorder that lasts for at least two weeks but is very devastating. Some children may bounce between the lows of depression and the highs of mania, a disorder referred to as Bipolar Disorder (BD). Many children with BD will experience several mood swings (highs and lows) on a daily basis, a condition called *rapid cycling*.

Mood Problems Checklist

Type of Mood	Symptom Examples		
Depressed/ Withdrawn Syndrome	☐ Does not enjoy life ☐ Withdrawn socially ☐ Shy, keeps to self ☐ Talks of running away ☐ Complains of boredom	☐ Fatigued, no energy ☐ Sad ☐ Poor schoolwork ☐ Physical complaints ☐ Increased risk taking ☐ Loss of interest	☐ Irritable ☐ A loner ☐ Secretive ☐ Frequent absenteeism ☐ Overly sensitive ☐ Poor social skills
Adjustment Disorder with Depressed Mood *Temporary reaction to identified stressor (six months or less)*	☐ Recent family relocation ☐ Recent change in schools	☐ Recent family change ☐ Sad ☐ Irritable ☐ Withdrawn	☐ Keeps to self ☐ Sad ☐ Loss of energy ☐ Complains of not feeling well
Mood Disorders: DD & MDD Dysthymic Disorder (DD) *Lasting at least one year, two symptoms* Major Depressive Disorder (MDD) *Lasting at least two weeks, four symptoms*	☐ **Pervasive "Irritable" Mood (depressed mood state)** *or* ☐ **Loss of Interest or Pleasure** Plus two symptoms (DD) or four symptoms (MDD) from seven symptoms below:		
	☐ Failure to meet expected weight/height ratios; poor appetite ☐ Insomnia or hypersomnia	☐ Excessive thoughts of worthlessness/guilt; low self-esteem ☐ Poor concentration, attention, indecisive	☐ Psychomotor agitation or lethargy ☐ Fatigue; loss of energy ☐ Suicidal thoughts or feelings of hopelessness

Type of Mood	Symptom Examples		
Bipolar Disorder *Meet criteria for MDD (see above) + manic symptoms, at least one week*	**Abnormally elevated, expansive, or irritable mood** Plus three of the following seven symptoms:		
	☐ Heightened self-esteem, grandiosity ☐ Decreased need for sleep	☐ Flight of ideas ☐ Distractibility ☐ Increased goal-directed activity	☐ Excessive need to talk/ pressured speech ☐ Excessive high-risk activities (theft, spending)
Other Characteristics of Bipolar Disorder	☐ Aggression ☐ Goofy	☐ Giddy ☐ Loss of temper	☐ Mad/cranky ☐ Loss of emotional control

DISRUPTIVE BEHAVIOR DISORDERS

Children can experience a number of different behavior problems or disorders that can cause problems in the classroom, on the playground, and at home. Whereas some behaviors cause minor difficulties, other behaviors can be more severe, frequent, and longer lasting.

Behavior Problems Checklist

Type of Behavior Problem	Symptom Examples		
Aggressive Behavior	☐ Argues ☐ Gets into fights ☐ Talks back ☐ Overly critical of others ☐ Spreads rumors	☐ Mean ☐ Demands attention ☐ Bullies/threatens ☐ Loses temper often ☐ Teases ☐ Not liked by others	☐ Disobedient ☐ Disturbs others ☐ Easily excitable ☐ Loud ☐ Defiant
Oppositional Defiant Disorder (ODD)	**Persistent, hostile, defiant, disobedient, and negative pattern of behaviors against authority figures.** Plus four from the following eight symptoms:		
	☐ Loss of temper ☐ Argumentative with adults ☐ Defiant, noncompliant	☐ Deliberately annoying ☐ Blames others for mistakes or problems ☐ Touchy, easily irritated	☐ Angry, resentful ☐ Spiteful, vindictive
Conduct Disorder (CD) *Symptoms must be present for at least past twelve months, and one symptom within past six months* **Childhood-Onset** *At least one symptom prior to age ten* **Adolescent-Onset** *No problems prior to age ten*	**Violation of social norms or the rights of others.** Plus three of the following fifteen criteria:		

Aggression	*Property Destruction*	*Deceit or Theft*	*Rule Violations*
☐ Bullies/ threatens ☐ Initiates fights ☐ Use of weapon ☐ Cruelty to others ☐ Cruelty to animals ☐ Forced theft (mugging) ☐ Forced sex	☐ Fire setting ☐ Vandalism	☐ Break-in (house, car) ☐ Cons others ☐ Theft (shoplifting, forgery)	☐ Stayed out all night* ☐ Ran Away ☐ Frequent truancy* ** Evidence of occurrence prior to thirteen years of age*

SOCIAL PROBLEMS, SOCIAL SKILLS AND SOCIAL GOALS

Children can experience social difficulties for a variety of reasons discussed throughout this book, including having associated learning difficulties, a shy temperament, poor ability to regulate emotions, or acting impulsively. Social skills can be impaired by the misinterpretation of information at a variety of levels including the recognition, interpretation, and response to social cues. However, we know that many children can benefit from direct instruction, socially, to develop skills in specific problem areas. The following checklist will be very helpful in recognizing a child's strengths and weaknesses, socially, in order to develop specific goals and interventions to increase opportunities for social success.

Social Problems, Social Skills, and Social Goals

Recognizing, Interpreting and Responding to Social Situations: Social Information Processing

Place an X beside areas where the child is experiencing problems [X]

Place a ✓ beside areas of strength [✓]

Recognizing Social Cues	Interpreting Social Cues	Responding to Social Cues (Expression)
Visual cues ☐ Facial expression ☐ Body posture ☐ Appropriate dress ☐ Social distance Auditory cues ☐ Voice and tone ☐ Emphasis Motor cues ☐ Gestures ☐ Body language ☐ Tactile/touch	☐ Awareness of space and time ☐ Memory for situations ☐ Organizing information ☐ Sequencing information ☐ Cause and effect reasoning ☐ Empathy ☐ Group norms	☐ Timing (passivity/impulsivity) ☐ Intensity (over-/under-react) ☐ Expressivity (facial/oral/gestural) ☐ Social roles
Remedial Focus: ☐ Attention to detail ☐ Looking for cues ☐ Hearing the message	**Remedial Focus:** ☐ Attention to sequence ☐ Comparing situations ☐ Past experiences ☐ Organizing information ☐ What caused what?	**Remedial Focus: How to get your point across** ☐ Know your audience ☐ Size up the listener ☐ Affecting ☐ Slow down/think before acting ☐ Responding differently to peers/authority figures

Important Social Skills: Goals to Building Better Social Behaviors

Cooperation	Assertiveness	Self-Control
☐ Compliance with requests ☐ Sharing ☐ Saying please and thank-you ☐ Giving compliments ☐ Volunteering to help ☐ Sense of honesty and fairness	☐ Introduce oneself ☐ Make positive self-statements ☐ Invite others to join in ☐ Start conversations ☐ Give compliments	☐ Control temper ☐ Compromise ☐ Appropriate response to teasing ☐ Accept criticism

APPENDIX

C

SAMPLE 504 PLAN

This Section 504 plan was developed by the American Diabetes Association and the Disability Rights Education and Defense Fund, Inc.

MODEL 504 PLAN FOR A STUDENT WITH DIABETES

[*Note:* This model 504 plan lists a broad range of services and accommodations that might be needed by a child with diabetes in school. The plan should be individualized to meet the needs, abilities, and medical condition of each student and should *include only the items that are relevant to that student.* Some students will need additional services and accommodations that have not been included in this model plan.]

Section 504 Plan for _____
School: _____
School Year: _____

| _____ | _____ | _____ | type ____ diabetes |
| Student's Name | Birth Date | Grade | Disability |

Homeroom Teacher: _____   Bus Number: _____

OBJECTIVES/GOALS OF THIS PLAN

Diabetes can cause blood glucose (sugar) levels to be too high or too low, both of which affect the student's ability to learn as well as seriously endanger the student's health both immediately and in the long term. The goal of this plan is to provide the special education and/or related aids and services needed to maintain blood glucose within this student's target range and to respond appropriately to levels outside of this range in accordance with the instructions provided by the student's personal health care team.

REFERENCES

School accommodations, diabetes care, and other services set out by this Plan will be consistent with the information and protocols contained in the National Diabetes Education Program's *Helping the Student with Diabetes Succeed: A Guide for School Personnel* (June 2003).

Definitions Used in This Plan

- *Diabetes Medical Management Plan* (DMMP): A plan that describes the diabetes care regimen and identifies the health care needs of a student with diabetes. This plan is developed and approved by the student's personal health care team and family. Schools must do outreach to the parents and child's health care provider if a DMMP is not submitted by the family. [*Note:* School districts may have other names for the plan. If so, substitute the appropriate terminology throughout.]

- *Quick Reference Emergency Plan:* A plan that provides school personnel with essential information on how to recognize and treat hypoglycemia and hyperglycemia.

- *Trained Diabetes Personnel* (TDP): Non-medical school personnel who have been identified by the school nurse, school administrator, and parent who are willing to be trained in basic diabetes knowledge and have received training coordinated by the school nurse in diabetes care, including the performance of blood glucose monitoring, insulin and glucagon administration, recognition and treatment of hypoglycemia and hyperglycemia, and performance of ketone checks, and who will perform these diabetes care tasks in the absence of a school nurse.

1. PROVISION OF DIABETES CARE

1.1 At least ___ staff members will receive training to be Trained Diabetes Personnel (TDP), and either a school nurse or TDP will be available at the site where the student is *at all times* during school hours, during extracurricular activities, and on school-sponsored field trips to provide diabetes care in accordance with this Plan and as directed in the DMMP, including performing or overseeing administration of insulin or other diabetes medications (which for pump users includes programming and troubleshooting the student's insulin pump), blood glucose monitoring, ketone checks, and responding to hyperglycemia and hypoglycemia, including administering glucagon.

1.2 Any staff member who is not a TDP and who has primary care for the student at any time during school hours, extracurricular activities, or during field trips shall receive training that will include a general overview of diabetes and typical health care needs of a student with diabetes, recognition of high and low blood glucose levels, and how and when to immediately contact either a school nurse or a TDP.

1.3 Any bus driver who transports the student must be informed of symptoms of high or low blood glucose levels and provided with a copy of the student's Quick Reference Emergency Plan and be prepared to act in accordance with that Plan.

2. **TRAINED DIABETES PERSONNEL**

   The following school staff members will be trained to become TDPs by _____ (date):

   _____

   _____

   _____

3. **STUDENT'S LEVEL OF SELF-CARE AND LOCATION OF SUPPLIES AND EQUIPMENT**

   3.1 As stated in the attached DMMP:

   (a) The student is able to perform the following diabetes care tasks without help or supervision:

   _____

   _____

   _____

   and the student will be permitted to provide this self-care at any time and in any location at the school, on field trips, at sites of extracurricular activities, and on school buses.

   (b) The student needs assistance or supervision with the following diabetes health care tasks:

   _____

   _____

   _____

   (c) The student needs a school nurse or TDP to perform the following diabetes care tasks:

   _____

   _____

   _____

   3.2 The student will be permitted to carry the following diabetes supplies and equipment with him/her at all times and in all locations:

   _____

   _____

   _____

   3.3 Diabetes supplies and equipment that are not kept with the student and additional supplies will be kept at:

   _____

3.4 A parent is responsible for providing diabetes supplies and food to meet the needs of the student as prescribed in the DMMP.

4. SNACKS AND MEALS

4.1 The school nurse or TDP, if the school nurse is not available, will work with the student and his/her parents/guardians to coordinate a meal and snack schedule in accordance with the attached DMMP that will coincide with the schedule of classmates to the closest extent possible. The student shall eat lunch at the same time each day, or earlier if experiencing hypoglycemia. The student shall have enough time to finish lunch. A snack and quick-acting source of glucose must always be immediately available to the student.

4.2 The attached DMMP sets out the regular time(s) for snacks, what constitutes a snack, and when the student should have additional snacks. The student will be permitted to eat a snack no matter where the student is.

4.3 The parent/guardian will supply snacks needed in addition to or instead of any snacks supplied to all students.

4.4 The parent/guardian will provide carbohydrate content information for snacks and meals brought from home.

4.5 The school nurse or TDP will ensure that the student takes snacks and meals at the specified time(s) each day.

4.6 Adjustments to snack and meal times will be permitted in response to changes in schedule upon request of parent/guardian.

5. EXERCISE AND PHYSICAL ACTIVITY

5.1 The student shall be permitted to participate fully in physical education classes and team sports, except as set out in the student's DMMP.

5.2 Physical education instructors and sports coaches must have a copy of the emergency action plan and be able to recognize and assist with the treatment of low blood glucose levels.

5.3 Responsible school staff members will make sure that the student's blood glucose meter, a quick-acting source of glucose, and water is always available at the site of physical education class and team sports practices and games.

6. WATER AND BATHROOM ACCESS

6.1 The student shall be permitted to have immediate access to water by keeping a water bottle in the student's possession and at the student's desk and by permitting the student to use the drinking fountain without restriction.

6.2 The student shall be permitted to use the bathroom without restriction.

7. CHECKING BLOOD GLUCOSE LEVELS, INSULIN AND MEDICATION ADMINISTRATION, AND TREATING HIGH OR LOW BLOOD GLUCOSE LEVELS

7.1 The student's level of self-care is set out in section 3 above, including which tasks the student can do by himself/herself and which must be done with the assistance of or wholly by either a school nurse or a TDP.

7.2 Blood glucose monitoring will be done at the times designated in the student's DMMP, whenever the student feels her/his blood glucose level may be high or low, or when symptoms of high or low blood glucose levels are observed.

7.3 Insulin and/or other diabetes medication will be administered at the times and through the means (e.g., syringe, pen, or pump) designated in the student's DMMP for both scheduled doses and doses needed to correct for high blood glucose levels.

7.4 The student shall be provided with privacy for blood glucose monitoring and insulin administration if the student desires.

7.5 The student's usual symptoms of high and low blood glucose levels and how to respond to these levels are set out in the attached DMMP.

7.6 When the student asks for assistance or any staff member believes the student is showing signs of high or low blood glucose levels, the staff member will immediately seek assistance from the school nurse or TDP while making sure an adult stays with the student at all times. Never send a student with actual—or suspected—high or low blood glucose levels anywhere alone.

7.7 Any staff member who finds the student unconscious will immediately contact the school office. The office will immediately do the following in the order listed:

(a) Contact the school nurse or a TDP (if the school nurse is not on site and immediately available) who will confirm the blood glucose level with a monitor and immediately administer glucagon (glucagon should be administered if no monitor is available);

(b) Call 911 (office staff will do this without waiting for the school nurse or TDP to administer glucagon); and

(c) Contact the student's parent/guardian and physician at the emergency numbers provided below.

7.8 School staff, including physical education instructors and coaches, will provide a safe location for the storage of the student's insulin pump if the student chooses not to wear it during physical activity or any other activity.

8. FIELD TRIPS AND EXTRACURRICULAR ACTIVITIES

8.1 The student will be permitted to participate in all school-sponsored field trips and extracurricular activities (such as sports, clubs, and enrichment programs) without restriction and with all of the accommodations and modifications, including necessary supervision by identified school personnel, set out in this Plan. The student's parent/guardian will not be required to accompany the student on field trips or any other school activity.

8.2 The school nurse or TDP will be available on site at all school-sponsored field trips and extracurricular activities, will provide all usual aspects of diabetes care (including but not limited to blood glucose monitoring, responding to hyperglycemia and hypoglycemia, providing snacks and access to water and the bathroom, and administering insulin and glucagon), and will make sure that the student's diabetes supplies travel with the student.

9. TESTS AND CLASSROOM WORK

9.1 If the student is affected by high or low blood glucose levels at the time of regular testing, the student will be permitted to take the test at another time without penalty.

9.2 If the student needs to take breaks to use the water fountain or bathroom, check blood glucose, or to treat hypoglycemia or hyperglycemia during a test or other activity, the student will be given extra time to finish the test or other activity without penalty.

9.3 The student shall be given instruction to help him/her make up any classroom instruction missed due to diabetes care without penalty.

9.4   The student shall not be penalized for absences required for medical appointments and/or for illness. The parent will provide documentation from the treating health care professional if otherwise required by school policy.

10. COMMUNICATION

10.1   The school nurse, TDP, and other staff will keep the student's diabetes confidential, except to the extent that the student decides to openly communicate about it with others.

10.2   Encouragement is essential. The student should be treated in a way that encourages the student to eat snacks on time and to progress toward self-care with his/her diabetes management skills.

10.3   The teacher, school nurse, or TDP will provide reasonable notice to the parent/guardian when there will be a change in planned activities such as exercise, playground time, field trips, parties, or lunch schedule so that the lunch, snack plan, and insulin dosage can be adjusted accordingly.

10.4   Each substitute teacher and substitute school nurse will be provided with written instructions regarding the student's diabetes care and a list of all school nurses and TDPs at the school.

11. EMERGENCY EVACUATION AND SHELTER-IN-PLACE

11.1   In the event of an emergency evacuation or a shelter-in-place situation, the student's 504 Plan and DMMP will remain in full force and effect.

11.2   The school nurse or TDP will provide diabetes care to the student as outlined by this Plan and the student's DMMP, will be responsible for transporting the student's diabetes supplies and equipment, will attempt to establish contact with the student's parents/guardians and provide updates, and will receive information from parents/guardians regarding the student's diabetes care.

12. PARENTAL NOTIFICATION

12.1   *NOTIFY PARENTS/GUARDIANS IMMEDIATELY IN THE FOLLOWING SITUATIONS:*

- Symptoms of severe low blood sugar such as continuous crying, extreme tiredness, seizure, or loss of consciousness.
- The student's blood glucose test results are below _____ or are below _____ 15 minutes after consuming juice or glucose tablets.

- Symptoms of severe high blood sugar such as frequent urination, presence of ketones, vomiting, or blood glucose level above _____.

- The student refuses to eat or take insulin injection or bolus.
- Any injury.
- Insulin pump malfunctions cannot be remedied.
- Other:

  _____

  _____

12.2. *EMERGENCY CONTACT INSTRUCTIONS*

Call the parent/guardian at the numbers listed below. If you are unable to reach the parent/guardian, call the other emergency contacts or student's health care providers listed below.

EMERGENCY CONTACTS:

Parent's/Guardian's Name	Home Phone Number	Work Phone Number	Cell Phone Number

Parent's/Guardian's Name	Home Phone Number	Work Phone Number	Cell Phone Number

Other Emergency Contacts:

Name	Home Phone Number	Work Phone Number	Cell Phone Number

Name	Home Phone Number	Work Phone Number	Cell Phone Number

Student's Health Care Provider(s):

Name	Phone Number

Name	Phone Number

This Plan shall be reviewed and amended at the beginning of each school year or more often if necessary.

Approved and received:

_____   _____
Parent/Guardian   Date

Approved and received:

_____   _____
School Administrator and Title   Date

_____   _____
School Nurse   Date

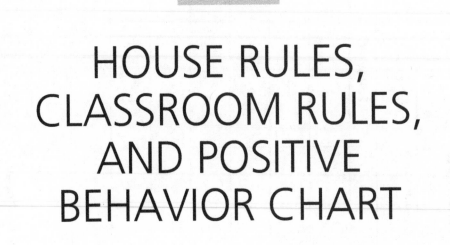

HOUSE RULES, CLASSROOM RULES, AND POSITIVE BEHAVIOR CHART

House Rules

_____
(Day of the Week)

Rule	Followed	Not Followed

Your Totals for Today _____

Classroom Rules

_____
(Day of the Week)

Rule	Followed	Not Followed

Your Totals for Today _____ _____

Positive Behavior Chart for

_____

(Day of the Week)

Goal		☺	☹

Your Totals for Today _____   _____

APPENDIX

PROCEDURAL
SAFEGUARDS

Procedures that safeguard the rights of children with disabilities and their parents must be developed by every state education agency or local school district that receives assistance under IDEA 2004, and information about the safeguards must be disseminated to parents of children with disabilities. Throughout this book, we have presented examples of the protections and rights accorded to children under IDEA 2004. For your convenience, we have collected most of the information that relates to the safeguards in this section. IDEA 2004 states that these procedures must be established and maintained in order to ensure protection of the rights of children with disabilities and their parents with respect to the provision of free appropriate public education. The rights of children with disabilities who are wards of the state must also be protected.

The procedural safeguards for children covered under Part B of IDEA 2004 can be found in Section 615 of the law, while for infants and toddlers covered under Part C, the safeguards are found in Section 639.

The following discussion represents a general overview of the safeguards as presented in IDEA 2004. Because each state is responsible for developing its own set of procedural safeguards, parents should contact their state's department of education or local school district to request a copy of these procedures for their state. See Appendix G for contact information for state departments of special education. The procedural safeguards spell out the rights of children with disabilities and their parents with respect to such issues as notice of and consent for certain actions by a school district, independent educational evaluations, records, hearings, and appeals. In this section, we will also discuss how parental and student rights pertaining to access to educational records are protected under the Family Educational Rights and Privacy Act of 1974 (FERPA).

According to IDEA 2004, the procedural safeguards notice shall include a full explanation of the procedural safeguards, written in the native language of the parents, unless it clearly is not feasible to do so, and written in an easily understandable manner, relating to:

- Independent educational evaluations

- Prior written notice of specified district actions

- Parental consent for certain district actions

- Access to educational records

- The process for presenting and resolving complaints, including

    - The time period in which to make a complaint
    - The procedure for the agency's response to the complaint
    - The availability of mediation

- The child's placement during pending due process proceedings

- Procedures for students who are subject to placement in an interim alternative educational setting

- Requirements for unilateral placement by parents of children in private schools at public expense

- Due process hearings, including requirements for disclosure of evaluation results and recommendations

- State-level appeals (if applicable in that state)

- Civil actions, including the time period in which to file such actions

- Attorneys' fees

NOTICE

Under IDEA 2004, a copy of the procedural safeguards must be made available to the parents of a child with a disability once each year. A copy of the safeguards must also be provided to parents under the following circumstances: upon an initial referral or parent request for evaluation, upon the filing of a complaint, and upon a parent's request for a copy of the procedural safeguards.

Parents have the right to prior written notice, provided in their native language (unless it clearly is not feasible to do so), whenever the school district

- Proposes the identification or evaluation of their child for a special education program or proposes placement of the child in a special education program

- Provides a free appropriate public education (FAPE) to their child

- Proposes to initiate or change their child's special education program

- Refuses to initiate or change their child's special education program

The notice should include

- A description of the action proposed or refused by the school district

- An explanation of why the school district proposes or refuses to take the action

- A description of any other options that the school district considered and the reasons why those options were not selected

- A description of each evaluation procedure, test, record, or report the school district will use or used as a basis for their decisions

- A description of any other factors that are relevant to the school district's proposal or refusal

- A statement that the parents of a child with a disability have protection under the procedural safeguards and, if this notice is not an initial referral for evaluation, the means by which a description of the procedural safeguards can be obtained

- Sources for the parents to contact in order to obtain assistance in understanding their rights under IDEA

CONSENT

Informed parental consent is required before a school district can conduct an initial evaluation to determine whether a child qualifies as a child with a disability under IDEA 2004. In addition, IDEA 2004 specifies that

- Parental consent for evaluation is not to be construed as consent for receipt of special education and related services.

- If parents refuse to consent for evaluation, the school can pursue an evaluation through mediation and due process procedures.

- If a parent refuses special education and related services or fails to respond, the school will not be responsible for providing an FAPE or developing an IEP.

- Parental consent is required prior to conducting a re-evaluation for a child with a disability unless the school district can demonstrate that they have taken reasonable measures to obtain consent and that the parents failed to respond.

RECORDS

The Family Educational Rights and Privacy Act of 1974 (FERPA) is a federal statute that applies to all agencies and institutions that receive federal funds, including elementary and secondary schools, colleges, and universities. The primary purposes of FERPA are

- To ensure that parents have access to their children's educational records

- To protect the privacy rights of parents and children by limiting access to these records without parental consent

Therefore, information in the procedural safeguards pertaining to parents' and students' rights concerning student educational records will comply with the rights and privacy statements that are set out in FERPA. These rights transfer to the student when he reaches the age of eighteen or attends a postsecondary institution. FERPA covers these topics:

- Access to educational records

- Parents' rights to inspect and review educational records

- Guidelines for the amendment of educational records

- Guidelines for the destruction of educational records

FERPA protects the privacy interests of parents in their children's education records and generally prevents an educational institution from disclosing the education records of students or personally identifiable information contained in education records without the written consent of a parent. The term *education records* is defined as all records, files, documents, and other materials that contain information directly related to a student and are maintained by the educational agency or institution or by a person acting for such agency or institution.

Following is a summary of important guidelines for release of educational records under FERPA:

- Parents or students age eighteen and older have the right to inspect and review the education records that are maintained by the school on a student. Most times, parents who wish to review the records will be invited to do so at the school, given that schools are not required to provide copies of records to parents. When a parent does request a copy of the records, the school may charge a fee for copies.

- Parents or eligible students have the right to request that a school amend records that they believe to be inaccurate or misleading. If the school declines the request to change the record, the parent or eligible student then has the right to a formal hearing. After the hearing, if the school decides not to amend the record, the parent or eligible student has the right to place a statement with the record to voice her view about the disputed information.

- Generally, schools must have written permission from a parent or eligible student in order to release any information from the student's education record. However, FERPA allows schools to disclose those records, without consent, to certain parties, such as:
  - School officials
  - Other schools to which a student is transferring
  - Officials who are conducting an audit
  - Individuals or entities as necessary in order to comply with a judicial order or lawfully issued subpoena
  - State and local authorities within a juvenile justice system, pursuant to state law

Schools must notify parents and eligible students annually of their rights under FERPA. How the notification takes place—for example, through a special letter or inclusion in a PTA bulletin, student handbook, or newspaper article—is left to the discretion of each school or district. Parents who wish to obtain further information about FERPA can contact the Family Policy Compliance Office, U.S. Department of Education, 400 Maryland Avenue, S.W., Washington, DC 20202; 202-260-3887.

DISCIPLINARY HEARINGS AND PLACEMENTS IN ALTERNATIVE EDUCATIONAL SETTINGS

IDEA 2004 has provided local school districts with more authority and guidance in managing students with disabilities who violate codes of student conduct. Disciplinary measures for children with disabilities and children who may be deemed in the process of being considered eligible under IDEA 2004 are discussed elsewhere in the book. In this section, we present a brief overview of some of the changes in the law that have affected the decision-making process in regard to disciplinary issues. IDEA 2004 addresses the need for local school districts to balance the need to protect the safety of the student body at large with the individual needs of students with disabilities through the following guidelines:

- Schools may address the unique circumstances of students with disabilities on a case-by-case basis when determining whether alternative school placement is advised in cases of student conduct violations.

- Students with disabilities who violate codes of student conduct may be disciplined in a manner similar to their nondisabled peers for a period of not more than ten school days, whether the disciplinary action involves an alternative educational setting or suspension.

- If a child is removed to an alternative setting, he will continue to receive services that allow him to progress toward meeting the goals of his IEP, and a functional behavioral assessment and a behavior intervention plan will be developed or, if these items already exist, modified in order to address the inappropriate behavior.

- If the alternative placement exceeds ten days and the behavior is deemed not to be a function of the child's disability, then the child may be disciplined in a manner similar to his nondisabled peers (suspension or expulsion); however, under this condition, FAPE will continue for the student with disabilities.

- A student with a disability who commits a violation involving serious bodily harm to another at school or a weapons or drug violation may be removed to an alternative educational setting for up to forty-five school days without a hearing and without parental permission. It is up to parents to appeal such a decision.

- Protective rights for children who are not yet eligible under IDEA 2004 extend to students whose parents have submitted to the school district a written statement that their child is in need of services under IDEA 2004.

- Protective rights are not extended to children whose parents have refused evaluation or placement or to children who have been declared to not have a disability under IDEA 2004.

INDEPENDENT EDUCATIONAL EVALUATION

Parents have the right to have an independent evaluation of their child at their own expense at any time. An independent educational evaluation (IEE) is an evaluation that is conducted by a qualified person who is not an employee of the school district. As we have discussed elsewhere, parents should be knowledgeable about what their school district requires in regard to an assessment for eligibility determination and who is qualified by the state to conduct the assessment.

If parents do not agree with an evaluation conducted by the school district, they have the right to request that an IEE be conducted at public expense and at no cost to the parents. Under these conditions, the school district may ask parents to provide a reason for dissatisfaction with the school-based evaluation; however, parents are not obligated to provide one. Following receipt of the request for an IEE, the school district must either respond with a due process hearing or ensure that an IEE is conducted at public expense, provided that district criteria for the location of the evaluation and the qualifications of the examiner are met.

MEDIATION

IDEA 2004 requires that parents and school districts have an opportunity for mediation so that either party can present complaints with respect to the identification, evaluation, or placement of a child for special education services or the provision of a free appropriate public education for a child. Mediation is an informal procedure that can be used to resolve disagreements between parents and a school district. IDEA 2004 requires that states develop procedures for mediation that ensure that the process is

- Voluntary for both parties
- Conducted by qualified and impartial mediators
- Conducted at a time and place that is convenient for all parties

- Confidential

- Conducted in a manner that will not delay or obstruct rights to a due process hearing

Under IDEA 2004, mediation may now be used without having to file for a hearing. IDEA 2004 also encourages the use of a preliminary meeting in order to discuss issues and perhaps reach a consensus and resolution without having to proceed to a due process hearing.

DUE PROCESS COMPLAINT NOTICE

IDEA 2004 requires that each state develop and disseminate procedures outlining how parents or a school district (or the attorney representing one of these parties) can render a due process complaint notice to the other party and forward a copy of the notice to the state educational agency. Furthermore, IDEA 2004 requires the state educational agency to develop a model form to assist parents in filing a complaint and due process complaint notice in accordance with procedures; the form should include

- The name of the child, the child's address (or, in the case of a homeless child or youth, available contact information for the child), and the name of the school the child is attending

- A description of the child's problem as it relates to the proposed initiation or change, including facts about the problem

- A proposed resolution of the problem

In addition, under IDEA 2004, neither party may engage in a due process hearing until notice is filed as outlined here.

RESPONSE TO A DUE PROCESS COMPLAINT NOTICE

Once a due process complaint notice is filed according to the procedures stated in the preceding section, the school district must respond within ten days of receiving the complaint, addressing these points:

- Why the school district proposed or did not take the action cited in the complaint

- Other options considered by the IEP team and why those options were not endorsed

- Evaluation procedures, reports, and all information used by the school district to reach a decision

- All other factors relevant to the decision-making process

EDUCATIONAL PLACEMENT PENDING OUTCOME OF MEDIATION OR HEARINGS

According to IDEA 2004, during the course of the proceedings, unless otherwise agreed to by the parents and the school district, the child shall remain in the educational placement that preceded the complaint procedure.

APPEAL OF DUE PROCESS HEARINGS

Either party (school or parent) may file an appeal and request a trial in the appropriate federal district court if they are not satisfied with the outcome of the due process hearing.

ATTORNEY'S FEES

IDEA 2004 continues to make provisions for awarding attorney's fees to a parent who prevails in a hearing. However, under IDEA 2004, the court may also award reasonable attorney's fees to the prevailing state or local school against the parent's attorney or parent, if the complaint is considered frivolous, unreasonable, and without foundation (or in the case of repeated litigation, if it has become frivolous, unreasonable, and without foundation) or if the complaint was presented for improper reasons, such as to harass, to cause unnecessary delay, or to needlessly increase litigation costs.

APPENDIX

SAMPLE RESPONSE-TO-INTERVENTION (RTI) MATERIALS

Exhibit F.1 shows the information that the Bartow County School System shares with parents about its response-to-intervention (RTI) program. The information is based on Georgia's four-tier RTI model; however, most states use a three-tier model.

EXHIBIT F.1   *A Parent's Guide to RTI*

What Is Response to Intervention?

Parents and educators alike are concerned when children experience difficulty learning in school. Response to intervention (RTI) is an education model that promotes early identification of students who may be at risk for learning difficulties. For students who are identified as struggling, the RTI process includes a multi-step approach for providing services and interventions at increasing levels of intensity. Federal laws (No Child Left Behind and Individuals with Disabilities Education Improvement Act of 2004) emphasize the importance of providing high-quality, scientifically based instruction and interventions for all students, as well as those who are struggling to meet grade-level standards. RTI is a method for measuring how students respond to academic and behavior interventions in regular education prior to identifying a disability.

The **essential elements** include:

- *Universal screenings* of academics and behavior in order to determine which students need closer monitoring or additional interventions;

- *Differentiation of instruction and use of scientific, research-based* instruction and interventions;

- *Multiple tiers* of increasingly intense scientific, research-based interventions that are matched to student needs;

- *Monitoring student progress* in response to the instruction and interventions

- *Use of progress-monitoring data* to shape instruction and make educational decisions;

- *Parent involvement* throughout the entire process.

In Georgia, a four-tier RTI model has been adopted for early intervention and to determine the student's response as required by Georgia Exceptional Student regulations (160-4-7). Students receive instruction based on their needs and may move within the pyramid as data supports.

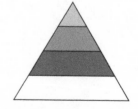

Tier 1 consists of a standards-based classroom with all students participating in instruction that is differentiated, research-based, and guided by progress monitoring and balanced assessments.

EXHIBIT F.1 *A Parent's Guide to RTI (Continued)*

Students who are identified as struggling participate in Tier 1 and **Tier 2** instruction, which consists of needs-based instruction with standard intervention protocols. Tier 2 uses established intervention protocols such as research-based reading or math programs, which provide enhanced opportunities for extended learning, using flexible, small groups, and include more frequent progress monitoring.

Students who are found to be in need of more intense instruction continue to participate in Tier 2 interventions in addition to Tier 3. **Tier 3** includes individual assessments, tailored interventions to respond to their needs, frequent formative assessments, and consideration for specially designed instruction when data indicates a need.

Students found eligible for specially designed instruction participate in **Tier 4** with specialized programs that implement adapted content, methodology, or instructional delivery with access to Georgia Performance Standards.

Important Terms:

Response to Intervention (RTI)—addressed through federal and state law and refers to a tiered approach to instruction. Students who do not make adequate academic progress and who are at risk for reading and other learning difficulties receive increasingly intensive instructional and behavioral interventions.

Differentiation of Instruction—instruction tailored to meet the needs of diverse learners in the general education classroom.

Progress Monitoring—is a scientifically based practice of assessing students' performance on a regular basis. Progress monitoring helps school teams make decisions about instruction.

Universal Screening—is a step taken by school personnel early in the school year to determine which students are at risk for not meeting grade-level standards. Universal screenings can be accomplished by reviewing recent results of state tests, or by administering an academic screening test to all children in a given grade level. Students whose test scores fall below a certain cutoff are identified as needing more specialized academic interventions.

Scientific, Research-Based Instruction—specific curriculum, educational, and behavioral interventions that have been proven to be effective through scientific peer-reviewed journals.

EXHIBIT F.1 *A Parent's Guide to RTI (Continued)*

Parent's Role in RTI:

- Be involved and proactive in the education of your child.

- Feel free to request to visit your child's classroom and ask for ways to assist your child to improve his or her performance.

- Work with your child at home on particular skills identified through screenings.

- If concerns arise, request a parent conference with your child's teacher or the administration.

Additional Information:	
Technical Assistance Alliance for Parent Centers http://www.taalliance.org	**National Center for Learning Disabilities** http://www.ld.org
Learning Disability Association of America http://www.ldaamerica.us/	**SchwabLearning.org** http://www.schwablearning.org/
LD Online http://www.ldonline.org/	**National Association of School Psychologists** http://www.nasponline.org/
Bartow County Schools Psychologists http://www2.bartow.k12.ga.us/psych/psych.html/	**Georgia Dept. of Education** http://www.doe.k12.ga.us/

TIER 2 INTERVENTION FORM

Exhibit F.2 shows a form that is used to gather information about students who are having academic or behavioral difficulties and then to plan and monitor interventions to help them. The form is based on Georgia's four-tier RTI model. In states that use a three-tier model, this intervention plan might be used at Tier 1 or Tier 2.

EXHIBIT F.2 *Tier 2 Intervention Plan*

Secondary Tier 2: Student Intervention Plan

Student: _____ **Grade:** _____ **Teacher:** _____ **Date:** _____

Area of Difficulty: _____
(1 per page) Reading, Math, Behavior,
Communication, etc.

Skill Deficit: _____
(Segmenting, computation, attending
to tasks, etc.)

Reading	**Math**	**Written Expression**
☐ Phonics	☐ Calculation	☐ Spelling skills
☐ Fluency	☐ Math reasoning	☐ Writing fluency skills
☐ Vocabulary	☐ Problem solving	☐ Capitalization skills
☐ Comprehension	☐ Other (explain)	☐ Punctuation skills
☐ Other (explain)	_____	☐ Organizational skills
_____		☐ Other (explain)
		_____

Speech/Language	**Behavior**
☐ Articulation	☐ Frequency
☐ Oral expression	☐ Duration
☐ Listening	☐ Intensity
comprehension	☐ Function:
☐ Fluency	____Escape
☐ Other (explain)	____Avoid
_____	____Attention
	____Power

Research-Based Intervention:

Standard Protocol: Choose one

Reading	**Math**
____Read 180	____Study Island
____Partner Reading	____Cover/Copy/Compare (Flue)
____Six Minute Solution	____CRA (Concrete, Rep/Abs)
____Reader's Theater	____Peer-Assisted Learning
____Click or Clunk	Strategies (PALS)
____Writing Destinations	____Schema-based Instruction
____RAP (Paraphrasing)	____Incremental Rehearsal
____Story Mapping	____FAST Draw (mnemonic)
____DISSECT	____QAR (Quest/Ans/Relat)
____Word Building	____CAI–Computer-Assisted
____Other (be specific) _____	Instruction

EXHIBIT F.2 *Tier 2 Intervention Plan (Continued)*

Behavior	**Communication**
___Check in/Check out	___Language for Learning
___Good Behavior Game	
___Mystery Motivator	___Earobics
___Visual Cues	___Speedy Speech
___Self-Monitoring	___Articu Check
___Rubber Band Plan	___Bridge of Vocabulary
___Points for Grumpy	
___Talk Ticket	___Story Schedules
___Response/Cost	
___Group Control	
___Positive Peer Reporting	
___Counselor Groups (name of group)	
___Other (be specific)_____	

Problem Solving: (be specific) www.interventioncentral.org

_____

_____

Plan for Implementation:

Date Begun	Baseline Data	Interventionist and Group Size (4–8 preferred)	Frequency/ Duration (weekly/ 30 min., etc.)	Progress Monitoring Prob/Freq	Criteria for Progress			Date Ended	Comments
					Date	Date	Date		

Recommended Action:

___Continue current intervention   ___ Alternative intervention

___Return to universal instruction   (describe reason for change)

                                         ___ Other (describe below)

                                         ___ Fidelity Check_____Signature/Date

EXHIBIT F.2 *Tier 2 Intervention Plan (Continued)*

Tier 2: Conference Summary

Student: _____ **Grade:** _____ **Teacher:** _____ **Date:** _____

Parent Notification: _____ **Date(s):** _____

Phone call _____ Note home ___ E-mail _____ Conference _____ Other (list) _____

What are the student's strengths, talents, or specific interests?

1. _____
2. _____
3. _____

Area of concern: _____
Specific concern: _____

Data collected:

Grades		R-MAZE	M-CAP	M-CBM: CD	Behavior RC	Other
ELA	Reading					
Math	Spelling					

Student attendance to date: Absences: _____ Unex. ___ Ex. ___ Tardies/checkouts: _____

Behavior: Satisfactory_____ Needs improvement _____ Unsatisfactory _____
Comments: _____

Conference summary/Recommendations:
_____
_____
_____
_____

Parent's concerns:
_____
_____
_____

Persons present in conference: (Name/Title)

_____   _____
_____   _____
_____   _____

On the first page of this form, the student support team (SST) identifies a specific area of concern: reading, math, written expression, speech/language, or behavior. (More than one of these pages can be used if there is more than one area of concern.) The team also indicates which research-based interventions have been attempted. Teachers may have used some of the standard research-based interventions listed on the form, or they may have used interventions from other sources. The plan for implementation includes information such as the start date of the intervention, the student's current performance (baseline data), who will be implementing the intervention, how frequently and for how long the intervention will be implemented, the ways in which progress will be monitored, the criteria that will be used to make a determination about whether progress has been demonstrated, and when the intervention will end.

The second page of the form allows schools to document the results of their conference meeting. The student's strengths, talents, and interests are identified, the data collected are specified, recommendations are made, and the parent's concerns are listed. More than one conference may occur at Tier 2.

TIER 3 INTERVENTION FORM

If a student needs more specialized interventions, he will be moved to Tier 3 in Georgia's four-tier RTI model (or Tier 2 intervention in a three-tier model) (see Exhibit F.3).

On the first page of this form, the student support team (SST) comes up with a specific plan to address academic or behavioral problems. The team lists the date when the interventions are to be implemented, the strategy or strategies to be used, who will be responsible for the implementation of the intervention, how progress will be evaluated (refer to the bottom of the form for possible methods), and the date when the specific intervention was ended.

On the second page of the form, the team graphs the progress of the student. Baseline data will be listed first, to facilitate comparison with future performance. Each time data are collected, they will be mapped on the graph and the date will be included at the bottom. The numbers will vary depending on what is being measured. It may be words read in a sixty-second period, the number of words written within a three-minute period, and so on. The numbers are simply included as a guide. This process allows the SST to see whether a student is making progress and over what period of time the progress has occurred. The two rows in the "Data Points" table are given if the team wants to track different types of data.

EXHIBIT F.3 *Tier 3 Intervention Plan*

Tier 3: Student Intervention Plan

SST _____ IAP/504 _____ IEP _____

Student: _____
School: _____

Teacher: _____
Grade: _____

Date: _____

Specific concern: _____
Goal: _____

Date Implemented	Strategy	Person(s) Responsible	Method(s) of Evaluation	Date Ended	Comments

Possible Method(s) of Evaluation

CBA = Curriculum-Based Assessment   ELT = End-of-Level Test
CRT = Criterion Reference Test   TO = Teacher Observation
DC = Data Collection Performance   LS = Language Sample
DIBELS = DIBELS   WS = Work Samples

Must specify any other methods used.

EXHIBIT F.3 *Tier 3 Intervention Plan (Continued)*

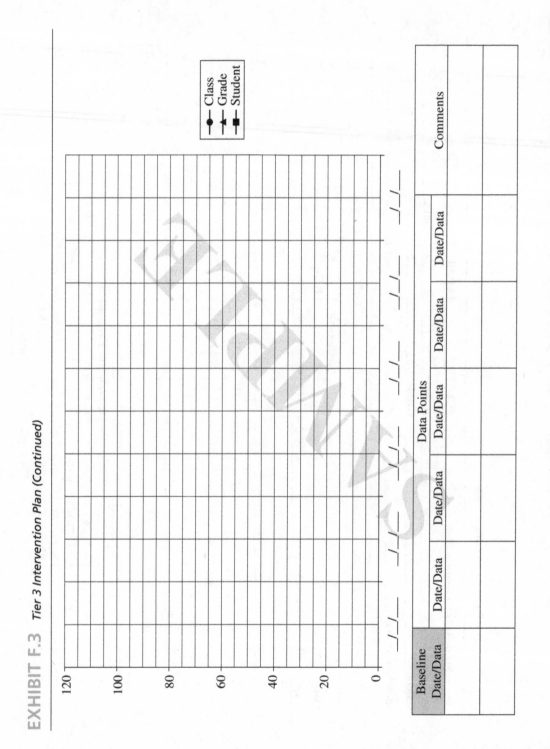

Legend:
● — Class
▲ — Grade
■ — Student

	Data Points				
Baseline Date/Data	Date/Data	Date/Data	Date/Data	Date/Data	Comments

APPENDIX

STATE DEPARTMENTS OF SPECIAL EDUCATION

Alabama Department of Special Education
    50 N. Ripley Street
    Montgomery, AL 36104
    334-242-9700
    http://www.alsde.edu/html/sections/section_detail.asp?section=65

Alaska Department of Special Education
    801 W. Tenth Street, Suite 200
    Juneau, AK 99801
    907-465-2972
    http://www.eed.state.ak.us/tls/sped/

Arizona Department of Exceptional Student Services
    1535 W. Jefferson Street, Bin 24
    Phoenix, AZ 85007
    602-542-4013
    http://www.ade.az.gov/ess/

Arkansas Department of Special Education
    1401 W. Capitol Avenue, Suite 450
    Little Rock, AR 72201
    501-682-4221
    http://arksped.k12.ar.us/

California Special Education Division
    1430 "N" Street, Suite 2401
    Sacramento, CA 95814
    916-445-4613
    http://www.cde.ca.gov/

Colorado Exceptional Student Leadership Unit
    1560 Broadway, Suite 1175
    Denver, CO 80202
    303-866-6694
    http://www.cde.state.co.us/index_special.htm

Connecticut Bureau of Special Education
    P.O. Box 2219
    Hartford, CT 06145
    860-713-6912
    http://www.sde.ct.gov/sde/cwp/view.asp?a=2678&Q=320730

Delaware Exceptional Children Group
    401 Federal Street, Suite 2
    Dover, DE 19901
    302-735-4000
    http://www.doe.k12.de.us/infosuites/students_family/specialed/

Department of Defense Education Activity
Office of Special Education
    4040 N. Fairfax Drive
    Arlington, VA 22203
    703-588-3147
    http://www.dodea.edu/curriculum/specialEduc.cfm

Florida Bureau of Exceptional Education and Student Services
    325 W. Gaines Street, Suite 614
    Tallahassee, FL 32399
    850-245-0475
    http://www.fldoe.org/ese/

Georgia Office of Standards, Instruction and
Assessment—Exceptional Students
    1870 Twin Towers East
    Atlanta, GA 30334
    404-656-3963
    http://public.doe.k12.ga.us/ci_exceptional.aspx

Hawaii Special Education Services Branch
    475—22nd Avenue, Room 115
    Honolulu, HI 96816
    808-203-5560
    http://doe.k12.hi.us/specialeducation/

Idaho Department of Special Education
    650 W. State Street
    Boise, ID 83720
    208-332-6911
    http://www.sde.idaho.gov/site/special_edu/

Illinois Department of Special Education Services
    100 N. First Street
    Springfield, IL 62777
    217-782-4321
    http://www.isbe.net/SPEC-ED/DEFAULT.HTM

Indiana Office of Special Education
    151 W. Ohio Street
    Indianapolis, IN 46204
    317-232-0570
    http://www.doe.in.gov/exceptional/speced/welcome.html

Iowa Department of Special Education
    400 E. 14th Street
    Des Moines, IA 50319
    515-281-5294
    http://www.iowa.gov/educate/index.php?option=com_content&view=
    article&id=574&Itemid=2126

Kansas Department of Special Education Services
   120 S.E. 10th Avenue
   Topeka, KS 66612
   800-203-9462
   http://www.ksde.org/Default.aspx?tabid=101

Kentucky Division of Exceptional Children Services
   500 Mero Street, 8th Floor CPT
   Frankfort, KY 40601
   502-564-4970
   http://www.education.ky.gov/KDE/Instructional+Resources/
   Exceptional+Children/

Louisiana Division of Special Populations
   1201 N. 3rd Street
   Baton Rouge, LA 70804
   225-342-3730
   http://www.doe.state.la.us/lde/eia/home.html

Maine Department of Special Services
   23 State House Station
   Augusta, ME 04333
   207-624-6600
   http://www.maine.gov/education/speced/index.htm

Maryland Division of Special Education/Early Intervention Services
   200 W. Baltimore Street, 9th Floor
   Baltimore, MD 21201
   410-767-0238
   http://www.marylandpublicschools.org/MSDE/DIVISIONS/
   EARLYINTERV/SPECIAL_ED_INFO.HTM

Massachusetts Department of Special Education
   75 Pleasant Street
   Malden, MA 02148
   781-338-3000
   http://www.doe.mass.edu/sped/

Michigan Office of Special Education and Early Intervention Services
608 W. Allegan Street
Lansing, MI 48909
517-373-0923
http://www.michigan.gov/mde/0,1607,7-140-6530_6598---,00.html

Minnesota Division of Special Education
1500 Highway 36 West
Roseville, MN 55113
651-582-8614
http://education.state.mn.us/mde/Learning_Support/Special_Education/
index.html

Mississippi Office of Special Education
359 N. West Street, Suite 301
Jackson, MS 39205
601-359-3498
http://www.mde.k12.ms.us/SPECIAL_EDUCATION/

Missouri Division of Special Education
P.O. Box 480
Jefferson City, MO 65102
573-751-5739
http://dese.mo.gov/divspeced/

Montana Department of Special Education
P.O. Box 202501
Helena, MT 59620
406-444-3095
http://www.opi.state.mt.us/SPECED/

Nebraska Office of Special Education
301 Centennial Mall South
Lincoln, NE 68509
402-471-2471
http://www.nde.state.ne.us/sped/index.html

Nevada Department of Special Education, Elementary
and Secondary Education, and School Improvement
    700 E. Fifth Street
    Carson City, NV 89701
    775-687-9200
    http://www.doe.nv.gov/SE_ESE_SI.htm

New Hampshire Bureau of Special Education
    101 Pleasant Street
    Concord, NH 03301
    603-271-3494
    http://www.ed.state.nh.us/education/doe/organization/instruction/bose.htm

New Jersey Office of Special Education Programs
    P.O. Box 500
    Trenton, NJ 08625
    609-292-0147
    http://www.nj.gov/education/specialed/

New Mexico Special Education Bureau
    120 S. Federal Place, Room 206
    Santa Fe, NM 87501
    505-827-1457
    http://www.ped.state.nm.us/seo/index.htm

New York Office of Vocational and Educational Services for Individuals with
Disabilities
    One Commerce Plaza, Room 1606
    Albany, NY 12234
    518-474-3852
    http://www.vesid.nysed.gov/specialed/

North Carolina Exceptional Children Division
    301 N. Wilmington Street, 6th Floor
    Raleigh, NC 27601
    919-807-3300
    http://www.ncpublicschools.org/ec/

North Dakota Department of Special Education
600 E. Boulevard Avenue
Bismarck, ND 58505
701-328-2260
http://www.dpi.state.nd.us/SPECED/INDEX.SHTM

Ohio Office of Exceptional Children
25 S. Front Street
Columbus, OH 43215
877-644-6338
http://www.ode.state.oh.us/GD/Templates/Pages/ODE/ODEPrimary.aspx?
page=2&TopicRelationID=967

Oklahoma Department of Education
2500 N. Lincoln Boulevard
Oklahoma City, OK 73105
405-522-3248
http://sde.state.ok.us/Curriculum/SpecEd/Assessment.html

Oregon Special Education Unit
255 Capitol Street, N.E.
Salem, OR 97301
503-947-5782
http://www.ode.state.or.us/search/results/?id=40

Pennsylvania Bureau of Special Education
333 Market Street, 7th Floor
Harrisburg, PA 17126
717-783-6913
http://www.pde.state.pa.us/SPECIAL_EDU/site/default.asp

Rhode Island Office for Diverse Learners
255 Westminster Street
Providence, RI 02903
401-222-4600
http://www.ride.ri.gov/Special_populations/default.aspx

South Carolina Office of Exceptional Children
    1429 Senate Street, Room 808
    Columbia, SC 29201
    803-734-8806
    http://ed.sc.gov/agency/Standards-and-Learning/Exceptional-Children/

South Dakota Office of Educational Services and Support
    700 Governors Drive
    Pierre, SD 57501
    605-773-3134
    http://doe.sd.gov/oess/specialed/index.asp

Tennessee Division of Special Education
    710 James Robertson Parkway
    Nashville, TN 37243
    615-741-2851
    http://www.state.tn.us/education/speced/

Texas Special Education Unit
    1701 N. Congress Avenue
    Austin, TX 78701
    512-463-9414
    http://ritter.tea.state.tx.us/special.ed/index.html

Utah Special Education Services Unit
    250 E. 500 South
    Salt Lake City, UT 84114
    801-538-7587
    http://www.schools.utah.gov/sars/

Vermont Department of Special Education
    120 State Street
    Montpelier, VT 05620
    802-828-3135
    http://education.vermont.gov/new/html/pgm_sped.html

Virginia Division of Special Education and Student Services
P.O. Box 2120
Richmond, VA 23218
800-292-3820
http://www.doe.virginia.gov/VDOE/sess/

Washington Special Education Section
600 Washington Street, S.E.
Olympia, WA 98504
360-725-6000
http://www.k12.wa.us/SPECIALED/DEFAULT.ASPX

West Virginia Office of Special Programs, Extended and Early Learning
1900 Kanawha Boulevard
Charleston, WV 25305
304-558-2696
http://wvde.state.wv.us/osp/

Wisconsin Division for Learning Support: Equity and Advocacy
125 S. Webster Street
Madison, WI 53707
800-441-4563
http://dpi.wi.gov/dlsea/

Wyoming Office of Special Education
320 W. Main Street
Riverton, WY 82501
307-777-2555
http://www.k12.wy.us/se.asp

APPENDIX

HELPFUL WEB SITES FOR PARENTS AND TEACHERS

The Access Center: Improving Outcomes for All Students K–8
    American Institutes for Research
    1000 Thomas Jefferson Street, N.W.
    Washington, DC 20007
    202-944-5300
    http://www.k8accesscenter.org

Alexander Graham Bell Association for the Deaf and Hard of Hearing
    3417 Volta Place, N.W.
    Washington, DC 20007
    202-337-5220
    202-337-5221 (TTY)
    http://www.agbell.org

American Academy of Child and Adolescent Psychiatry (AACAP)
    3615 Wisconsin Avenue, N.W.
    Washington, DC 20016
    202-966-7300
    http://www.aacap.org

American Association of the Deaf-Blind (AADB)
    8630 Fenton Street, Suite 121
    Silver Spring, MD 20910
    301-495-4402
    http://www.aadb.org

American Association on Intellectual and Developmental Disabilities (AAIDD)
    444 North Capitol Street, N.W., Suite 846
    Washington, DC 20001
    800-424-3688
    http://www.aaidd.org

American Brain Tumor Association (ABTA)
    2720 River Road
    Des Plaines, IL 60018
    800-886-2282
    http://www.abta.org

American Council of the Blind (ACB)
    2200 Wilson Boulevard, Suite 650
    Arlington, VA 22201
    800-424-8666
    http://www.acb.org

American Counseling Association (ACA)
    5999 Stevenson Avenue
    Alexandria, VA 22304
    800-347-6647
    http://www.counseling.org

American Diabetes Association
    1701 N. Beauregard Street
    Alexandria, VA 22311
    800-342-2383
    http://www.diabetes.org

American Federation of Teachers (AFT)
    555 New Jersey Avenue, N.W.
    Washington, DC 20001
    202-897-4400
    http://www.aft.org

American Foundation for the Blind (AFB)
   11 Penn Plaza, Suite 300
   New York, NY 10001
   800-232-5463
   http://www.afb.org

American Occupational Therapy Association (AOTA)
   4720 Montgomery Lane
   P.O. Box 31220
   Bethesda, MD 20824
   301-652-2682
   http://www.aota.org

American Physical Therapy Association (APTA)
   1111 N. Fairfax Street
   Alexandria, VA 22314
   800-999-2782
   http://www.apta.org

American Psychological Association (APA)
   750 First Street, N.E.
   Washington, DC 20002
   800-374-2721
   http://www.apa.org

American School Counselor Association (ASCA)
   1101 King Street, Suite 625
   Alexandria, VA 22314
   800-306-4722
   http://www.schoolcounselor.org

American Society for Deaf Children (ASDC)
   800 Florida Avenue, N.E.
   Washington, DC 20002
   800-942-2732
   http://www.deafchildren.org

American Speech-Language-Hearing-Association (ASHA)
   2200 Research Boulevard
   Rockville, MD 20850
   800-638-8255
   http://www.asha.org

Anxiety Disorders Association of America (ADAA)
    8730 Georgia Avenue, Suite 600
    Silver Spring, MD 20910
    240-485-1001
    http://www.adaa.org

Association of Educational Therapists (AET)
    11300 W. Olympic Boulevard, Suite 600
    Los Angeles, CA 90064
    800-286-4267
    http://www.aetonline.org

Association on Higher Education and Disability (AHEAD)
    107 Commerce Center Drive, Suite 204
    Huntersville, NC 28078
    704-947-7779
    http://www.ahead.org

Asthma and Allergy Foundation of America (AAFA)
    8201 Corporate Drive, Suite 1000
    Landover, MD 20785
    800-727-8462
    http://www.aafa.org

Attention Deficit Disorder Association (ADDA)
    P.O. Box 7557
    Wilmington, DE 19803
    800-939-1019
    http://www.add.org

Autism Society (AS)
    7910 Woodmont Avenue, Suite 300
    Bethesda, MD 20814
    800-328-8476
    http://www.autism-society.org

Brain Injury Association of America
    1608 Spring Hill Road, Suite 110
    Vienna, VA 22182
    703-761-0750
    http://www.biausa.org

Center for Mental Health in Schools
    Department of Psychology
    University of California, Los Angeles
    P.O. Box 951563
    Los Angeles, CA 90095
    866-846-4843
    http://smhp.psych.ucla.edu

Center on Positive Behavioral Interventions and Supports (PBIS)
    1235 University of Oregon
    1761 Alder Street
    Eugene, OR 97403
    541-346-2505
    http://www.pbis.org

Children and Adults with Attention-Deficit/Hyperactivity Disorder (CHADD)
    8181 Professional Place, Suite 150
    Landover, MD 20785
    301-306-7070
    http://www.chadd.org

Children's Tumor Foundation (CTF)
    95 Pine Street, 16th Floor
    New York, NY 10005
    800-323-7938
    http://www.ctf.org

Consortium for Appropriate Dispute Resolution
in Special Education (CADRE)
    Direction Service, Inc.
    P.O. Box 51360
    Eugene, OR 97405
    541-686-5060
    http://www.directionservice.org/cadre

Council for Exceptional Children (CEC)
    1110 N. Glebe Road, Suite 300
    Arlington, VA 22201-5704
    888-232-7733
    http://www.cec.sped.org

Council for Learning Disabilities (CLD)
   11184 Antioch Road, Box 405
   Overland Park, KS 66210
   913-491-1011
   http://www.cldinternational.org

Depression and Bipolar Support Alliance (DBSA)
   730 N. Franklin Street, Suite 501
   Chicago, IL 60610
   800-826-3632
   http://www.dbsalliance.org

Educational Resources Information Center (ERIC)
   ERIC Project
   c/o Computer Sciences Corporation
   655—15th Street, N.W., Suite 500
   Washington, DC 20005
   800-538-3742
   http://www.eric.ed.gov

ERIC is a national information system that is funded by the U.S. Department of
Education in order to provide access to education literature and resources.

Epilepsy Foundation
   8301 Professional Place
   Landover, MD 20785
   800-332-1000
   http://www.epilepsyfoundation.org

Families of Spinal Muscular Atrophy (FSMA)
   925 Busse Road
   Elk Grove Village, IL 60007
   800-886-1762
   http://www.fsma.org

Institute of Education Sciences (IES)
   U.S. Department of Education
   555 New Jersey Avenue, N.W.
   Washington, DC 20208
   202-219-2239
   http://www.ed.gov/about/offices/list/ies/index.html

International Dyslexia Association (IDA)
    40 York Road, 4th Floor
    Baltimore, MD 21204
    410-296-0232
    http://www.interdys.org

International Reading Association (IRA)
    800 Barksdale Road
    P.O. Box 8139
    Newark, DE 19714
    800-336-7323
    http://www.reading.org

Learning Disabilities Association of America (LDA)
    4156 Library Road
    Pittsburgh, PA 15234
    412-341-1515
    http://www.ldanatl.org

March of Dimes
    1275 Mamaroneck Avenue
    White Plains, NY 10605
    914-997-4488
    http://www.modimes.org

Muscular Dystrophy Association (MDA)
    3300 E. Sunrise Drive
    Tucson, AZ 85718
    800-572-1717
    http://www.mdausa.org

National Alliance of Black School Educators (NABSE)
    310 Pennsylvania Avenue, S.E.
    Washington, DC 20003
    800-221-2654
    http://www.nabse.org

National Alliance on Mental Illness (NAMI)
    3803 N. Fairfax Drive, Suite 100
    Arlington, VA 22203
    703-524-7600
    http://www.nami.org

National Association for Bilingual Education (NABE)
    1313 L Street, N.W., Suite 210
    Washington, DC 20005
    202-898-1829
    http://www.nabe.org

National Association of School Nurses (NASN)
    8484 Georgia Avenue, Suite 420
    Silver Spring, MD 20910
    866-627-6767
    http://www.nasn.org

National Association of School Psychologists (NASP)
    4340 East West Highway, Suite 402
    Bethesda, MD 20814
    866-331-6277
    http://www.nasponline.org

National Association of the Deaf (NAD)
    8630 Fenton Street, Suite 820
    Silver Spring, MD 20910
    301-587-1788
    301-587-1789 (TTY)
    http://www.nad.org

National Brain Tumor Foundation (NBTF)
    22 Battery Street, Suite 612
    San Francisco, CA 94111
    800-770-8287
    http://www.braintumor.org

National Center for Learning Disabilities (NCLD)
    381 Park Avenue South, Suite 1401
    New York, NY 10016
    888-575-7373
    http://www.ncld.org

National Center for Special Education Accountability Monitoring (NCSEAM)
    Human Development Center
    Louisiana State University Health Sciences Center
    1900 Gravier Street, Room 823 (8B9)
    New Orleans, LA 70112
    504-556-7559
    http://www.monitoringcenter.lsuhsc.edu

National Center on Education, Disability, and Juvenile Justice (EDJJ)
    University of Maryland
    1224 Benjamin Building
    College Park, MD 20742
    301-405-6462
    http://www.edjj.org

National Center on Secondary Education and Transition (NCSET)
    University of Minnesota
    6 Pattee Hall
    150 Pillsbury Drive, S.E.
    Minneapolis, MN 55455
    612-624-2097
    http://www.ncset.org

National Consortium on Deaf-Blindness (NCDB)
    345 N. Monmouth Avenue
    Monmouth, OR 97361
    800-438-9376
    http://www.dblink.org

National Dissemination Center for Children with Disabilities (NICHCY)
    1825 Connecticut Avenue, N.W., Suite 700
    Washington, DC 20009
    800-695-0285
    http://www.nichcy.org

National Down Syndrome Society (NDSS)
    666 Broadway, 8th Floor
    New York, NY 10012
    800-221-4602
    http://www.ndss.org

National Early Childhood Technical Assistance Center (NECTAC)
    University of North Carolina
    Campus Box 8040
    Chapel Hill, NC 27599
    919-962-2001
    http://www.nectac.org

National Education Association (NEA)
    1201 — 16th Street, N.W.
    Washington, DC 20036
    202-833-4000
    http://www.nea.org

National Fragile X Foundation
P.O. Box 190488
San Francisco, CA 94119
800-688-8765
http://www.fragilex.org

National Institute on Deafness and Other Communication Disorders (NIDCD)
National Institutes of Health
31 Center Drive, MSC 2320
Bethesda, MD 20892
301-496-7243
http://www.nidcd.nih.gov

National Multiple Sclerosis Society (NMSS)
733 Third Avenue
New York, NY 10017
800-344-4867
http://www.nmss.org

National Organization on Fetal Alcohol Syndrome (NOFAS)
900—17th Street, N.W., Suite 910
Washington, DC 20006
800-666-6327
http://www.nofas.org

National Research Center on Learning Disabilities (NRCLD)
Vanderbilt University
P.O. Box 328
Peabody College
Nashville, TN 37103
http://www.nrcld.org

National Spinal Cord Injury Association
1 Church Street #600
Rockville, MD 20850
800-962-9629
http://www.spinalcord.org

National Stuttering Association (NSA)
119 W. 40th Street, 14th Floor
New York, NY 10018
800-937-8888
http://www.nsastutter.org

National Urban Alliance for Effective Education (NUA)
   33 Queens Street, Suite 100
   Syosset, NY 11791
   800-682-4556
   http://www.nuatc.org

Obsessive-Compulsive Foundation (OCF)
   P.O. Box 961029
   Boston, MA 02196
   617-973-5801
   http://www.ocfoundation.org

Office of Special Education Programs (OSEP)
   Office of Special Education and Rehabilitative Services
   U.S. Department of Education
   400 Maryland Avenue, S.W.
   Washington, DC 20202
   202-205-5507
   http://www.ed.gov/about/offices/list/osers/osep/index.html

Parent Advocacy Center Coalition for Educational Rights (PACER)
   8161 Normandale Boulevard
   Minneapolis, MN 55437
   952-838-9000
   http://www.pacer.org

Prader-Willi Syndrome Association (PWSA)
   8588 Potter Park Drive, Suite 500
   Sarasota, FL 34238
   800-926-4797
   http://www.pwsausa.org

Recording for the Blind & Dyslexic (RFB&D)
   20 Roszel Road
   Princeton, NJ 08540
   866-732-3585
   http://www.rfbd.org

Registry of Interpreters for the Deaf (RID)
   333 Commerce Street
   Alexandria, VA 22314
   703-838-0030
   http://www.rid.org

Research and Training Center on Family Support and Children's Mental Health
    Portland State University
    P.O. Box 751
    Portland, OR 97207
    503-725-4040
    http://www.rtc.pdx.edu

Special Olympics
    1133—19th Street, N.W.
    Washington, DC 20036
    800-700-8585
    http://www.specialolympics.org

Spina Bifida Association of America (SBAA)
    4590 MacArthur Boulevard, N.W., Suite 250
    Washington, DC 20007
    800-621-3141
    http://www.spinabifidaassociation.org

Tourette Syndrome Association (TSA)
    42-40 Bell Boulevard
    Bayside, NY 11361
    718-224-2999
    http://www.tsa-usa.org

United Cerebral Palsy Association (UCP)
    1660 L Street, N.W., Suite 700
    Washington, DC 20036
    800-872-5827
    http://www.ucp.org

Williams Syndrome Association (WSA)
    570 Kirts Boulevard, Suite 223
    Troy, MI 48084
    800-806-1871
    http://www.williams-syndrome.org

INDEX